W. B. Yeats
Interviews and Recollections
Volume I

Also by E. H. Mikhail

The Social and Cultural Setting of the 1890s
John Galsworthy the Dramatist
Comedy and Tragedy
Sean O'Casey: A Bibliography of Criticism
A Bibliography of Modern Irish Drama 1899–1970
Dissertations on Anglo-Irish Drama
The Sting and the Twinkle: Conversations with Sean O'Casey
(co-editor with John O'Riordan)
J. M. Synge: A Bibliography of Criticism
J. M. Synge: Interviews and Recollections *(editor)*
British Drama 1900–1950
Contemporary British Drama 1950–1976

W. B. YEATS

Interviews and Recollections

Volume I

Edited by
E. H. Mikhail

With a Foreword by
A. Norman Jeffares

M

First published 1977 by
THE MACMILLAN PRESS LTD
London and Basingstoke
Associated companies in New York
Dublin Melbourne Johannesburg and Madras

SBN 333 19711 9

Printed in Great Britain by
BILLING AND SONS LTD
Guildford, Worcester and London

cC

To my wife

Contents

Foreword

This collection of interviews and recollections of Yeats throws light upon the authors as well as the poet himself. His brilliant school fellow Charles Johnston writes appreciatively out of a cautious, perhaps less brilliant early middle age – his marriage to Madame Blavatsky's niece having probably subdued his wilder questing for the philosopher's stone – summarising the elements of culture which informed Yeats's early work. The attraction of the Ireland Yeats was presenting in his work and into which he was trying to bring a new attitude of mind, a regard for the Gaelic past and a richer, independent intellectual future is shown in the article by Cornelius Weygandt, who gives a lyrical account of the 'druid charm' he found in the west of Ireland. There is the inevitable contrast: reports and interviews: the Abbey row over *The Playboy of the Western World* where Yeats reveals himself as a good, pugnacious propagandist, generalising on the special dramatic genius and capacity for fantasy of the Irish, notably in an interview with Robert Lynd. Yeats's interviews in America show his ability to alter his approach to suit a different audience, and his interview with 'F. H.' conveys something of the meditative monologue that converted his conversations into a complex commentary on life.

Yeats's difficulty in talking easily on common topics seemed to St John Ervine to arise out of his being uncomfortable with individuals, and yet having trained himself to an elegance of demeanour, an elaborate courteousness. His effect on other writers comes clearly through this commentary, and, though his praise of St John Ervine's *The Magnanimous Lover* and *John Ferguson* stimulated and encouraged the Ulster playwright, it was the adverse criticism of *Mrs Martin's Man* which seemed especially valuable. This long piece slowly puts together Yeats's power to attract – and repel. Both St John Ervine and Montrose J. Moses convey the reaction of lesser writers to Yeats's eloquence: there was 'no trace of social intercourse about it' writes the latter, thoroughly confident that Yeats would never remember that Moses had called upon him. But what emerges from those articles, and, particularly, Marguerite Wilkinson's, is Yeats's very real interest in other writers' work, and his awareness as a Senator, of what was happening in Ireland. And in his interview in the *Irish Press*, on his seventieth birthday, he welcomed the absence of the bitter partisanship which 'spoiled everything' when he was a young man.

The recollections of other writers fill in the picture. Ernest Rhys remarked, when Yeats missed a train, that he did not mind at all and 'seemed to regard trains as things that came and went at random'. Sir William Rothenstein, W. J. Turner, Oliver St John Gogarty, Lennox Robinson, and E. R. Walsh give us their very different views of him. His practicality appealed to Lennox Robinson, and his criticisms of plays—especially realistic plays. 'Smear cow dung on their faces,' he exclaimed when the actresses playing some farmer's daughters were too clean.

Frank O'Connor felt that in Yeats's relations with F. R. Higgins and himself 'a circuitous and brilliant strategy was performing complicated manoeuvres about non existent armies'. His piece about Yeats and AE (whose friendship he understood) and his subsequent article written in 1964 entitled 'Quarreling with Yeats: a friendly recollection', though they convey his admiration for the poet (so notably communicated in the lectures which he gave on him in Trinity College Dublin), also contain enough of Dublin's literary sharpness to show the reader the kind of milieu Yeats enjoyed, avoided and occasionally manipulated.

Hugh Kingsmill's article illustrates some of Yeats's 'set piece' remarks, and L. A. G. Strong records his Monday evenings with reverence. Richard Eberhart's memory of meeting Yeats is delightful, full of acute comedy, not least his description of how they left Gogarty's house, and walked in an eloquence of silence through the Dublin streets. Gabriel Fallon produces an interior view of life in the world of the later Abbey, Arthur Power adds to our sense of the Dublin background, as does Thomas MacGreevy with an awareness of Yeats's sense of fun, while V. S. Pritchett rightly records his detestation of Irish attitudes of mockery of Yeats.

This book of varied views reinforces our awareness of the largeness of Yeats. Some aspects of his personality patently puzzled smaller men. But even their doubts and occasional disparagement add to the dimension of his achievement, for they show how he preserved his inner vision while playing a powerful part in contemporary life, the extent of which is slowly being realised in his own country. And some of the writers included here knew what it was like to work with Yeats. Theirs are probably the most interesting contributions to our knowledge of a very complex creative character.

Stirling   A. NORMAN JEFFARES

Acknowledgements

This book would never have taken its present shape without the constant help and perceptive criticism of Professor A. Norman Jeffares. Considerable research has been done for me in Dublin by Miss Carol Coulter; in London by Research Assistance Routledge Associates; and in New York by Mrs Nellie Jones. At various stages I also received useful comments, information or assistance from Professor Robert O'Driscoll, Professor Lorna Reynolds, Professor Ronald Ayling, Senator Michael Yeats and Dr F. F. Farag. I am grateful to Mr Robert Jameson of Microfilming Executors and Methods Organisation Ltd, Dublin, for the reproduction of photoprints; to Mr R. O Farachain of Radio Telefis Eireann for the useful information supplied; to Miss Bea Ramtej for her patience and skill in typing and preparing the final manuscript; to Mr Tim Farmiloe of Macmillan for his enthusiasm and encouragement; to Mr Stan Steinger and his staff of the same firm for their help in seeing the book through the press; and to Mr John Prince for compiling the index.

Thanks are due to the Canada Council for a research grant, and to the University of Lethbridge for a teaching-free semester during the academic year 1974–5.

It is also a pleasant duty to record my appreciation to the staff of the University of Lethbridge Library; the British Library, London; the National Library of Ireland, Dublin; Trinity College Library, Dublin; the British Drama League Library, London; and the New York Public Library.

The editor and publishers wish to thank the following who have kindly given permission for the use of copyright material.

Reprinted from the *Literary Review*, Autumn 1957, Vol. 1, No. 1 and published by Fairleigh Dickinson University, Rutherford, New Jersey.
Faber and Faber Ltd for the extract from *My Brother's Keeper*, by Stanislaus Joyce.
Leslie Frewin Publishers Ltd for the extract 'Did you Know Yeats', by Denis Johnston, from *A Paler Shade of Green*, edited by Des Hickey and Gus Smith.
Harper's Magazine Co. for the extract 'Personal Impressions of W. B. Yeats', by Charles Johnston, from *Harper's Weekly*, XLVIII, 20 Feb 1904.
A. M. Heath & Co. Ltd on behalf of the Estate of the late Diarmuid Russell for George W. Russell's letter to Joyce.
William Heinemann Ltd, for Mrs Eva Reichman, and Alfred A. Knopf Inc. for the extract 'First Meetings with W. B. Yeats' from *Mainly on the Air*, by Max Beerbohm.
Irish Independent Newspapers Ltd for extracts from newspaper articles.
The Irish Times for the newspaper review, 'The Plough and the Stars: Mr Sean O'Casey's New Play', in *The Irish Times*, 12 Jan 1926.
J. B. Lippincott Company for 'With Mr W. B. Yeats in the Woods of Coole' by Cornelius Weygandt from *Lippincott's Magazine*, LXXIII, Apr 1904.
Macmillan Publishing Co. Inc., New York, for the extract 'With The Poet in Merrion Square' from *Inishfallen, Fare Thee Well (Autobiographies)* by Sean O'Casey, copyright 1949.
Meanjin Quarterly, University of Melbourne, for the extract 'Conversations with W. B. Yeats' by Louis Esson from *Louis Esson and the Australian Theatre* by Vance Palmer.
Methuen & Co. Ltd for the extract 'Yeats at the Arts Club' from *The Dublin of Yesterday* by P. L. Dickinson.
Modern Drama for the article 'Profiles of a Poet', by Gabriel Fallon from *Modern Drama*, Vol. VII, No. 3, Dec 1964.
New Republic for the extract 'Meeting Yeats' by F. H. from *Books and Things*, *New Republic*, XIII, 24 Nov 1917.
The *New York Times* for 'The Early Days of the Irish National Theatre' by P. J. Kelly, 1 June 1919, © 1919, reprinted by permission.
The *North American Review* for 'Some Impressions of My Elders: William Butler Yeats' by St John Ervine from *North American Review*, CCXI, Feb/Mar 1920. Reprinted with the permission of the University of Northern Iowa.
A. D. Peters & Co., on behalf of Clifford Bax, for 'Yeats at Woburn' from *Inland Far* by Clifford Bax, published by William Heinemann Ltd.
Roche Son & Neale, executors for Henry W. Nevinson, for the extract 'Vacillation' from *Fire of Life*.
Sir John and Michael Rothenstein for the extract 'Sonnets and Revolutions' by William Rothenstein, from *Men and Memories: Recollections 1872–1900*.
The Society of Authors, as the literary representative of the Estate of John Masefield and Macmillan Publishing Co. Inc., New York, for 'My First

Meeting with Yeats' from *Some Memories of W. B. Yeats*, copyright 1940 by John Masefield, renewed 1968 by Judith Masefield.

The *Spectator* for the article 'Sidelight' by Compton MacKenzie from the *Spectator*, CXCIII, 1 Oct 1954.

Mrs Sylvia Strong for the extract 'Reminiscences of W. B. Yeats' by L. A. G. Strong from the *Listener*, LI, 22 Apr 1954, and 'Yeats at His Ease' from the *London Magazine*, II, No. 3, Mar 1955.

A. P. Watt & Son on behalf of M. B. Yeats and Miss Anne Yeats for the extract 'What We Try To Do' by W. B. Yeats from *Sunday Record Herald*, 4 Feb 1912, and for the letter to James Joyce from W. B. Yeats.

The publishers have made every effort to trace the copyright holders but if they have inadvertently overlooked any, they will be pleased to make the necessary arrangements at the first opportunity.

Introduction

A definitive biography of W. B. Yeats does not exist. There are already at least three books in print which are properly classified as biographies of Yeats. Joseph Hone's *W. B. Yeats: 1865–1939* was published in 1943,[1] and it was the result of considerable discussion with the poet's widow, his family and friends. Naturally, a high degree of tact had to be maintained, and a good deal of detail excluded, lest anyone's feelings be wounded. So there are many vacant places in Hone's book. The same applies, though perhaps in different measure, to Professor A. Norman Jeffares's *W. B. Yeats: Man and Poet* and Professor Richard Ellmann's *Yeats: The Man and the Masks*, both published in 1949. Mrs Yeats gave both Professor Jeffares and Professor Ellmann access to some materials. Still, certain things were not made available for publication, and both biographers must have accepted this restriction in good spirit. So, in effect, an authorised biography in the full sense of that phrase, a biography with any claim to the quality of being definitive, such as Professor Ellmann's life of James Joyce, could not with decency have been proposed until after Mrs Yeats's death in 1968.

Nearly six years ago the Oxford University Press suggested to Senator Michael Yeats that the time had come for such a biography of his father, and proposed Professor Denis Donoghue as the person to write it. This was warmly welcomed by Senator Yeats and the press's subsequent invitation to Professor Donoghue to write the 'authorised, definitive Life of Yeats' was gladly taken up. Professor Donoghue was not immediately free to start on the work but contracts were signed. Some time ago, however, certain problems arose which, despite the good will in all of the interested parties, could not be resolved to Professor Donoghue's satisfaction, and he has recently asked the publisher to release him from his contract.

Professor Donoghue's attitude was that if the phrase 'authorised biographer' meant anything, it meant that he should have sole access to unpublished materials, and sole use of them during the years in which he would be at work on the biography. 'My position was that . . . the entire Yeats industry, so far as unpublished biographical material was in question, should have been closed down on the day on which I signed the contract as authorized biographer.'[2]

Senator Yeats's attitude, on the other hand, was that while he would do everything possible to help Professor Donoghue in the work, he could not 'close down the entire "Yeats industry" for an indefinite period'. On 29 November 1972, he wrote to the Oxford University Press that he had now adopted, in giving scholars access to unpublished materials, the following form of warning: 'I should perhaps warn you, however, that I may not be in a position to allow publication of any of this material, until Denis Donoghue's "authorized biography" has been published.' This, however, did not satisfy Professor Donoghue, who felt that its only effect was to convince him that he was not to have sole access to anything.

Yeatsian scholars, therefore, have to wait for the official biography of the poet.[3] In the meantime, the much augmented edition of Yeats's letters, at present in the capable editorial hands of John Kelly and Eric Domville, will not appear for some years and the separate publication of individual unpublished letters has been proscribed. Such letters, however, would surely produce many new interesting details of the poet's life and perhaps reveal more of his views. Admirers of Yeats will also be pleased to learn of the publication of his unfinished novel *The Speckled Bird*, which is in several respects autobiographical and at which Yeats worried sporadically in the late 1890s.

The present collection of interviews and recollections is a small effort to contribute to Yeats scholarship. It is hoped that it will constitute an added source of material for future biographical research.

E. H. MIKHAIL

NOTES

1. This edition was misdated 1942.
2. Denis Donoghue, 'Viewpoint', *Times Literary Supplement* (London), 16 Feb 1973, p. 178.
3. The Provost of Trinity College Dublin, Professor F. S. L. Lyons, has been commissioned to write it.

Interviews and Recollections

W. B. Yeats at School*

I have just been glancing at the recently published volume entitled 'Plays for an Irish Theatre,' by W. B. Yeats. I use the word 'glancing' advisedly, for I must confess to being a member of that vulgar herd who can neither read nor understand the writings of my gifted fellow-countryman. As I closed the book quite a host of boyish memories crossed my mind of the days when I was a classmate of the Irish poet, as if it were but yesterday, although it is over five-and-twenty years ago since Yeats entered the High School, Dublin. As he took his seat, as was customary for new pupils to do, near the head-master's desk, while prayers were being said, we found ourselves wondering at the strange appearance of the 'new boy,' and speculating as to what class he would be sent into. It so happened that he came into mine—the Upper Fourth—and for nearly four years I was the class-fellow of one who perhaps, of all the brilliant boys the school has turned out, was the most brilliant, or at all events has achieved most fame. In appearance he was thin and gaunt-looking, with long, dark locks and a vacant expression, and at once we unanimously put him down as being of the 'clever' type. At all events, we felt that in the newcomer we had obtained no acquisition to either our cricket or our football ranks, and valued him accordingly. He took his seat demurely at the end of the class, and in the shyness of his disposition seemed to shrink within himself. He certainly, I remember well, took little interest in what was going on around him, and I can see him now, looking dreamingly out of the opposite window, which offered no more enticing vision than a cobbled yard with a grim-looking washed wall for a background. He then must have been about sixteen years of age, but tall at that, and his altogether 'lanky' appearance made him appear even more so. With that perception which schoolboys are rarely lacking in in summing up their fellows, we soon grew to understand and feel that there was an 'unusual' amongst us; but little did we dream of the embryo genius we barely tolerated in our midst.

As a task-learner Yeats was, I may say without exaggeration, a failure, and in some respects a hopeless failure. I can readily recall to mind his floundering through the routine tasks set for every day, oftentime bringing down upon himself the censure, and sometimes the ridicule of his masters. This was particularly true of him where mathematics were concerned; that is to say, mathematics as we schoolboys understood them. Although in this connection I may mention that there was in the class at the time I refer to a youngster, not more than fourteen years of age, who was brilliant in this

* _T. P.' s Weekly_ (London) XIX, no. 500, 7 June 1912, 709 (reminiscences by a classmate).

particular, as indeed he was in all his studies. I refer to the now well-known scientist and physicist, Professor Thrift, of Dublin University, who, before he had attained to manhood, had achieved a remarkably brilliant collegiate career. I do not think that the now famous poet ever cared or took the trouble to understand the mysteries of algebra, geometry, or Euclid. At all events, I have seen him floundering hopelessly before the blackboard, and I believe that he never once accomplished the task of solving a quadratic equation, as he certainly never achieved the distinction of doing a cut from Euclid. In classics he held his own fairly well, while in history he displayed not a little superiority to all of us. But he generally impressed one as being quite uninterested in all about him, with a vacancy of manner that amounted to even absent-mindedness. He made few friends, for although mild and docile—rarely his voice was heard except when answering a question—there was something quietly repellent in his manner which affected even his relations with his masters. At playtime he almost invariably kept to himself, reading, as we then thought, the day's tasks that were yet unfinished, but probably some of those old folk-lore stories that have influenced his mind and writings so much. He was, as all such boys in a big school must be, the victim of much careless banter, and many a thoughtless schoolboy joke, which he suffered uncomplainingly. As time progressed, we got to know and understand him better, and permitted him to go his way undisturbed. Oftentimes we saw traces of what we now know to have been his genius, but which we then mistook for eccentricity. In the matter of prize-winning Yeats was by no means a success, a natural result of his desultory study, and was rarely ever near 'the top of the class.' On more than one occasion I have seen him the recipient of what was known as a 'detention card,' the result of unsuccessful answering in any subject, and which carried with it the humiliation of its owner having to bring it home to be signed by his parent or guardian, and which further entailed the loss of the Saturday half-holiday. His leaving the school was as uneventful as his coming. At the opening of the new term his place in the class was vacant, and we soon forgot all about him.

During the time I speak of Yeats was a most ardent entomologist, although I must confess, if any of us boys had been so informed at the time we would have had but vague ideas of what was meant. We knew him better by the more homely 'insect collector,' and as such he was more or less looked down upon by those connoisseurs of birds' eggs and postage stamps amongst us. He always carried in his pockets—and I quite remember that he had a number of those boyish necessities—several little cardboard boxes and pill-boxes, filled with his victims, and sometimes the more favoured few were permitted to gaze at (to him, at all events) their wonderful contents. On one occasion this hobby got him into dire disgrace. One day while in class—history, I think, was the subject—a beetle had the temerity to cross the floor. Nobody made any attempt to interrupt its progress. Suddenly, however, Yeats's eye rested on it. With one bound he was off his seat, sprawling on the floor, and soon had his captive in his possession. The master was outraged at this unseemly interruption to his discourse, and poor Yeats paid the penalty of having to report himself to the head-master, who severely admonished him, and set him a task which occupied him for several hours after school-time.

Only the other day I met an old schoolfellow, now a doctor in a London suburb. We fell to talking over old times, and those most pleasant of all old times—our schooldays. 'Tell me,' he said, 'isn't Yeats the poet the Yeats who was in class with us at school, and whom we always regarded as being such a "queer" chap.' 'He is,' I said.

Yeats at the High School*

JOHN EGLINTON

Yeats in the High School was a kind of super-boy, who enjoyed an enviable immunity from the various ignominies of school-discipline. After days of absence, he would suddenly slide into his seat—beside me as it happened for some time—and apply himself diligently to his work; I remember him chiefly in the mathematical class, and his quick reply 'Oh, yes!' to my incredulous enquiry whether he actually *liked* geometry and algebra. His privileged standing among the boys was due, no doubt, to some arrangement with his father, who had applied certain educational principles to his children's upbringing, of which spontaneous development was the essential; and Yeats was really an unusually well-read young man of about 19, with a conscious literary ambition. Some knowledge of classics and 'grammar' were graces to be added, and there was a singular charm in his deference to those who in these respects were better equipped than himself.

I used to feel flattered when he would mention Huxley or Herbert Spencer, names which had hardly come within my ken, and avowed himself a complete 'evolutionist.' From his talk and his allusions to his doings out in Howth, where he lived, I thought of him chiefly as a naturalist; he looked like my notion of one, with his sallow skin and a certain grey coat he wore which hung loosely about his lithe figure. One morning he came in full of the project of starting a school field-club, and strove to persuade the Head-Master, who listened to him with a quizzical smile. It must be said that Mr. Wilkins had neither then nor subsequently a very high opinion of Yeats: 'the flighty poet,' he used to call him, though he admitted later that Yeats was able to 'get about.' The truth is that it was

* *Erasmian* (Dublin) xxx (June 1939) 11 – 12.

only in later life that Yeats became a serious student of books, and especially of philosophy; with the result that he had a great 'second period,' in which he wrote poems weighted almost overmuch with reflection and recondite allusion.

The Head-Master's brother, George Wilkins, to whose room we had to adjourn for a formidable hour of instruction in the classics, had an even less favourable opinion of Yeats. The patience and docility required in the early stages of the study of Greek and Latin were not his characteristics, and he had his crib spread out inside his text-book when called upon to translate. Years afterwards, when George Wilkins was a Fellow of Trinity College, he took me to task one day outside the College gate for my association with the new Irish Literary Movement. 'I hear,' he said, 'you are in with Yeats and his crowd—the Irish language and all that! There is nothing in it, as you ought to know, or anyone who has been into a really great literature like the Greek!' This was not quite accurate. In those days Yeats used to greet me genially as 'the enemy,' and he himself had only entered into an alliance with the Language movement, with a view to the 'encirclement' of the old Anglo-Irish culture, against which he was himself a rebel.

One rather trifling recollection I have of Yeats at the High School, which is perhaps worth mentioning. There was a certain boy whom no one liked and who was left a good deal to himself; a 'sneak' someone called him, not for anything he had done but as a name for a certain type of unpopular boy. I do not think that otherwise there was anything of special interest in this one. During the play-hour one day I was surprised to see Yeats walking up and down with this boy, in grave conversation. The sight impressed me at the time and I think now it showed that in the youthful Yeats we had amongst us not only a poet but a student of souls.

NOTE

'John Eglinton' (William Kirkpatrick Magee) (1868–1961) was an Irish essayist and poet. He appears in George Moore's *Hail and Farewell* and James Joyce's *Ulysses*. His works include *Two Essays on the Remnant* (1896), *Pebbles from a Brook* (1901), *Bards and Saints* (1906), *Anglo-Irish Essays* (1917), *Irish Literary Portraits* (1935), *A Memoir of A.E.* (1937) and *Confidential; or, Take It or Leave It* (1951). Eglinton was a school friend of Yeats.

Portrait of Yeats*

JOHN EGLINTON

My acquaintance with Yeats began in the High School in Dublin, where for some time I sat next to him in class. He lived out at Howth, and came and went as he pleased, a yellow-skinned, lank, loose-coated figure, for he was several years older than any of us, and even had the beginnings of a beard. He was remarkable for the manner in which he attached himself to the most unlikely boys, even those who were avoided by the others, as if they presented a problem to him, and I think we all felt it a kind of distinction to be seen walking with him. Certainly I remembered feeling honoured when he borrowed a copy of Gray's poems from me, and returned it scrupulously next day. He was strong in algebra and Euclid, and I recollect the readiness with which, during an examination, he would shift his position so as to make it convenient for me to 'cog' from him. It is true that in another class-room, the classical master's, our relations were reversed, and I think I was able to be of some small assistance to him in translating Demosthenes. Yeats's manner of translating, with the crib laid inside his book for all to see, was an unfailing delight to the classical master—a cruel man to the rest of us—who sat quivering in all his fat while Yeats did his turn, and I can still see the doubtful look which would come over Yeats's face when he became aware of how his efforts were being received. 'So that is your notion of Demosthenic fire?' our tyrant would ask amid the general relaxation. We had to read aloud our weekly compositions, and I think Yeats's were a little above us all, the English master not excepted (I recollect a cryptic one beginning 'The Norway Rat has a litter of five'), and once there was a constrained pause in the proceedings when Yeats informed us that 'no one could write an essay now except Matthew Arnold'. He held his manuscript thrust out in front of him and declaimed his sentences, just as he did with those of Demosthenes, and curiously I don't think anyone laughed. One week the master took it into his head to make us write our essays in verse, and we looked forward to Yeats's—it was already circulated that he was a poet—but on that day he was careful to be absent, though I remember that next day he enquired kindly about my own.

When Yeats left us at the High School, with 'small Latin and less Greek', we did not quite lose sight of him; presently we began to hear that he was a great poet, and read with wonder his contributions to the *Dublin University*

* Extracted from *Irish Literary Portraits* (London: Macmillan, 1935) pp. 20–2.

Review. The loan of a book by him to one of the boys at the top of the school was an event, as it turned out, of some importance in certain developments in Irish literature: this was Sinnett's *Esoteric Buddhism,* a book which captured the intelligence of half a dozen youths who were preparing to enter Trinity College. The Head Master beheld with dismay the ravages of this spiritual infection, which touched his most promising pupils with the indifference of the Orient to such things as college distinctions and mundane success. I do not know whether Yeats actually had a share in founding a branch of the Theosophical Society, of which he once said that 'it had produced more in literature than Trinity College', but I am quite sure that the Dionysiac spark was kindled about this time in Irish literature.

Yeats in the Making*

CHARLES JOHNSTON

Willie Yeats first comes into the story as a new boy at Harcourt Street school. I remember him as a lanky youth, with shaggy black hair, markedly good-looking and very talkative. He fitted in at once; Irish school-boys are far gentler and more hospitable to the newcomer than boys in England. Willie Yeats and I gravitated together. We had both recently come from English schools. We were about of an age. We both had a passion for experimental science. So we sat together, worked together, gossiped together, paraded the playground together, and, on half-holidays, went on long rambles in the country. The school had once been Dean Swift's mansion; the torch-extinguishers still stand at either side of the doorway, and the vast garden has been turned into a playground, strewn with gravel and overshadowed by huge, ragged elms.

Willie Yeats was strong in mathematics, especially Euclid, and he had a gift for chemistry, but he was no good at all at languages, whether ancient or modern. He just managed to stumble through his Homer, partly with his father's scholarly help, partly by aid of a bad translation. Here, in the tale of Odysseus and the Cyclops, he found the wonderful word 'yeanling' for a young lamb, and presently brought it out triumphantly in class, rendering a famous passage: 'And he placed a yeanling under each!' This won him the title of Yeatling, which stuck for awhile, but for most of the time he was simply Willie Yeats. A day school has not the same opportunities for nicknames as a boarding school. At Derby, for instance, where I passed the three preceding years, a string of boys, and some of the

* Extracted from *Poet Lore* (Boston) XVII, no. 2 (June 1906) 102-12.]

manliest in the number, bore girls' names habitually, and one heard calls for Katie and Amy in the football field and the boathouse, with gruff, unconscious response.

Willie Yeats was even then one of the best and most willing talkers I have ever known. He began by relating all kinds of wonderful things he had accomplished at school in London, with cells and batteries. There was a burglar alarm, distributing shocks from his doorknob. There was the story of a fight. A bigger boy, one of two handsome athletic brothers, had coached him for weeks, sending him in with a final 'You'll do!' to lick his bully. There were fascinating yarns, too, of the days when he was commodore of a model yacht-club, sailing his boat on the Round Pond in Kensington Garden, where the white sails and the ample chestnut branches were reflected together in the rippled mirror of the water. He was a keen critic of the lines of a boat, and expounded the theory of the in keel.

Yeats made his first mark at school as an essayist and revolutionary. He had just discovered Darwinism, and was brimful of the Descent of Man. We had to write on our Favorite study, and Willie Yeats, with malice prepense, chose Evolutionary Botany. That was the first of his writings to win fame, though I doubt if he remembers it today. For weeks after it was handed in, the class-room was full of suppressed lightning. The master, 'Tommy' Foster, was advanced in some ways, glorying greatly in the mathematics of the infinities; but to countenance Yeats' heresy was quite another matter. Nor had he any idea of letting the enormity be debated in class. He decided to suppress Yeats, and Yeats decided not to be suppressed; so the flashes crackled out every now and then among the elements of Euclid.

To one of the boys, whose name may have been Rowbotham, Yeats' evolutionary ideas caused real pain and grief. Rowbotham was a devoted literalist, and between the two, the conflict of science and religion raged for a whole term. Yeats, when he should have been studying the Olynthiacs, pored instead over Grant Allen and Edward Clodd, gathering arrows for the fray, while poor Rowbotham split his head and grieved his heart with the interpretation of the Pentateuch. Yeats, who is now so great a mystic, was frankly a materialist in those days, and it was just a little bit painful to listen to his arguments with his antagonist, for whom all spiritual life depended on the six days of Genesis.

The conflict raged daily beneath the surface, in the class rooms and about the playground, and at last the combatants carried it down to the museum. There Yeats sought missing links, while Rowbotham found irrefragable evidences of special creation. Yeats comes up before the inner eye, as he was in those days: lean, graceful, impetuous, his arms swinging in long curved gestures, his eyes flashing, as he brushed the long black lock from his white forehead. He pointed out adaptations, bridges between kingdoms, the plesiosaurus, the archeopteryx, the duck-billed platypus. His slower opponent, handicapped by religious sensibility, and therefore

easily wounded, doggedly fought all arguments, found objections to all
theories, declared that probable was not proven, and resisted stubbornly,
as one who felt his soul at stake. It was rather a painful battle that thus
raged along the cases of stuffed birds and beasts, and among the remains of
chalky monsters. Finally Yeats was pressed to give positive facts instead of
mere plausible fancies. He quoted paleolithic man, older far than the four
thousand and four years before the nativity to which Rowbotham
passionately clung; and Rowbotham desperately declared that, though
these things might indeed be found, yet 'only in isolated instances,' which
proved nothing. So the matter closed.

Think it not strange that schoolboys should engage in so deep spiritual
matters. It is very likely that never in later life do we feel so keenly the
burden and importunity of immaterial issues; never again are principles so
all important. There were other pathetic spiritual dramas. One boy
confessed that he spent whole nights in prayer, seeking proof of spiritual
realities, and watching for a sign till the dawn broke in grey and rose. Yet
he was by daylight the most inveterate practical joker, and the wittiest;
once he gathered a great crowd in St. Stephen's Green[1] to see the meridian,
which revealed itself as a telegraph wire across a white sky. But Willie
Yeats was not interested in spiritual things; another side of his nature was
being developed. He and I went for long walks on Saturday afternoons,
along the Dodder's amiable, idyllic banks, or over the green foot-hills that
lead to the matted heather of the Dublin mountains, or down by the shore
where fought Brian the Brave,[2] of whom in those days we had never even
heard. Yeats was always the chief speaker, telling, with endless flow of
words, the last thoughts he had gleaned from The Evolutionist at Large,
and plucking a big ox-eye daisy or a bunch of sycamore seeds, with their
pink wings, or a jointed mare's tail to illustrate his view.

'Look at this daisy!' he would say, his big, dark eyes aglow with
enthusiasm, 'you can prove the whole of Evolution from it! It finds it more
advantageous to gather all its flowers in a single colony at the top of the
stalk, and then the flowerets divide into two families, the white flags round
the edge, and the yellow trumpets over the round cushion in the center!'

'Oh, but how can you talk of a daisy deciding to form a colony?'

'That's only a figure of course! The flowers that were more con-
spicuously grouped, attracted more bees, got fertilized soonest, and so
propagated their kind. Among these, some were better fitted than others,
and so it goes on, till the new form is reached!'

Yes, there is the whole of the Origin of Species, in a single daisy, and in
these studies, among fields and woods and by the seashore, the future poet
learned to see the natural world with keen and individual vision. To these
days of wandering and study he owes the wonderful nature touches that fill
his poems; such lines as these:

> 'Autumn is over the long leaves that love us,
>   And over the mice in the barley sheaves;
> Yellow the leaves of the rowan above us,
>   And yellow the wet wild-strawberry leaves.'[3]

I think I could point out the very rowan trees, with their fringed, delicate leaves, by a roadside near the Dublin mountains, that gave him this image. What fresh beauty is given, too, by the individual vision of natural life in lines like these:

> 'And I shall have some peace there, for peace comes dropping slow,
>   Dropping from the veils of the morning to where the cricket sings;
> There midnight's all a glimmer, and noon a purple glow,
>   And evening full of the linnet's wings.'[4]

Nor are these vivid nature-images used for beauty only. From the market of souls, in the 'Countess Cathleen,' one may take lines like these:

> 'Now people throng to sell,
> Noisy as seagulls tearing a dead fish.'

The simile may have come from the strand of Sandymount, or the green, wet boulders of Clontarf, or from Howth, perhaps, a year or so later. The poet transfigures what the evolutionist saw.

II

Then came the period when science began to be humanized and touched with culture. The strongest influence came from the studio of Yeats' father, who with rare wisdom and sympathy aided his son's spiritual growth. Mr. Yeats was, and happily I can still say, is, a rare idealist, a pure worshipper of beauty; full of enthusiasm, full of generous unworldliness, gifted with great artistic insight and power. Somewhat late in life, he determined to devote himself to painting. He has done many admirably sympathetic portraits, and much fine work in black and white; yet he has always felt what he would have gained by an earlier start, and was, therefore, tenderly solicitous of his son's beginnings. A little tale he told me himself will serve to paint him. He had been asked to paint the portrait of some dignitary, who sat, rather solemn and impressive, in his arm-chair. Finally Mr. Yeats came to a stop, his palette and brushes in his hand, and his fine, gentle eyes lit with humorous pathos.

'This won't do at all!' he protested. 'You must praise me! If you don't praise me, I cannot paint you!'

Many of the finer qualities of Willie Yeats' mind were formed in the studio on St. Stephen's Green, in long talks on art and life, on man and God, with his sensitive, enthusiastic father. One remembers the long room, with its skylight, the walls of pale green, frames and canvasses massed along them; a sofa and a big armchair or two; the stout iron stove with its tube; and, filling the whole with his spirit, the artist stepping forward along a strip of carpet to touch his work with tentative brush, then stepping back again, always in movement, always meditating high themes, and now and then breaking into talk on the second part of 'Faust,' or the Hesperian apples, or the relation of villainy to genius.

'The same surcharge of energy makes both,' I remember him saying; 'you must have high positive force to be a successful pirate; a change in environment would have made the same man a great creative artist!'

'Transmutation of energy!' broke in Willie, brushing the shaggy black hair from his eyes, and still hovering in thought between science and art.

'Precisely! That is it exactly!' cried Mr. Yeats, enthusiastic over his son's phrase; 'And now let us have tea!'

The black kettle was brought forth from the cupboard, and set on the stove; a big loaf was duly divided into hunches, liberally buttered; the kettle boiled, the tea was made, and tempered with condensed milk, and the talk on art and life went on.

In those days, Yeats had thoughts of following in his father's footsteps, and becoming an artist in color and form, and much of the view he then held breaks forth in his criticism, for instance, of the pictures of William Blake. He drew well, with sensitive impressionism, and studied hard for some months at the Art Schools in Merrion Square. Indeed, he left school about this time, and gave himself up wholly to drawing, and I saw him more frequently at home, and in the studio. The happiest atmosphere filled his home life, gay, artistic, disinterested, full of generous impracticability. The Yeatses lived in Northumberland Terrace in those days, on the road between Harold's Cross and Terenure, and the artistic spirit radiated out from everything in the house, sketches, pictures, books, and the perpetual themes of conversation. Mr. Yeats loved to read aloud to his children, and I remember many a humorous scene when Mrs. Yeats, who used to take a little nap during the reading, was called on suddenly to tell the subject. She invariably repeated the last sentence, with a quaint little smile, though an instant earlier she had been fast asleep. Willie Yeats was full of Swinburne in those days, and recited to me many of the Poems and Ballads; chanted them, rather; and even now, phrases came back, ringing with his voice, and lit with his dark eyes: 'A girdle of arms for the queen's daughter;' and then, in the closing line: 'The pains of hell for the queen's daughter.'

While still determinedly drawing from the white plaster models in Merrion Square, Willie Yeats began to write verse also. He used to read or repeat to me his earliest poems, as we sat in his little room, or walked on our interminable rambles, towards the mountains or the sea. The first verses came forth out of a vast murmurous gloom of dreams, and were full of vague, enormous shapes of some supernatural forest. In the later days of precise enameling, of dainty word-music, I have many a time regretted the largeness and epic sweep of the earliest work, much of which was never published. I remember a few lines of that early date:

> 'Dwelt the princess great Wiagin
> Fairest child of Sweden old,
> In her castle by the Baltic
> In her towers calm and cold' . . .

There were also 'a timid folk who dwelt among the pines' . . . and a majestic Sintram, 'a great twin brother,' who revealed himself a shining form, in the gold and crimson of sunset, and who was bound by mysterious destiny with his earthly counterpart.

In the work of the earliest days, there was nothing to reveal or even suggest the poet of mystical Ireland; no consciousness, even, of any special poetical material to be drawn from mystic Eire. One can realize this by turning over the leaves of the earlier book of verse, or, better still, by noting the order of first publication in the rare folios of the *Dublin University Review*. There were Princesses of Sweden, there were Greek islands with a mystical people of statues; there were Moorish magicians, Spanish Inquisitors, and Indian Sages; nothing peculiarly Celtic or Irish; yet everywhere a largeness, a vague gloom, an imaginative and dreamy depth, a sense of cavernous things, of overhanging deeps, from which were presently to issue the more purely Celtic forms of vision and of dream.

The determining force was doubtless found in the friendship of John O'Leary,[5] the old man eloquent, who had returned from years of exile to his native land. For the artistic visionaries and dreamers, who were always meditating large, vague actions, there was something fascinating and irresistible in the man of action, who had not only dreamed but dared; who had staked his life on an ideal, and sacrificed his youth and manhood for a forlorn hope. Yet man of actions as he was, John O'Leary was the greatest dreamer of them all. He was full of large philosophic thought, a lover of the Neoplatonists, a devotee of Ideas. It was either from him or through his influence that Willie Yeats now got the poems of Sir Samuel Ferguson,[6] which finally crystalized his shadowy purposes and dreams, and made him from henceforth the chosen singer of Gaelic mysticism. He pored over the dusty volumes of the Royal Irish Academy, and the versions of the Gaelic Text Society, saturating himself with legends and traditions, and delightedly perceiving that all that he had noted of natural beauty in his own land was available for his new themes.

From these mingled influences came 'The Wanderings of Oisin,' which was printed, if I mistake not, in the *Dublin University Review*, in the autumn of 1884 or the spring of 1885. For me, it is subject of regret that he has retouched the name and many a passage in the body of the work; yet this epical story ever fills me with wonder and delight; and it is especially dear to me, as holding more of the swift movement and large multitudinous action which I miss in much of his later work, but which was so powerful a part of the first unpublished writings. Here is a passage from the first Book:

'Caolte, and Conan, and Finn were there,
When we followed a deer with our baying hounds,
With Bran, Sgeolan, and Lomair,
And passing the Firbolgs' burial mounds,
Came to the cairn-heaped grassy hill
Where passionate Maive is stony still;
And found on the dove-gray edge of the sea
A pearl-pale, high-born lady, who rode
On a horse with bridle of findrinny;
And like a sunset were her lips,
A stormy sunset on doomed ships;
A citron colour gloomed in her hair,
But down to her feet white vesture flowed,
And with the glimmering crimson glowed
Of many a figured embroidery' . . .

More characteristic, both in movement and rhythm, is the following from the third Book:

'Fled foam underneath us, and round us a wandering and milky smoke,
High as the saddle-girth, covering away from our glances the tide;
And those that fled, and that followed, from the foam-pale distance broke;
The immortal desire of immortals we saw in their faces, and sighed.'

NOTES

Between 1884 and 1888 Yeats wanted to find intellectual support for his vague feelings of rebellion. With George Russell, who wrote under the pseudonym AE, he was soon deep in occult study. Around the two eager young men gathered several others; one was Yeats's schoolfellow Charles Johnston (1867–1931), son of a well-known Protestant Member of Parliament from Ulster, who decided to give up his idea of becoming a missionary for once he became converted to esoteric Buddhism. Johnston made a summary of the theosophists' theories of spiritual evolution in the *Dublin University Review* in July 1885. According to Johnston, the soul passes through seven rounds, each being a passage round the seven planets and through all the races. This article was a paper he had read to a new group known as the Dublin Hermetic Society. The Society was started, according to a note in the same issue of the magazine, 'to promote oriental religions and theosophy generally'. In 1886, Johnston crossed to London to interview Madame Blavatsky, and returned to form the famous Dublin Theosophical Lodge, which for many years had rooms in Ely Place. Yeats was never a member of the Lodge, though he was in and out of the rooms a great deal, chiefly to see George Russell, who quickly assumed leadership of the little community. Johnston went to Russia to marry Madame Blavatsky's niece.

1. St Stephen's Green is a park in Dublin.
2. Brian Boru, the semi-mythical chief and High King of Ireland, was killed at the battle of Clontarf in 1014.
3. W. B. Yeats, 'The Falling of the Leaves', *Crossways* (1889).
4. W. B. Yeats, 'The Lake Isle of Innisfree', *The Rose* (1893).
5. John O'Leary (1830–1907) turned to revolutionary journalism under the influence of Davis; edited the *Irish People;* was arrested in 1865 in the great wake of Fenian arrests and

sentenced to twenty years, but served only nine; exiled, he chose Paris for a home until allowed to return to Ireland in 1885. There he made friends with the Yeats family and deeply impressed the young W. B., who later wrote of 'O'Leary's noble head'. His principal books are *Young Ireland* (1885), *What Irishmen Should Read* (1889) and *Recollections of Fenians and Fenianism* (1896). It was at the Contemporary Club that Yeats met O'Leary, who became a chief stimulating impact upon his life and awakened in him the desire of intellectual leadership in Ireland. When O'Leary lent Yeats the poems of Davis and of other patriots, of whom he knew nothing, he read them eagerly. Yeats's *The Wanderings of Oisin, and Other Poems* (1889) was published chiefly by O'Leary's effort; he scraped together most of the subscriptions which induced Kegan Paul to launch a new poet.

6. Sir Samuel Ferguson (1810–86), Irish poet and antiquary; published *Congal, an Epic Poem* (1872) and *Lays of the Western Gael* (1885). Yeats's first published piece of criticism was an article on Ferguson in the *Dublin University Review* in 1886. The article was an eulogy of a poet lately dead, whose work had been the largest effort yet made to interpret through the medium of English the history and the spirit of Gaelic Ireland. It was rhetorical, and Yeats did not stand by it at a later date.

Personal Impressions of W. B. Yeats*

CHARLES JOHNSTON

I knew W. B. Yeats before he had discovered in himself the divine faculty of verse, though his life was already full of vision. In those early days his tendency was toward science, and we carried out together a number of more or less ingenious and unsuccessful experiments in physics, chemistry, and electricity, with home-made contrivances often destined for quite other uses. Our researches soon took a different field, which, I have always thought, was of high importance for Yeats's poetry. He was a rabid Darwinian, and, like all new proselytes, longed for a convert; and I, as his school chum, was the natural prey. So Yeats spent the hours that should have gone to Homer and Horace in pursuit of test cases and missing links, with which I was in due time to be belabored; and many a delightful afternoon we spent roaming over the Dublin hills, or the cliffs of Howth, Yeats holding forth on evolutionary botany, while I listened, commented, and at the end of ends, declared myself still unconvinced. Unconvinced of the materialism that so often goes with Darwinism, that is; though accepting the idea of growth and development.

Then came the first poems. And I remember some, never so far published, I believe, which filled my imagination with a large and sombre magnificence, and had in many ways a broader sweep, a larger handling than any of his later works.

* *Harper's Weekly* (New York) XLVIII, 20 Feb 1904, p. 291.

And soon after this came poems for the first time printed, in the newly founded and ill-starred *Dublin University Review*,[1] which was presently to be disowned by its *alma mater* for printing one of the burning idyls of Theocritus.[2] Among these first-printed works, I remember 'Mosada,'[3] a dramatic poem of mediaeval Spain, with Moors and witchcraft; and 'The Island of Statues,'[4] Greek in coloring, but after the Greece of Keats rather than the authentic Hellas.

Thus Yeats's early work was drawn, as to its subject, from the universal material of romance, from many European lands; and it was only after he had already written a good deal, that he found his proper subject-matter in Gaelic tradition, learning it first under the mentorship of Sir Samuel Ferguson,[5] who has written so well, with such genuine bardic fervor, of the heroes of Gaelic eld. 'The Wanderings of Oisin'[6] was among the first-fruits of this new inspiration.

Then came an Oriental period, full of the study of Eastern religion and Indian books. There are traces of it in poems like 'Anashuya and Vijaya,'[7] and in the two·Sermons of Kanva the Indian.[8] From India and her philosophy, Yeats presently came to the Western mystics, from Jakob Boehme[9] to William Blake; and all through his later work, whether as theory or as symbolism, his mystical studies have left their mark.

Here, then, we may say, are certain of the elements of culture which make up the poetical substance of Yeats's work: the mediaeval romance of all lands, the Gaelic tradition, the teaching of India, the mystics of the West. Whatever be his substance, whatever his form, lyric, epic, drama, the magical music, the fineness and distinction, the transmutation through passion and thought are there always; perhaps in their perfection in 'The Lake Isle of Innisfree':

I will arise and go now, and go to Innisfree,
   And a small cabin build there, of clay and wattles made;
Nine bean rows will I have there, a hive for the honey bee,
   And live alone in the bee-loud glade.

And I shall have some peace there, for peace comes dropping slow,
   Dropping from the veils of the morning to where the cricket sings.
There midnight's all a glimmer, and noon a purple glow,
   And evening full of the linnet's wings.

I will arise and go now, for always night and day
   I hear lake water lapping with low sounds by the shore;
While I stand on the roadway, or on the pavement gray,
   I hear it in the deep heart's core.

NOTES

1. The *Dublin University Review* was published between 1885 and 1887.
2. Greek pastoral poet of the third century BC; little is known of his life history. Regarded as creator of pastoral poetry, of his work about thirty idylls and a number of epigrams are extant.
3. W. B. Yeats, *Mosada: A Dramatic Poem* (Dublin: Sealy, Bryers and Walker, 1886).
4. W. B. Yeats, 'The Island of Statues', *Dublin University Review*, (Apr –July 1885).
5. For a note on Sir Samuel Ferguson see p. 13.
6. W. B. Yeats, *The Wanderings of Oisin and Other Poems* (London: Kegan Paul, Trench, 1889).
7. W. B. Yeats, 'Anashuya and Vijaya', *Crossways* (1889).
8. W. B. Yeats, 'The Indian upon God' and 'The Indian to His Love', *Crossways* (1889).
9. Jakob Boehme (1575– 1624), German theosophist and mystic, author of *Aurora, oder die Morgenröte im Aufgang*, manuscript of which was condemned as heretical by ecclesiastical authorities. Yeats read him in William Law's book on Boehme, *An Illustration of the Deep Principles of Jacob Boehme, the Teutonic Philosopher* (1763).

With Mr W. B. Yeats in the Woods of Coole*

CORNELIUS WEYGANDT

Three experiences come into my mind oftenest when I think of our three weeks in Ireland. I think of the earnest faces of the young actors that I saw rehearsing plays of Ireland's old wars and older dream in a bare hall back of a produce shop in a Dublin suburb; I think of the Arctic hare that ran before me as I climbed Knocknarea, that long green mountain that lies like the keel of a great ship, driven in from the Atlantic, overturned and stranded, between Sligo Bay and Ballisadare Bay; and I think of a walk with a dream-wrapt poet in the Woods of Coole.[1] There were other experiences as new to me as these three: there was the ballad that broke my first sleep in Ireland, a ballad sung at midnight under my window in Queenstown by a street singer who wove into twenty stanzas praise of Ireland's heroes and England's foes from Brian Boru to DeWet; there was that dinner at the little inn at Inchegeela, topped off with brown bread and heather-honey from the Kerry mountains; there were the voteens[2] doing the Stations of the Cross around a holy well at the base of Croagh Patrick preparatory to their long journey up into the clouds that capped the top of that sacred mountain; there was the spectral procession of men and ponies through the mists that clung to the summits of the Meenawn cliffs, mists so deep that the foals that followed hung close to their dams' heels, and even

* *Lippincott's Magazine* (Philadelphia) LXXIII (Apr. 1904) 484 –7.

the collies were afraid to range through the white heather; there were the wild-eyed men and women that, huddled together in silent groups, watched us sharply as we halted in the weird twilight of a sullen August evening in Doagh, that little fishing village all but at the uttermost end of bare Achill, men that still go to sea in skin-covered curraghs[3] such as their fathers used in Cæsar's time, women that still stain their skirts garnet-red with the sea-stain that their mothers used when they toiled as slaves in the raths of the sea-rovers out of far Lochlin; there was the far vision of the past that opened before me as I saw the stone circle and trilithons of Leacht-Con-mic-Ruis under a stormy black-gold sky, while the rabbits scurried into holes sunk in earth once red with the blood of sacrifice, while the lapwings called plaintively as they lifted and beat their way across the ruins of a great stone fort and on towards Lough Gill and the storied Mountains of the Ox to the southward;—these and many other things I shall remember, but longer than these the earnest faces of the young actors in the half-light, the white hare among the purple ling,[4] and longest the poet telling me of the other world the peasants know and chanting his own visionary songs.

It was a dull, gray morning that we drove over the Galway plain from Ardrahan to Coole, where Mr. Yeats was one of a house party, a morning when such shafts of light as broke through the leaden clouds served only to make harsher the gray tone of the landscape. The aspect of earth and sky had not changed except to take on something of the eeriness of twilight when that afternoon I walked with Mr. Yeats in the Woods of Coole. All morning we had talked in the great library of Lady Gregory's home of the old far-off things of Ireland's past, that past that until yesterday was all but forgotten by the lettered and that Mr. Yeats has done so much to recall; and of the very near things of Ireland's present, of the men that are giving to English literature legends as fascinating as any in 'Morte d'Arthur' or 'Mabinogion'[5] and imaginings of a rare and fresh beauty that our age had thought men could hardly make again. We had talked too of the English poets, of the great men gone, of the men among us that may be great. But always the talk turned again to the many phases of the movement that is striving to give Ireland a national life—to the Celtic art in Loughrea Cathedral; to Irish painting; to Irish music and to Mr. Yeats's own theories of the chanting of verse to the psaltery; and to 'The Irish Literary Theatre,' whose work, then ended, was to be so successfully carried on later by 'The Irish National Theatre Society.'[6]

Six years before Mr. Yeats had written me, 'The chief influences on my work have been Irish folk-lore and mythology and certain mystics of the Middle Ages.' Of these things we had not yet spoken, and I forgot to speak at all of Ruysbroeck[7] and Paracelsus[8] and Boehme,[9] as I had thought to, but Mr. Yeats told me much of Irish folk-lore that afternoon as we walked in the old garden, cut off from the woods by its great wall, and on into the woods themselves, and by the shore of Coole Lake. It is but a few miles from Coole to the sea, so few that the great gales from the Atlantic beat southeastward all but the stoutest of the oaks and ashes and firs that push above the general level of the woods. This day, as on so many days, the gray Atlantic clouds banked up over the woods, painting all the world gray. As we stood on the shore of the lake all above us and about us was gray, gray sky over gray water amid gray-green trees—even the grass of the lake's margin was grayer than green. It is a mysterious place at any time; on this gray afternoon it was eerie, and as the day went out in flashes of bewildering light from a broad band of winter-yellow on the western horizon it was more than eerie—it was portentous.

It was very quiet as we walked between the shore and the wood; there was no wind; our footfalls on the soft turf were all but noiseless; the faint skirling of the gulls as they changed position to rest more comfortably on the rocks on the far side of the lake, and the murmur of the water meeting the land, that murmur Mr. Yeats has caught in imperishable phrase—'lake-water lapping with low sounds by the shore,'[10] only emphasized the gray stillness. Sir Bedevere's words to his Lord Arthur on the shore of the lake this side Avalon would come to mind—'the waters wappe and the wawes wanne.' This gray, flat landscape, very like that which a day before had from the train seemed so monotonous and so unromantic, was now, by the presence of water and brooding skies, made quick with the very spirit of wonder. It no longer seemed strange that after walking here the poet should dream in following nights of the phantom shapes of Forgael and Dectora[11] that move through the mists of 'The Shadowy Waters,' or that here and in the lonely villages about he should think out the strange life of Paul Ruttledge that he was now fashioning into the play that has come to be called 'Where There is Nothing.' Mr. Yeats as we walked chanted snatches of the verses he was making. Now it would be the refrain of a song, such as

> 'All that's beautiful drifts away
> Like the waters,'[12]

that he had made the day before and could no more get out of his head than had it been an old tune; now a line that was the heart of a deep thoughted poem, as 'quiet wanders eating her wild heart.'[13] As I to-day read the poems of 'In the Seven Woods' I come upon many lines I recall from Mr. Yeats's chanting that gray August afternoon. Most beautiful of all these are the lines of the title poem itself that prove how 'the green quiet' of these woods dimmed his memory until he could forget

> 'Tara uprooted, and new commonness
> Upon the throne and crying about the streets
> And hanging its paper flowers from post to post,
> Because it is alone of all things happy.'[14]

Mr. Yeats had none of his poems by heart, but he could and did tell me folk-tales with the detail of incident of their peasant repeaters. These old stories, told in his haunting voice by that gray lakeside, carried me all but past the portals of this world to the very verge of that eerie land into which he is so often wrapt away.

Mr. Yeats had never himself seen 'The Other People' in the Woods of Coole, he said, but many of the neighboring peasants had. That the country people had a thorough conviction of the reality of the visions that appeared to them he believed, and he could not believe that some visions they spoke of were imaginings. Perhaps this would be an explanation—just as the highest poetry appealed to some part of a man superior to what Blake called the 'corporeal understanding,' so people of 'The Other World' may appear to those who inherit or develop some special insight the many do not possess. Strange visions had come to him, he said, after walking in these woods, visions of 'immortal, mild, proud shadows,'[15] but always as dreams, and not as objective realities. At times, however, he had seen visions in waking dreams, and he felt the border of the unseen so near that no man should say that no man had crossed it.

Mr. Yeats sometimes wonders if, when a poem stirs us as by magic, there is not an upwelling in us of the universal memory and imagination that have been since the beginning of time and of so little of which we are ordinarily aware. Perhaps it is a real magic that compels this upwelling and that floats upon its flood visions of the past and of the unseen that else we should never see. He thinks that we perhaps feel and see, when reading such a poem, as our pagan ancestors felt and saw as their priest celebrated his magical rites before them. The poet is now maker of magic and seer, as was in old time the priest. If so it is, surely the religion that anteceded Mr. Yeats's poetry celebrated its rites in temples of gray stone builded among desolate gray woods and moors and open to the sky. Surely it was a religion as mysterious as Druidism,[16] only that, unlike that cruel creed, it claimed no victims at blood-red sunrise, but practised its gentler rites on gray days, and reserved its high ceremonials for pale sunsets, whose weird light glitters yet in the eyes of the western Gaels. As I had read Mr. Yeats's poetry I had thought often of the priests of prehistoric Ireland, for everywhere it took me to the borders of the unseen world, whether it was folk-lyric, or old legend retold, or dream remembered long enough to put into words—of the past and the unseen with which these priests by means of their magic were the communicants, as the poets are now with their magic. Now I knew what Mr. Yeats meant by 'Druid charm' and 'Druid light.' I felt the 'Druid charm' that was potent in gray skies over gray water and gray rock and gray-green woods; the bewildering 'Druid light' flashed on me as the sun flickered out in the wintry yellow afterglow at day's end in the Woods of Coole.

NOTES

Cornelius Weygandt (1871–1957) was author of *Irish Plays and Playwrights* (1913), *A Century of the English Novel* (1925), *The Time of Tennyson: English Victorian Poetry As It Affected America* (1936) and *The Time of Yeats: English Poetry of Today against an American Background* (1937).

1. When Yeats met Lady Gregory, the co-founder of the Abbey Theatre, in 1896, she asked him to visit Coole the following summer, and this old house was to become almost a second home to him through many years of his life. Yeats's first poem on Coole was 'In the Seven Woods'.

2. Voteens (Irish)=devotees; very religious persons.

3. Curraghs (Irish)=light boats made of tarred canvas or leather stretched upon wooden ribs.

4. Ling=kind of fish.

5. A collection of Welsh stories of the 1200s and 1300s.

6. In 1902 the Irish National Theatre Society, which eventually became the Abbey Theatre, was founded, with Yeats as President and George Russell (AE) as Vice-President, to continue on a more permanent basis the work begun by the Irish Literary Theatre under the directorship of Yeats, Edward Martyn and George Moore.

7. Jan van Ruysbroeck (1293–1381), Flemish mystical theologian, known as 'the Ecstatic Doctor'.

8. Phillipus Aureolus Paracelsus (1493?–1541), Swiss alchemist, physician and author of medical and occult works.

9. See footnote p. 15.

10. W. B. Yeats, 'The Lake Isle of Innisfree', *The Rose* (1893).

11. Forgael and Dectora are characters in Yeats's play *The Shadowy Waters* (1911).

12. W. B. Yeats, 'The Old Men Admiring Themselves in the Water', *In the Seven Woods* (1904).

13. W. B. Yeats, 'In the Seven Woods', *In the Seven Woods* (1904).

14. Ibid.

15. W. B. Yeats, 'I Walked among the Seven Woods of Coole', *The Shadowy Waters* (1906).

16. The religious and philosophical system of the Druids ('an order of men among the ancient Celts of Gaul and Britain, who, according to Caesar were priests or religious ministers and teachers, but who figure in native Irish and Welsh legend as magicians, sorcerers, soothsayers, and the like'. – *O.E.D.*

Interview with
Mr. W. B. Yeats*

D. N. D[UNLOP]

A few evenings ago I called on my friend, Mr. W. B. Yeats, and found him alone, seated in his arm-chair, smoking his cigarette, with a volume of Homer before him. The whole room indicated the style and taste peculiar to its presiding genius. Upon the walls hung various designs by Blake and other less well-known symbolic artists; everywhere books and papers, in apparently endless profusion.

* *Irish Theosophist* (Dublin) II, no. 1, 15 Oct 1893, 147-9.

In his usual genial way he invited me to have a cup of tea with him. During this pleasant ceremony little was said, but sufficient to impress me more than ever with the fact that my host was supremely an artist, much in love with his art. With a passion deep and entrancing he adores his art: 'his bread is from her lips; his exhilaration from the taste of her.' The Muse finds in him a tongue to respond to her most subtle beauties. In song was handed down the great Solar Religions that advanced the people of antiquity; in song those of a later day received that which caused them to emerge from their cold isolation and kiss 'the warm lips of Hellos'; and in these days, too, we look to the poets for that inspiration which will

> 'Overflow mankind with true desires.
> And guide new Ages on by flights of living lyres'

Tea over, I disclosed the object of my visit. 'Mr. Yeats,' I said, 'I understand that you saw a great deal of Madame Blavatsky[1] in the earlier days of the Theosophical movement in England, and so I thought you might have something to say regarding her, which would interest the readers of the IRISH THEOSOPHIST.'

'Yes,' replied Mr. Yeats, 'I had the privilege of seeing Madame Blavatsky frequently at that time, and so many interesting little incidents crowd in upon me, that I find some difficulty in selecting what might be most interesting to your readers.'

'Well,' I replied, 'suppose you begin by giving your personal impressions.'

'Madame Blavatsky' said Mr. Yeats, 'struck me as being a very strong character. In her ordinary moods, rather combative, and inclined to rub people's prejudices the other way. When depressed she dropped her combativeness, and, thrown back on herself, as it were, became most interesting, and talked about her own life. A clever American, who was not a Theosophist, said to me once: 'Madame Blavatsky has become the most famous woman in the whole world, by sitting in her arm-chair, and getting people to talk to her.'

'I have heard it stated,' said I, 'in connection with the Coloumb incidents,[2] that Madame Blavatsky showed great lack of insight into character.'

'For so powerful a personality,' replied Mr. Yeats, 'she did seem to lack something in that respect. I remember, for instance, on one occasion she introduced me to a French occultist, whom she spoke of very highly, and even urged me to read his books. Within a short time he was expelled from the Society for what appeared excellent reasons. "I have had to expel him," said Madame Blavatsky to me; "he sold a love elixir for two francs; had it been forty francs I might have overlooked the fact." On another occasion she told me, quite seriously, that I would have a severe illness within six months, and I am waiting for that illness still. Attempts are made by people very often,' continued Mr. Yeats, 'to wash humanity out of their

leaders. Madame Blavatsky made mistakes; she was human, and to me
that fact makes her, if possible, the more interesting. Another peculiarity
was her evident lack of proportion. An attack on the Theosophical
movement (she did not seem to mind personal attacks) in some obscure
little paper, was to her of as much importance as if it appeared in the
Times.'

In reply to another question, Mr. Yeats remarked that she had met
Demussét [*sic*][3] a few times, and Balzac[4] once. She had worked a little at
occultism with George Sands [*sic*],[5] but, to use her own words, both were
'mere dabblers' at the time.

'What did you think of Madame Blavatsky as a talker?' I asked.

'It has been said of Dr. Johnson,' replied Mr. Yeats, 'that the effeminate
reader is repelled by him; and the same might be said of Madame
Blavatsky as a talker. She had that kind of faculty which repelled the weak,
and attracted those of a stronger temperament. She hated paradox, and
yet she gave utterance to the most magnificent paradox I ever heard.'

'As you heard her talk a good deal, perhaps you will kindly relate to me
any interesting sayings that occur to you,' said I.

'With pleasure,' replied Mr. Yeats, lighting another cigarette. 'I called
on Madame Blavatsky one day, with a friend—a T. C. D.[6] man. She was
trying to explain to us the nature of the Akas,[7] and was entering into an
exceedingly subtle metaphysical analysis of the difference between
foreknowledge and predestination—a problem which has interested
theologians of ancient, as well as modern times—showing the way in which
the whole question was mixed up with the question of the Akas, when
suddenly she broke off—my friend not following, and said, turning round,
and pointing to one of her followers who was present: "You with your
spectacles and your impudence, you will be sitting there in the Akas to all
eternity—no not to all eternity, for a day will come when even the Akas
will pass away, and then there shall be nothing but God—Chaos—that
which every man is seeking in his heart."'

'At another time, when I called, she seemed rather depressed. "Ah!" she
said, "there is no solidarity among the good; there is only solidarity among
the evil. There was a time when I used to blame and pity the people who
sold their souls to the devil, now I only pity them; I know why they do it;
they do it to have somebody on their side." "As for me I write, write, write,
as the Wandering Jew walks, walks, walks."'

'On one occasion, too,' said Mr. Yeats, continuing, 'she referred to the
Greek Church as the church of her childhood, saying: "The Greek Church,
like all true religions, was a triangle, but it spread out and became a
bramble bush, and that is the Church of Rome; then they came and lopped
off the branches, and turned it into a broomstick, and that is Pro-
testantism."'

In reply to a question, Mr. Yeats said, quoting her own words, with
reference to Col. Olcott: 'Ah! *he* is an honest man; *I* am an old Russian

savage'; and, referring to Mr. Old, she said, with a hearty enthusiasm that, in certain respects, he was above all those about her at that time.

'Can you remember anything in the nature of a prophecy, Mr. Yeats, made by Madame Blavatsky, that might be of interest to record, notwithstanding the fact that you are yet awaiting your prophesied illness?' I asked.

'The only thing of that nature,' replied Mr. Yeats, 'was a reference to England.' 'The Master told me,' said she, 'that the power of England would not outlive the century, and the Master never deceived me.'

'I am very much obliged to you, Mr. Yeats,' said I, 'for the kind manner in which you have responded to my enquiries regarding Madame Blavatsky; perhaps you will pardon me if I ask you one or two questions about your own work now. Do you intend, at any time, publishing a book on "Mysticism"?'

'Yes; at no very distant date I hope to publish a work dealing with mystics I have seen, and stories I have heard, but it will be as an artist, not as a controversialist.'

'And what about your present work?' I asked.

' "Celtic Twilight,"[8] a work dealing with ghosts, goblins, and faeries, will be out shortly; also a small selection of "Blake's Poems," '[9] he replied. 'Then, I am getting ready for publication, next spring, a book of poems, which I intend calling, "The Wind among the Reeds";[10] and, as soon afterwards as possible, a collection of essays, and lectures dealing with Irish nationality and literature, which will probably appear under the title of the "Watch Fire." '

After due apologies for my intrusion, I bade my host good evening, and withdrew feeling more than satisfied with the result of my interview.

Mr. Yeats has often been spoken of as a dreamer, and many strange stories are afloat which go a long way to bear out such a statement. But, in my opinion, he combines the man of thought with the man of action; he is 'whole of heart and sound of head,' and Ireland may, indeed, be proud of one who promises to rank among her most worthy sons.

NOTES

By early 1886 Yeats was involved in occult research, and was particularly interested in the new movement which was called theosophy and which seemed likely to help him to develop his latent possibilities. He needed help to change his personality, to purify himself of timidity, and to learn to control others and himself. He was brought into contact with a system based on opposition to materialism and on support of secret and ancient wisdom, and was encouraged to believe that he would be able to bring together all the fairy tales and folklore he had heard in childhood, the poetry he had read in adolescence, and his dreams. The theosophists gave him support because they accepted and incorporated into their system ghosts and fairies, and regarded dreams and symbols as supernatural manifestations. Whether these ideas took immediate effect or remained latent in his mind, they gave his thought a basis, and the work in which he afterwards embodied his philosophy and theology, *A Vision* (1925), is full of connections with theosophy and is recommended as a text by present day theosophists. On

Yeats and theosophy see Harbans Rai Bachchan, *W. B. Yeats and Occultism* (Delhi, Varanasi, Patna: Motilal Banarsidass, 1965).

1. Elena Petrovna Blavatsky (1831–91), Russian traveller and theosophist. She travelled widely, visiting India and Tibet, and became interested in spiritualism and in the occult. In 1873 she went to the United States, where with Colonel Henry Steel Olcott she founded the Theosophical Society in New York in 1875. She wrote extensively on the esoteric doctrines of India, translated from the Sanskrit, and established the official journal of her movement, the *Theosophist*. At the time of her death, in London, her followers numbered nearly 100,000. Yeats was still hesitating about becoming a theosophist when he moved with his family to London in May 1887. Madame Blavatsky had arrived a month before and within two weeks of her landing had founded a Blavatsky Lodge. Yeats went to call on her with a letter of introduction from his friend Charles Johnston and was immediately persuaded to dismiss his doubts and join the Lodge. Troubled by his self-consciousness and lack of spontaneity, he was especially taken with her because she was so fully herself. While with her he escaped from the restlessness of his own mind, and he was reassured of the validity of his anti-materialist theories by the certainty and erudition with which she expounded them. The tenets of *The Secret Doctrine* (1888), her chief work, are of interest because they brought Yeats for the first time a comprehensive cosmology. See Yeats's allusions to her in his *Autobiographies* (London: Macmillan, 1955) pp. 173–82.

2. Many of Madame Blavatsky's so-called miracles were demonstrated as fraudulent by the Society for Physical Research in 1884.

3. Louis Charles Alfred de Musset (1810–57), French poet and dramatist who conceived a grand passion for George Sand ending in their angry parting in Venice. This breakdown of the great love affair of his life led to his best poetry, some of the most memorable in French romantic literature.

4. Honoré de Balzac (1799–1850), considered the greatest novelist of France. His work is essentially romantic, but so detailed as to make it appear that he is a realist.

5. George Sand is the pseudonym of Amandine Aurore Lucie Duphin, Baronne Dudevant (1804–76), who was a French novelist. She became well known in the literary circles of the Bohemian kind, adopting men's dress smoking pipes and cigars, and being decently promiscuous. More famous and long-lasting than her affair with Alfred de Musset was her liaison with Chopin.

6. Trinity College Dublin.

7. Akasa=a concept by which the mind is enabled to distinguish objects in external perception. In Chinese Buddhism it means dwelling in empty space or a fabulous Buddha living somewhere to the south of our universe.

8. W. B. Yeats, *The Celtic Twilight* (London: Lawrence and Bullen, 1893).

9. W. B. Yeats and E. J. Ellis, eds, *The Works of William Blake, Poetic Symbolic and Critical* (London: Quaritch, 1893).

10. W. B. Yeats, *The Wind among the Reeds* (London: Elkin Mathews, 1899).

Joyce's First Meeting with Yeats*

STANISLAUS JOYCE

The manner of his first meeting with Yeats, of which Gogarty gives a wrong account, has been much discussed, and Yeats himself has given an account of it 'fabled by the daughters of memory'. My brother introduced himself to Yeats, accosting him in the vicinity of the National Library. It is reported that at their first meeting my brother said to Yeats: 'I regret that you are too old to be influenced by me'; and it seems that my brother always denied the story. To the best of my recollection, it is at least substantially correct, though perhaps Jim may have phrased it somewhat differently. As it stands, it sounds rather like one of Yeats's good stories; what is certain is that at that meeting my brother told Yeats how much he admired two stories of his, 'The Tables of the Law', and 'The Adoration of the Magi',[1] and urged him to reprint them. In 'The Day of the Rabblement'[2] my brother had already spoken of them as 'stories which one of the great Russians might have written'. Yeats did reprint them a couple of years later, and in the few lines of preface to the reprint, he said that he had met a young man in Ireland 'the other day', who admired these stories very much and nothing else that he (Yeats) had written. That young man was my brother, unless some other young man told him exactly the same thing, which is improbable, for in that case there would have been at least two 'young men in Ireland' who told him so. The words 'and nothing else that he had written', have been added for dramatic effect. I believe that the other phrase has been similarly edited. I do not think that Yeats ever cared much about pointing a moral, but he undoubtedly liked to adorn a tale.

Already at that time when Yeats was regarded in Dublin as a minor poet and a poseur, and even his friends, except Moore, treated him as an eccentric, whose poetry was likely to find favour only with literary cliques, my brother had claimed for him that his poetry was of the highest order. He considered him to be the greatest poet Ireland had produced, with only Mangan[3] worthy to be his predecessor, and the greatest of contemporary English poets. I have no doubt that he said so to Yeats. He was not the kind of youth to stint his praise of work he admired, and more than once (in the case of Italo Svevo,[4] for example, and to some extent of Dujardin)[5] he

* Stanislaus Joyce, *My Brother's Keeper* (London: Faber and Faber, 1957) pp. 182–6.

astonished writers by the claims he made for their work, claims which at the time seemed even to the writers themselves to be wildly extravagant. But he regarded with disdain Yeats's attempt to write popular drama and to win the favour of an Irish mob and its leaders, who derided him openly. He could not understand Yeats's avowed intention of singing 'to lighten Ireland's woe'.

A couple of years later Yeats wrote *The King's Threshold*, in which he magnified the poet and his importance in the state. It is among the least of his works, a weak and unconvincing play, because words alone are not certain good.[6] My brother, too, believed in words (that, at least, was common ground) but not *pour s'en payer*.[7] He regarded psychology, which he was then studying, as the basis of philosophy, and words in the hands of an artist as the medium of paramount importance for a right understanding of the inmost life of the soul. The revelation of that inmost life was, my brother firmly believed, the poet's high office, spurning recognition by the state, and to traffic in words was a kind of literary simony.

In fact, my brother's opinion of Yeats then was not very unlike Yeats's own judgement of himself when, as an ageing poet, he regarded himself in retrospect. When he died on the Riviera, the wreath my brother sent for the funeral was a token of sincere homage. What my brother said, or meant to say, at their first meeting was in plain words that Yeats did not hold his head high enough for a poet of his stature, that he made himself too cheap with people who were not worthy to dust his boots. But he was aware of the futility of trying to ingraft into the elder man any of his own pride or arrogance as a poet—the choice of the words matters little. Jim had written this criticism in 'The Day of the Rabblement',[8] and said it to me a dozen times, and to the best of my recollection that is what he told me after the meeting that he had said to Yeats.

Yeats may have had some inkling of the real respect underlying the crude phrases, for he took no offence and always remained willing to help Jim practically and with advice. He was about to start for London when my brother introduced himself; when he returned, my brother brought him his poems and 'epiphanies'. Yeats read them carefully and then wrote him a long, four-page letter, urging him to devote himself to literature. In that letter he said among other things: 'You have a very delicate talent, I cannot yet say whether for prose or verse'.

It was Yeats, too, who introduced my brother to Lady Gregory, one of the founders of the Irish Literary Theatre and one of the principal figures in the literary movement, in which the theatre was the dominant factor. Eglinton tells a different story, describing, as if he had been an eye-witness, how my brother gate-crashed his way into a reception given by Lady Gregory, who did not want to invite him. I was not present, but I have two letters which are hardly reconcilable with Eglinton's story. One is from Russell and seems to have been written after Yeats's return to Dublin. It is undated.

My dear Joyce,
Yeats will be in Dublin all this week and will be at the Antient Concert
Rooms every night. He would like to meet you, and if you could come here
on Tuesday at 5 o'c. I will bring you to his hotel. I told him I would try to
get you to come at that hour if possible. If this will not suit you you could
call some other time on him yourself with this letter. He is staying at Nassau
Hotel, South Frederic Street. He will be glad to see you.

GEO. W. RUSSELL

The other is from Yeats and is also undated.

Dear Mr. Joyce,
Lady Gregory begs me to ask you to come and dine with her at the
Nassau Hotel tomorrow (Monday) at 6.45 to meet my father.

Yours sincerely,
W. B. YEATS

Nassau Hotel
South Frederic St.
Dublin

However unconventional his way of introducing himself may have been, it
is plain that he had aroused no little curiosity among the leaders of the Irish
literary movement.

NOTES

Stanislaus Joyce (1884–1955) joined his brother James Joyce (1882–1941) in Trieste in
1905, taught in the Berlitz School there, and became Professor at the University of Trieste. He
was expelled from Italy in 1936 for opposing the Fascists. His relations with James cooled after
1914, and from 1920 onwards they rarely met. His *Recollections of James Joyce by His Brother*,
first written in Italian, were translated and published by S. J. in New York in 1950. *My
Brother's Keeper* (1957) and *The Dublin Diary of Stanislaus Joyce* (1962) have an interest of their
own, apart from their information about James Joyce. 'I have had [James] Joyce with me for
a day,' wrote Yeats to Lady Gregory on 4 December 1902, 'He was unexpectedly amiable and
did not knock at the gate with his old Ibsenite fury. I am trying to get him work on the *Academy*
and *Speaker* and I have brought him to Arthur Symons.' During World War I Yeats also
supported James Joyce, then in a very unhappy condition in Zurich, where he was almost
totally excluded from his ordinary means of livelihood, the teaching of languages.

   1. W. B. Yeats, *The Tables of the Law: The Adoration of Magi* (London: privately printed,
1897).

   2. A pamphlet James Joyce wrote in 1901.

   3. James Clarence Mangan (1803–49), author of *Poets and Poetry of Munster* and *The Tribes
of Ireland*. A bronze bust of the Irish poet stands in St Stephen's Green, Dublin. See Yeats's
article on him, 'Clarence Mangan's Love Affair', *United Ireland* (Aug 1891).

   4. Pseudonym of Ettore Schmitz (1861–1928). Italian fiction writer.

   5. Edouard Dujardin (1861–1949). French journalist and writer associated with the
Symbolists.

   6. 'Words alone are certain good.' W. B. Yeats, 'The Song of the Happy Shepherd',
Crossways (1889).

   7. For having a good time.

   8. James Joyce, himself a Catholic, had not read the Protestant Anglo-Irish writers before
he went to Belvedere College. He then discovered Yeats and admired him to the point of

committing his stories as well as his poems to memory. *A Portrait of the Artist as a Young Man* tells how at the opening night of *The Countess Cathleen* Stephen refuses to join the rioting nationalists and takes care in his diary to dissociate himself from Yeats. However, in *The Day of the Rabblement* Yeats's theatre is condemned for coming to terms with the rioters. For more details and numerous other essays see James Joyce, *The Critical Writings*, ed. Ellsworth Mason and Richard Ellmann (New York: Viking Press, 1959).

First Meetings with W. B. Yeats*

MAX BEERBOHM

I often had the pleasure of meeting Yeats, and I liked him. But merely to like so remarkable, so mystic and intense a creature, to be not utterly under his spell whenever one was in his presence—seemed to argue a lack in oneself and to imply an insult to that presence. Thus the pleasure of meeting Yeats was not for me an unmixed one. I felt always rather uncomfortable, as though I had submitted myself to a mesmerist who somehow didn't mesmerise me. I hoped against hope that I should feel my volition slipping away from me—my cheap little independence fading into a drowsy enchantment where visions would come thronging presently . . . Nothing of the sort happened . . .

Perhaps because I had formed no expectations, my first sight of Yeats was the deepest impression I had of him. That was in the winter of '93. Aubrey Beardsley had done a poster for the Avenue Theatre and had received two stalls for the first night of Dr. Todhunter's play 'The Black Cat'; and he had asked me to go with him. Before the main play there was to be a 'curtain-raiser'—'The Land of Heart's Desire'. Yeats was not more than a name to us then; nor were we sure that it beseemed us, as men of the world, to hurry over our dinner. We did so, however, and arrived in good time. The beautiful little play was acted in a very nerveless and inaudible manner, casting rather a gloom over the house. When at length the two curtains of the proscenium swept down and met in the middle of the stage; the applause was fainter than it would be nowadays. There were, however, a few sporadic and compatriotic cries for 'Author'. I saw a slight convulsion of the curtains where they joined each other, and then I saw a long fissure, revealing (as I for a moment supposed) unlit blackness behind the curtains. But lo! there were two streaks of white in the upper portion of

* Extracted from a broadcast on the BBC Third Programme published in the *Listener* (London) LIII (6 Jan 1955) 15–16. It had been written, but not published, some forty years earlier.

this blackness—a white streak of shirt-front, and above that a white streak of face; and I was aware that what I had thought to be insubstantial murk was a dress-suit, with the Author in it. And the streak of Author's face was partly bisected by a lesser black streak, which was a lock of Author's raven hair . . . It was all very eerie and memorable.

More than a year passed before this vision was materialised for me in private life. A new publication, entitled *The Savoy*,[1] was afoot, with Arthur Symons for literary editor and Beardsley for art-editor. The publisher[2] was a strange and rather depressing person, a north-countryman, known to have been engaged in the sale of disreputable books. To celebrate the first number of the magazine, he invited the contributors to supper in a room at the New Lyric Club. Besides Symons and Beardsley, there were present Yeats, Mr. Rudolf Dircks, myself, and one or two other writers whom I forget. Also there was one lady: the publisher's wife. She had not previously been heard of by anyone. She was a surprise. She was touching—dreadfully touching. It was so evident that she had been brought out from some far suburb for this occasion only. One knew that the dress she wore had been ordered specially; and one felt that it might never be worn again. She was small, buxom, and self-possessed. She did the honours. She dropped little remarks. It did not seem that she was nervous: one only knew that she *was* nervous. She knew that she did not matter; but she would not give in; she was brave and good. Perhaps, if I had not been so preoccupied by the pity of her. I would have been more susceptible to Yeats's magic. I wished that I, not he, had been placed next to her at the table. I could have helped her more than he. The walls of the little room in which we supped were lined with bamboo instead of wall paper. 'Quite original, is it not?' she said to Yeats. But Yeats had no reply ready for that; only a courteous, lugubrious murmur. He had been staying in Paris, and was much engrossed in the cult of Diabolism, or Devil-worship, which appeared to have a vogue there. He had made a profound study of it: and he evidently guessed that Beardsley, whom he met now for the first time, was a confirmed worshipper in that line. So to Beardsley he talked, in deep, vibrant tones across the table, of the lore and rites of Diabolism—'Dyahbolism' he called it, thereby making it sound the more fearful. I daresay that Beardsley, who always seemed to know by instinctive erudition all about everything, knew all about Dyahbolism. Anyhow, I could see that he with that stony commonsense which always came upmost when anyone canvassed the fantastic in him, thought Dyahbolism rather silly. He was too polite not to go on saying at intervals, in his hard, quick voice, 'Oh really? How perfectly entrancing!' and 'Oh really? How perfectly sweet! But, had I been Yeats, I would have dropped the subject sooner than he did.'

At the other end of the table, Arthur Symons was talking of some foreign city, carrying in his waistcoat-pocket, as it were, the *genius loci*,[3] anon to be embalmed in Pateresque prose. I forget whether this time it was Romê or

Seville or Moscow or what; but I remember that the hostess said she had never been there. I liked Symons feigning some surprise at this, and for saying that she really ought to go. Presently I heard him saying he thought the nomadic life was the best of all lives for an artist. Yeats, in a pause of his own music, heard this too, and seemed a little pained by it. Shaking back the lock from his brow, he turned to Symons and declared that an artist worked best among his own folk and in the land of his fathers. Symons seemed rather daunted, but he stuck to his point. He argued that new sights and sounds and odours braced the whole intelligence of a man and quickened his powers of creation. Yeats, gently but firmly, would have none of this. His own arguments may not have been better than Symons'; but, in voice and manner and countenance, Symons was no match for him at all. And it was with an humane impulse that the hostess interposed.

'Mr. Symons', she said, 'is like myself. He likes a little change'.

This bathos was so sharp that it was like an actual and visible chasm: one could have sworn to a glimpse of Symons' heels, a faint cry, a thud. Yeats stood for an instant on the brink, stroking his chin enigmatically, and then turned to resume the dropped thread of Dyahbolism. I could not help wishing that he, not poor Symons, had been the victim. He would somehow have fallen on his feet: and his voice, issuing uninterruptedly from the depth of the chasm, would have been as impressive as ever.

'Une Ame Auguste'

I have said that my first and merely visual impression of Yeats was my deepest. Do not suppose that at other times he did not impress me with a feeling that I, had I been of finer clay, must have been more deeply impressed than I was. I always did feel that here was *une ame auguste*,[4] if ever there was one. His benign aloofness from whatever company I saw him in, whether he were inspired with language or with silence, made everyone else seem rather cheap. Often, at great receptions in great houses, with colonnaded rooms-full of beautiful women in all their jewels, and of eminent men ribanded and starred, it must have seemed to the quietly observant. Nobody there that the scene had its final note of distinction in the sober purple soutane of Monsignor So-and-So, yonder. Monsignor So-and-So himself may happen to be as worldly as you will, but nominally, officially, by hierarchic intention, he is apart from the rest. That is the secret of his effect. Something like that was for me the secret of Yeats's effect anywhere. He, not indeed in any nominal or official way, but by reason of himself, was apart from the rest. That was his strength. He was not primarily of this world.

But confound it! So soon as ever one has elaborated a theory, always there is some wretched flaw staring one in the face. Didn't Yeats's management of the Celtic Renascence prove him a practical man? The birth may not have been effected. But there the indefatigable *accoucheur* was. Pamphlets, letters to newspapers, lectures in America, speeches—that speech which I heard him deliver at the Shelbourne Hotel, Dublin: that fighting speech of which George Moore has gasped in 'Ave' some slight record for posterity. Yes, it made Moore gasp. Perhaps posterity will be equally stirred. At the Shelbourne Hotel it sounded very beautiful. But no Dans of Trinity, nor any of the Catholics either, were any more offended by it than they would have been by a Nocturne of Chopin. Mournfully, very beautifully, Yeats bombinated in the void, never for an instant in any vital relation to the audience. Moore likens him to Demosthenes. But I take it that Demosthenes swayed multitudes. Yeats swayed Moore. My memory of that speech does somewhat patch the flaw in my theory.

As years went by, the visual aspect of Yeats changed a little. His face grew gradually fuller in outline, and the sharp angles of his figure were smoothed away; and his hands—those hands which in his silences lay folded downward across his breast, but left each other and came forth and; as it were, stroked the air to and fro while he talked—those very long, fine hands did seem to have lost something of their insubstantiality. His dignity and his charm were as they had always been. But I found it less easy to draw caricatures of him. He seemed to have become subtly less like himself.

NOTES

Sir Max Beerbohm (1872–1956) was an English critic, essayist and caricaturist. He succeeded Bernard Shaw in 1898 as the dramatic critic of the *Saturday Review*. Among his works are *The Happy Hypocrite.* (1897), *More* (1899), *And Even Now* (1920), *Variety of Things* (1928), *Zuleika Dobson* (novel; 1911), *A Christmas Garland* (parodies; 1912) and *Around Theatres* (1953). His volumes of pictorial caricatures include *Twenty-Five Gentlemen* (1896), *The Poet's Corner* (1904), *Rosetti and His Circle* (1922) and *Observations* (1925).

1. The *Savoy* was founded by Arthur Symons in 1896 to carry on the tradition of the *Yellow Book*, which ran for thirteen volumes. It began as a quarterly, but became a monthly almost at once, to die at the end of the year.

2. Lenoard Smithers.

3. The tutelary spirit of a place.

4. An august soul.

Early Memories of Yeats*

JOHN EGLINTON

In his *Reveries over Childhood and Youth* Yeats gives his age as fifteen when for a short period he attended classes at the High School; but he was surely somewhat older, between seventeen and eighteen; he certainly seemed to us quite a young man, with a beard beginning on his sallow face. His father, who had views of his own on education, was content that in this way

* *Dublin Magazine*, XXVIII, no. 3 (July–Sep 1953) 22–6.

his son should pick up a little extra schooling, and, he used, when I came to know him later, to point to his own family as proving the wisdom of his method. It happened that during one term my place was beside Yeats in the Fourth Form. I had previously come into contact with him while spending a summer holiday in Howth, where, through my elder brother who had made his acquaintance, he directed us to a small quarry-pool above the demesne in which we could catch roach. Perhaps it was this that made me think of him for some time as a naturalist, and in fact his early interest was in natural science; and one of my recollections is of watching with curiosity an interview between him and our formidable Headmaster, whom he had approached with a proposal to start a school Field Club. I also remember him quoting his father's opinion of people who did not acknowledge Evolution. Boys accept everything, and the presence amongst us of this tall young man excited little comment, especially as he was not in the least stand-offish, and would even talk with boys whom the rest of us were disposed to leave to themselves. His favourite class was in mathematics; he was almost as good as our fellow-pupil Thrift, a future Provost of Trinity, in doing 'cuts' in Euclid; and during an examination he would most readily shift his position to provide me with a good view of his work. It was in the Greek and Latin class that he betrayed his weakness, and he defied all rules by consulting a crib laid inside his book as he declaimed his passage, while our master, a terror to the rest of us, sat quietly chuckling. In the English class he read out his compositions, as we all had to do, in the same declamatory manner, one of them I remember beginning with a cryptic passage about the 'Norway Rat'. I was pleased, I may say, when in later life he recalled something in an essay I had contributed. He absented himself as he pleased, and I envied him when he would mention casually 'I shan't be here to-morrow'. He did not join in any games, but sought the companionship of the young men of the Sixth Form, with some of whom he became intimate; and indeed the whole direction of the lives of more than one of them was altered through the influence of a book on Theosophy which he introduced among them.

I myself was too junior for him, and when he left the High School he passed out of my acquaintance for several years. I had a word with him once in the National Library,[1] still in its old quarters in Leinster House, where he sat with a volume of the old English dramatists propped up before him, while T. W. Lyster, who was to become an important figure in my own life, stepped about among the tables. His fame as a poet was still mainly local but had begun, together with some notoriety as a public speaker; so perhaps behind his studies he was immersed in dreams of a romantic Ireland, reigned over by the queenly figure of Miss Maud Gonne. In Trinity College I found a great friend in Edward Dowden,[2] of whom Yeats was soon to speak rather spitefully and indeed ungratefully; for Dowden far more than is generally known was the friend and confidant of many young Irish poets including Yeats himself. I once asked Dowden what he thought of Yeats's poems and he replied 'If I did not remember the boy who brought me his verses I should not think very much of them'. Yeats was to go from strength to strength, both as man and poet. Dowden, alas, was to fade rapidly into the past—the *Götterdämmerung*,[3] of the Anglo-Irish. They had never really owned a country. I remember Dowden telling me of a proposal that Sir Samuel Ferguson had once made to him, that Irish authors should adopt in their publications a certain gilt badge to be stamped on the covers of their books, thus distinguishing them from English authors. Dowden of course abhorred nationalism, and he received the proposal coldly; for him there was only one literature common to these islands, and Ferguson probably assumed a solidarity of Irish-born writers which did not exist. Yet there was perhaps something in the idea. There were several poets and thoughtful essayists, like Aubrey de Vere and Dowden himself, now mostly neglected, who might have been better remembered had they belonged to such a brotherhood of authors.

My chief friend in Trinity College amongst the under-graduates was Charles Weekes, himself a poet and the friend of poets, through whom I became acquainted with George Russell. Weekes had money, and when he decided to start a publishing business on his own account he looked no further than ourselves for authors. His first publication, *Homeward: songs by the way* at once gave Russell his standing as the well-known poet AE. His second, contributed by myself, I only mention because it attracted the interest of Yeats, and it was then that I began to be really intimate with him. We had a common friend in AE., to whose authentic vision he continued to defer, even though they soon began to indulge privately in rather acrimonious comments on one another. He even shared in some degree in Russell's feeling that in poetry he was deserting a higher vocation, and I remember him, as if thinking of something in his own experience, telling a story he had picked up of how Tennyson as a young man had been presented with the choice between fame as a poet and mystical knowledge. (Tennyson he was later to repudiate as 'brainless'). His talk in those days differed from the rather cynical candour of his later years: there was even a kind of abstertion in his presence, and I can recall the serious approval with which speaking once of sensuality, he quoted Burns's lines

> 'But och, it hardens a' within
> And petrifies the feelin's'.

He was much in London, and was impressive with his casual references to distinguished people there, particularly William Morris, whose opinions he often quoted: I remember one about Carlyle, of whom Morris said: 'Carlyle was all very well if there had been someone to come along now and then and punch his head'. Morris was, I think, a considerable influence with Yeats, and I remember how, when I had joined the staff of the National Library, Yeats would come in, complaining that he was tired and ask for 'one of Morris's'. The poets were of course everything to him, but I don't think he attached himself specially to any one of them. Like Keats, he 'looked on fine phrases like a lover', and he found these everywhere, often in the verses of his friends. Blake of course—whom he regarded as an Irishman—he knew well; Blake indeed, on whom he had done a good deal of work, was perhaps the only poet on whom he was really grounded. One might have expected in him a special devotion to Shelley, and at one time he carried in his pocket a copy of 'Prometheus Unbound', saying he was going over it word by word; yet it was possible to discover quite well-known poems of Shelley which he did not know. This was certainly the case with Wordsworth, whom on the whole he did not like: Wordsworth was for him as he said 'too much of the rural dean'. Yet once, when I had happened to quote to him the line:

'Armoury of the invincible knights of old'

he exclaimed: 'Oh, you must give me chapter and verse for that—it is just the kind of line I want'. The Wordsworthian feeling for nature, I think, seemed no more to him than a kind of English sentimentality. He seemed himself somewhat indifferent to natural beauty, as I noticed when walking with him in the country round Coole Park; or perhaps like a true countryman he took it for granted. In any case he had more in common with Wordsworth's pagan who 'had sight of Proteus rising from the sea'; certainly he came to a halt once when we suddenly saw, standing at the edge of the lake there a huge hog. A notable limitation in Yeats was a complete indifference to music, shared by him with his family, though I remember his father triumphantly identifying 'God save the Queen' when it was being played somewhere. The relation of poetry to the sister art of music is a fruitful subject for thought, and Yeats must have considered it when he once claimed that his peculiarity in this respect helped to give him what he called in a curious phrase his 'antiquity of mind'. Few poets have been without a sensibility to music, and if we are to consider Yeats as a national poet he was probably unique amongst national poets in his deafness to the national airs of his country. We have Shakespeare's authority for thinking of a man who hears no music as 'fit for treasons, stratagems and spoils', and without going so far as that in Yeats's case we may admit that there was a certain malicious vein in his nature, and that his worst personal fault was a lack of ordinary good nature. No one could say that he was without humour, but it was a saturnine humour, and he was certainly not one who suffered gladly the numerous people whom he considered fools. And he was not above a liking for malicious gossip. He had made a great mistake, from his own point of view in importing George Moore into the Irish scene. He had assigned to Moore the part of an 'Irish Aristophanes', pointing gleefully to Mahaffy, Dowden, and other champions of the West Britons as the obvious victims. Moore however had hardly looked round him in Dublin when he saw his chance of turning

Yeats himself, and even his temporary hero AE, into figures of fun for English and a good many Irish readers. Yeats meditated reprisals, and spoke of writing out all he knew about Moore. 'I will leave out nothing', he said. But I don't know whether anything of this kind was found among his papers.

These are scrappy and perhaps unworthy records of my early memories of an eminent poet, who also was possessed of a fascinating and influential personality. He brought a new importance to Irish literature. Yet he has shown by his example that Dowden was on the whole right in maintaining that so long as English is the accepted language of Ireland there can be only one literature for these islands.

NOTES

For a note on John Eglinton see p. 4.

1. John Eglinton became Assistant Librarian in the National Library in Dublin.

2. Professor Edward Dowden (1843–1913), the first holder of the Chair of English at Trinity College Dublin, was an opponent of Irish home rule and disbelieved in the possibility of a distinctive Irish literature in English. He had been a college friend of J. B. Yeats and used to invite father and son to breakfast with him, and criticised Willie's poetry without damping the ardours of the youth. Later, Yeats could never forgive him his attitude towards the prospects of an Irish literary movement, and in a chapter of his autobiography (1914) Dowden is pictured as a little unreal, a specious moral image, set up for contrast beside the real image of O'Leary.

3. Death of the Gods.

W. B. Yeats: Early Recollections*

ERNEST RHYS

It was at William Morris's house on the Mall in Hammersmith, one Sunday night all but fifty years ago that I met Willie Yeats (as we called him then) for the first time. There had been a Socialist League lecture in the long-hut at the top of Morris's garden, and I was invited to supper afterwards[1] by that hospitable poet—memorable occasion for a young newcomer from the north country. A raw recruit in the London literary campaign, I held the author of *The Earthly Paradise*[2] in some awe, and as he sat there at the top of the long supper-table he looked friendly but formidable. He might have passed for some great Norseman, and the setting with P.R.B.[3] pictures and old tapestry on the walls helped to bear

* *Fortnightly Review* (London) CXLIV, N.S. CXXXVIII (July 1935) 52–7.

out the effect of the host of this viking feast. The bare oak table was lavishly spread, and the guests were numerous and strangely varied, foreigners like Prince Kropotkin,[4] most urbane of revolutionaries, and opposite him a noticeably alert figure, ginger-bearded, Jaeger-clad—Bernard Shaw to wit (whose acquaintance I had just made in the lecture hut).

But the one figure that took my fancy was a very pale, exceedingly thin, young man with a raven lock over his forehead, his face so narrow that there was hardly room in it for his luminous black eyes. I was introduced to him after supper as an unknown Irish poet called Yeats whose first poems were soon to appear. We left Morris's door together when it was getting late and Yeats missed his train at Hammersmith station. But he did not mind that at all, and seemed to regard trains as things that came and went at random. He talked eagerly, continuously, in a soft Irish voice, quite content, late as it was, to walk on towards Chelsea with me. On the way he regaled me with two Irish stories in which I noticed how he relished the names, putting 'a leaf on his tongue' (as the Welsh say) and lengthening out words like *Tir-nan-ogue*. We stood talking until midnight under a lamp-post at the end of World's End Passage and when we parted he was uncertain which way to go.

A day or two later he turned up with a book of Irish Tales—Crofton Croker's[5] I believe, and we supped sparely on cold bacon and cider. He ate as if by magic, the viands disappeared before I had taken a mouthful. He talked of Indian mysticism—of a wonderful seer called Mohini, and of 'H. P. B.' (Madam Blavatsky);[6] or again of Irish folk like Paddy Flynn who had the secret of happiness, cooked mushrooms on a turf fire and smiled in his sleep under a hedge.

In return he asked me to supper at his father's house in Bedford Park—the first genuine Irish house I had ever been to—all the inmates thoroughly in character, and his two sisters delightful. The father, John B. Yeats, was not only a rare portrait-painter, but a vehement eloquent Irishman, hot on politics. That evening he and his son wrangled over Irish Nationalism, which rather spoilt our supper; but of all the household, it was the mother with her strange dark eyes who seemed nearest in mould to her unaccountable eldest son.

His room upstairs had a ceiling crudely painted by himself with signs of the Zodiac, and his writing-table I noticed was even crazier than mine. But he had the art of making any room he lived in 'a scene of himself'. He produced a copy of Sir Samuel Fergusson's [sic][7] poems, which he dearly prized, and gave me a little brown-paper-covered book *Songs [sic] and Ballads of Young Ireland*[8] in which some of his earliest poems appeared. He read out one ballad in a curious sing-song—the *Ballad of Father John O'Hart*—

> 'There was no human keening;
> The birds from Knocknarea

> And the woods Round Knocknashee,
> Came keening in that day.'

He reprinted it afterwards in a volume of Irish folk-lore, but it does not appear in his *Collected Poems*. His voice cast a *comether* over me, that and his faith in his poet's art. Compared with him I was but a undecided Celtic visionary, trying to adapt myself to the fashions of the moment. As he once said: 'I use all my great will power to keep me from reading the newspapers and spoiling my vocabulary'.

About this time I had started as 'Camelot'[9] editor, and was very glad to rope in an Irish recruit. We planned together a volume of Irish folk and fairy-tales,[10] which he did for the series—almost his first London commission. That was in 1888. In a letter[11] he said: 'Make plain to the mind of Scott (the publisher) that I have taken much trouble about the book, and there is original matter of value which no one else could have got—that is to say Douglas Hyde's stories—one of them the finest thing in the book, and some gathering of my own besides in notes, etc. . . .' It was one of the most original books in that original prose series in which so many young writers made their début. His own book *The Wanderings of Oisin* appeared within a year or two[12] of the Folk Tales, and it convinced me there was the making of a quite rare and unprecedented lyric poet in its writer.

> 'There was a green branch hung with many a bell,
> When her own people ruled in wave-worn Eire;
> And from its murmuring greenness calm of Faery,
> A Druid kindness on all hearers fell.'

In the following winter we set the Rhymers' Club going at the Old Cheshire Cheese in Fleet Street, whose founders and first members were T. W. Rolleston,[13] Yeats and myself. Other Rhymers soon joined up and when fully constituted, our rule was to sup downstairs then climb to a smoking-room at the top of the house, which we looked upon as the Club sanctum. There we smoked long clays or churchwardens, and cigarettes, and every man had a lyric or piece of verse in his pocket, which he read out, and we criticised afterwards. By far the best reader was Yeats, who intoned his verse with a drawn out haunting cadence. The one Rhymer we thought most of was Ernest Dowson, who usually came along with Lionel Johnson and one night read a poem with a refrain that became famous:

> 'I have been faithful to thee, Cynara, in my fashion.'

We had one formidable Scottish guest, John Davidson, author of *Fleet Street Eclogues*[14] who told me with an angry laugh: 'I hate the Irish nation'. Yeats was his *bête noire*—perhaps he envied W.B.Y. his black raven's lock, for he had lost his own black hair after an attack of typhoid and wore a wig, which he once switched off his head to startle his fellow-rhymers.

Along with his Irish idealism, Yeats in those early years had a congenial positive leaning to Theosophy. He was quite ready to draw one into the mystic circle, and his account of the High Priestess, Madame Blavatsky, left one full of curiosity about her and her secret doctrine. She lived then in Lansdowne Road, Kensington, and one evening we set off there together, and found a house not at all like my idea of a temple of mysticism. It was one of those well-to-do Victorian villas with large ugly rooms and an air suggesting a well-to-do bourgeoisie. When we arrived we were shown into a room from which the daylight was shut out by heavy curtains—in its midst a table covered with green baize at which four card players were seated under a powerful shaded lamp such as you see over billiard tables. Three of the players were extremely pale young men whose faces looked as if the ascetic discipline were affecting their health.

The fourth was the High Priestess herself, dressed in a plain loose black gown, with what looked like a black rope round the waist. Her powerful head, and face with Kalmuck[15] features and sallow complexion had, under that staring light, an effect which would have been forbidding except for its gleam of humour. As Yeats presented me she paused in her card-play, held out a left hand, then went on with the game. We sat down and watched silently, but not for long, because suddenly one of the young men cried out: 'H.P.B. you're cheating!'

At that she broke into a contemptuous laugh, throwing down her cards: 'Did you only find that out now? I've been cheating all along!'

Still at the card-table, she asked if I was a believer in the secret doctrine, meanwhile rolling a cigarette with her tobacco-stained fingers and tendering it to me. I must confess to a qualm; but the personality of the woman was all dominating and when she talked her words were touched with latent humour, or so one fancied. As we walked away, Yeats asked me how 'H.P.B.' impressed me. But I hesitated. Isis was not yet to be unveiled for me, nor was this strange Sybil to be the predestined seer, while for Yeats Theosophy meant a new revelation, a spiritual deliverance. It was only a phase, however, in his career, while the Mysticism it connoted was an ingrained part of his equipment.

But it was Ireland, not India, gave Yeats his poet's birthright and mystical bias. He often came to my Chelsea rooftree (two garrets in Cheyne Walk with windows scanning the Thames) and brought with him tales from Galway and County Sligo, or maybe the rough sketch of a play like *Countess Kathleen*. He could picture a character like Shemus Rua[16] to the life. 'Willie Yeats and the Abbey Theatre between them', it was once said, 'killed the stage Irishman!' But he conjured up a stage illusion just as wild, and in story-telling could be extravagant as the author of *King O'Toole and the Goose*,[17] humour that often served him when helping to coach the Irish players. He loved the surprise motive, whether sprung by a fairy-finder like Paddy O'Flynn, or by the County Sligo Man he once discovered binding corn, 'in the merest pocket-handkerchief of a field'! when the topic of

ghosts was started. 'Ghosts', said he; 'there are no such things at all, at all.
But the gentry, they stand to reason; for the devil, when he fell out of
heaven, took the weakminded ones with him, and they were put into the
waste places, and that's what the gentry are. But they are getting scarce
now, because their time's over, ye see, and they're going back. But ghost,
no! And I'll tell ye something more I don't believe in—the fire of hell'.

Like the Brontës, Yeats had a dual Celtic strain in him, Irish and
Cornish, and he was proud of his descent as both earlier and later poems of
his (e.g., in *The Tower*) tell:

> 'Having inherited a vigorous mind
> From my old fathers, I must nourish dreams
> And leave a woman and a man behind
> As vigorous of mind; and yet it seems
> Life scarce can cast a fragrance on the wind,
> Scarce spread a glory to the morning beams
> But the torn petals strew the garden plot
> And there's but common greenness after that.'

But *The Tower* and its ancestral memories must not blot out the London
scene in which I so often tracked him. The other day I went again to the
slummy Court behind St. Pancras, Woburn Buildings, where he had for
some years his abode, two or three staircases up above a cobbler's shop, to
find it much changed and chastened. The cobbler's shop was gone and
Liberty curtains hung in the discreet windows that had taken its place.
There once a week Yeats held a symposium, where one met poets and
players, and other cranks whom he knew how to set talking on sempiternal
and temporal topics. Thither came Florence Farr[18] with her psaltery to
which she intoned his poems,[19] Aubrey Beardsley,[20] Æ., Edmund Dulac[21]
and Augustus John.[22] One night I went down to the front door to let in a
late-comer, and it proved to be a singularly handsome young stranger,
Rupert Brooke,[23] then a poet unknown.

The most radiant apparition that visited the Woburn chambers was that
of an Irish Princess (for so she looked) who might have came straight from
Tara[24] on the evening I saw her—Maud Gonne. No taxis or motor-cars
then, and her chariot was an old four-wheeler. It was her first visit to that
strange slummy little court behind St. Pancras Church, which reminded
one of the purlieus of St. Patrick's Close in Dublin. It was a wretched wet
black winter's night, and Yeats had arranged a small party to meet her and
darted out of his doorway in the rain to receive his guest at the end of the
court. As she dismounted in dismay, a tall stately figure in green gown, a
gold torque round her neck, a troop of dirty little urchins had gathered
from nowhere attracted by this lovely 'lidy' and called out shrilly for half-
pennies. Useless to attempt painting the scene within that evening—the
low dusky room with its kitchen-grate and bright fire—Blake drawings on
the walls and tall silver-candlesticks on the table. The Irish illusion with

that superb Irish rebel as mistress of the hour would have been perfect if only her favourite Irish wolfhound could have been lying at her feet.

The last glimpse I had of W. B. Yeats in his Woburn Buildings interior was two or three years later, and that night I found him alone. He had been reading an Irish play sent to the Abbey Theatre—the worse he said he had ever read. But he had found one magnificent phrase in it, only two words which were haunting him: *Dreamy Dish*. When I left to catch a bus to Hampstead he accompanied me along the Euston Road, and as we parted murmured with absolute oblivion of the London hubbub around *Dreamy Dish!*

NOTES

Ernest Rhys (1859–1946) was a Welsh editor and writer. He edited 'The Camelot Series', 'The Lyric Poets' and 'Everyman's Library'. His writings include verse, as *Welsh Ballads* (1898), *Lays of the Round Table* (1908) and *Song of the Sun* (1937); novels, as *The Fiddler of Carne* (1896) and *Black Horse Pit* (1895); and autobiographical works, as *Everyman Remembers* (1931) and *Wales England Wed* (1940).

1. Some of the visitors to the socialist lectures at Morris's house used to be invited to remain for supper.

2. Published 1868–70.

3. Pre-Raphaelite Brotherhood.

4. Prince Pëtr Alekseevich Kropotkin (1842–1921), Russian geographer, revolutionist and social philosopher.

5. Thomas Crofton Croker (1789–1854), Irish antiquary; author of *Fairy Legends and Traditions of the South West of Ireland* (1825), *Legends of the Lakes* (1829) and *Popular Songs of Ireland* (1839).

6. See note on Madame Blavatsky p. 23.

7. See note on Samuel Ferguson p. 13.

8. *Poems and Ballads of Young Ireland* (Dublin: Gill, 1888). The Dublin firm of Gill and Son commissioned Yeats to make this selection from the work of contemporary Irish poets. He included from his own work 'The Madness of King Goll', 'The Old Fisherman', 'The Stolen Child', and a love song from the Gaelic.

9. The series ran from 1886 to 1891.

10. *Fairy and Folk Tales of the Irish Peasantry* (London: Walter Scott, 1888).

11. *The Letters of W. B. Yeats*, p. 91.

12. Published in 1889.

13. Thomas William Rolleston (1857–1920), Irish journalist and writer; editor of *A Treasury of Irish Poetry* (1900); and author of *Sea Spray* (verse, 1909) and *Myths and Legends of the Celtic Race* (1911). Yeats first met Rolleston at the Contemporary Club. Rolleston wrote a severe criticism of Yeats's *The Wanderings of Oisin*, which he found weak in the handling of the longer metres and defective in expression in many passages. In London Yeats prepared a scheme for the publication of a series of books on the lines of the old National Library Society, which Rolleston, with the assistance of Yeats, had lately founded. Unlike Yeats's Dublin organisation, the Irish Literary Society included Unionists and anti-Parnellites among its members, and presently Rolleston intervened and collected a group of learned men, many of them Yeats's political opponents, who decided that the one really necessary thing was to raise money for the publication of books of Irish scholarship. Not having set his thoughts on books for scholars but on popular imaginative literature, Yeats crossed to Ireland in a passion. For details of Rolleston's life see C. H. Rolleston, *Portrait of an Irishman; A Biographical Sketch of T. W. Rolleston* (1939).

14. If there was one thing the writers and artists of the 1890s loved pre-eminently, it was the city. John Davidson wrote *In a Music Hall and Other Poems* (1891) and *Fleet Street Eclogues*

(1893–6). Whistler revealed the beauty of London by night. W. E. Henley wrote *London Voluntaries* (1892). Arthur Symons wrote *Silhouettes* (1892) and *London Nights* (1895). Stephen Phillips set himself deliberately to express modern London in verse. Laurence Binyon wrote *London Visions* (1896–9). Lionel Johnson's most characteristic poem was suggested by a statue of King Charles at Charing Cross. Richard Le Gallienne hailed

> London, London, our delight,
> Great flower that opens but at night. . .

'There was a demure poetry about her,' said Max Beerbohm once of the London of his youth; 'one could think of her as "her"; nowadays she cannot be called "she": she is essentially "it". '

15. Of a Mongolian people living on the Caspian.

16. A character in *The Countess Cathleen* (1892).

17. By the Irish novelist Samuel Lover (1797–1868).

18. Florence Farr (1860–1917), British actress, producer and manager. Yeats's sense of the importance of the theatre was strengthened by two events: his meeting Maud Gonne, and his delight at the verse-speaking of Florence Farr, who produced his first acted play, *The Land of Heart's Desire*. In 1899 she created the part of Aleel the minstrel in *The Countess Cathleen* on its first production in Dublin, a role that allowed her and Yeats to test their theories of reading or intoning verse to the psaltery in a monotonous chant-like manner and 'a rhythmic dreaminess of movement and gesture'. See Clifford Bax, ed., *Florence Farr, Bernard Shaw and W. B. Yeats* (Dublin: Cuala Press, 1941) and *Florence Farr, Bernard Shaw, W. B. Yeats: Letters* (New York: Dodd, Mead, 1942; London: Home and Van Thal, 1946).

19. Yeats's theories on verse-speaking were amplified by Florence Farr's performances on the psaltery.

20. Aubrey Vincent Beardsley (1872–98), English artist in black and white; became ornamental illustrator of books, including *Morte d'Arthur*, *The Rape of the Lock*, *Mademoiselle de Maupin* and Wilde's *Salome;* art editor of the *Yellow Book* (1894). His contributions to this magazine had caught and irritated the eye of the great public, and when Blake's design, *Antaeus setting Virgil and Dante upon the verge of Cocytus*, appeared the magazine was excluded from the station bookstalls. The design illustrated an article by Yeats, who relates that his casual acquaintance, and even his comfort in public places, began to be affected. But he enjoyed taking part in the battle against moral and academical prejudice. As he says: 'Being all young we delighted in enemies and in everything that had an heroic air.'

21. Edmund Dulac (1882–1953), British (naturalised) artist, illustrator and stage designer; best-known for his illustrated editions of many classics. Dulac designed the masks and costumes for *At the Hawk's Well*, the first of Yeats's *Plays for Dancers*. In January 1918 Yeats asked Dulac to cut a medieval-looking woodcut of Giraldus Cambrensis, which would really be a portrait of Yeats, and later used this as a frontispiece for *A Vision*.

22. Augustus John (1878–1961), British painter; became known principally for his portraits of prominent people. His portraits are realistic, and are considered good interpretations of character. He also made etchings. Yeats first met John at Coole. In a letter to John Quinn dated 4 October 1907 he described him as a 'a delight, the most innocent-wicked man I have ever met'. Yeats's first portrait since his hair had turned from brindled grey to white was painted by Augustus John. Oliver Gogarty brought poet and painter together at Renoyle in Connemara, and John expressed the desire to do a 'serious portrait'. 'And to-day', Yeats wrote on 21 June 1930 (*Pages from a Diary Written in 1930*) 'I have been standing in front of the hotel mirror, noticing certain lines about my mouth and chin. . . . In those lines I see the marks of recent illness, marks of time, growing irresolution, perhaps some faults that I have long dreaded, but then my character is so little myself that all my life it has thwarted me. It has affected my poems, my true self, no more than the character of a dancer affects the movements of a dance.'

23. Rupert Brooke (1887–1915), English poet; author of *Poems* (1911), *1914 and Other Poems* (1915) and *Letters from America* (1916).

24. A village in Ireland, near Dublin; the Hill of Tara was the home of the ancient Irish kings.

Yeats and the Rhymers' Club*

ERNEST RHYS

It was in my fourth winter that the Rhymers' Club was set going at the old Cheshire Cheese in Fleet Street. The three first members were T. W. Rolleston, W. B. Yeats ('Willie' Yeats, which did not in any sense describe him), and myself. Each of us asked other Rhymers to come to the club suppers, and we soon reached the allotted number of ten. Our custom was to sup downstairs in the old coffee-house boxes, something like high double-seated pews with a table between. After supper at which we drank old ale and other time-honored liquors, we adjourned to a smoking-room at the top of the house, which we came to look upon as our sanctum. There long clays or churchwarden pipes were smoked, and the Rhymers were expected to bring rhymes in their pockets, to be read aloud to the club for criticism.

The best reader among the Rhymers, by far the best, was W. B. Yeats, who recited, or say intoned, his verse with a musical voice and very haunting cadence. Some of the other Rhymers, whether from shyness or because they had never learned to open their mouths, gave no sort of expression to their verse. Lionel Johnson had a demure, gentle voice, which one visitor to the Rhymers' Club said reminded him of a mouse's recitative. That was not a fair description, but compared with the incanting of Yeats or the plain military style of Rolleston, his melic mode was not in tune with churchwarden pipes and bowls of punch.

* *Everyman Remembers* (London: Dent; New York: Cosmopolitan Book Corporation, 1931) pp. 220–1.

Yeats, Pound and Ford at Woburn*

DOUGLAS GOLDRING

One of his [Ezra Pound's] greatest triumphs in London was the way in which he stormed 18 Woburn Buildings, the Celtic stronghold of W. B. Yeats, took charge of his famous 'Mondays', precisely as he took charge of the South Lodge tennis-parties, and succeeded in reducing him from master to disciple. The 'later Yeats', which is now so universally admired, was unmistakably influenced by Pound.[1] I shall never forget my surprise, when Ezra took me for the first time to one of Yeats's 'Mondays', at the way in which he dominated the room, distributed Yeats' cigarettes and Chianti, and laid down the law about poetry. Poor golden-bearded Sturge Moore, who sat in a corner with a large musical instrument by his side (on which he was never given a chance of performing) endeavoured to join in the discussion on prosody, a subject on which he believed himself not entirely ignorant, but Ezra promptly reduced him to a glum silence. My own emotions on this particular evening, since I did not possess Ezra's transatlantic *brio*,[2] were an equal blend of reverence and a desire to giggle. I was sitting next to Yeats on a settle when a young Indian woman[3] in a *sari* came and squatted at his feet and asked him to sing 'Innisfree', saying that she was certain he had composed it to an Irish air. Yeats was anxious to comply with this request but, unfortunately, like so many poets, he was completely unmusical, indeed almost tone deaf. He compromised by a sort of dirgelike incantation, calculated to send any unhappy giggler into hysterics. I bore it as long as I could, but at last the back of the settle began to shake and I received the impact of one of the poet's nasty glances from behind his pince-nez. Mercifully I recovered, but it was an awful experience.

Ford had printed three poems by Yeats in an early number of *The English Review*, out of respect for his reputation, but did not really appreciate him and used to be rather sarcastic at the expense of the over-praised 'Innisfree'. Ezra changed all that and soon converted Ford into an ardent admirer. I suppose Ford and Yeats knew one another and occasionally met, through Ezra's good offices, but I cannot imagine these

---

* *South Lodge: Reminiscences of Violet Hunt, Ford Madox Ford and 'The English Review' Circle* (London: Constable, 1943) pp. 48–9.

rival pontiffs getting on well together. Ford, however, had a romantic feeling for Southern Ireland, largely because it was a Catholic country oppressed by alien Protestants, sympathized with the Sinn Feiners as warmly as he did with the suffragettes, and always did his best to help Irish writers.

NOTES

Douglas Goldring (1887–1960) was an English editor and writer. His works include *Ways of Escape* (1911), *Streets: A Book of London Verses* (1912), *Margot's Progress* (1916), *Cuckoo* (1925), *The Facade* (1927), *The Coast of Illusion* (1932) and *Pot Luck in England* (1936). See also his references to Yeats in 'Irish Influences', *The Nineteen Twenties: A General Survey and Some Personal Memories* (London: Nicholson and Watson, 1945) pp. 115–35.

1. For Ezra Pound's influence on Yeats see Ernest Boyd, *Portraits: Real and Imaginary* (London: Jonathan Cape, 1924) p. 238.

2. Vivacity.

3. Yeats had many Indian friends at the time, including the poetess and nationalist Sarojini Naidu.

Yeats at Woburn*

CLIFFORD BAX

Throughout that Wednesday I went about London in a dazed delight. 'I am a person who is going to meet[1] Yeats',—that was the rhythm to which I worked at my drawing, and swallowed my exiguous lunch, and battled with humdrum humanity for a seat on the five-o'clock bus.

When at length I reached Woburn Buildings, a young man answered my knock: for Yeats had devised a rule that each visitor should go down to admit the next. I followed my guide up some narrow and ancient stairs. He brought me into a dusky room. It looked like a square black cave. A candle, stout as a lamp-post, threw an exaggerated chiaroscuro about the scene. Dim figures moved in its shadows; a dozen faces blinked and shone in its light. Yeats greeted me with a courtesy that would have befitted the palace at Urbino.[2] 'This man,' cried a voice in my brain, 'this man it was who wrote the story of "pearl-pale Niam",[3] and the lyric that begins

Impetuous heart, be still, be still,[4]

and a score of poems and a hundred phrases that could have been minted by no other mind in the world.' I was introduced to Lady Gregory. She was polite but frigid; and I had to assure myself that she had written some buoyant farces. For the rest, though I stayed for an hour, I remember little

* Extracted from *Inland Far; A Book of Thoughts and Impressions* (London: Heinemann, 1925) pp. 36–8.

that can be recorded. Somebody referred to the death, a few weeks earlier, of G. F. Watts,[5] whom he termed 'a Wesleyan Tintoretto'. Yeats took my breath away by declaring that the opening stanzas of 'Adonais' are cold, formal, unfelt, and not of a piece with the body of the poem. Every one seemed slightly pained, and a brief silence followed. It was broken by the sturdy voice of Ernest Rhys, who maintained, from a depth of shadow in which I had not discerned him, that 'taken by themselves, the stanzas have a noble movement'.

When I had risen to go, I paused for a moment to look closely at four or five little pictures, visionary in subject and like enamel in the brilliance of their colour. 'I did them', said Yeats, 'when I was at the art-school in Dublin.' Then taking me to the top of the stairs, he observed, 'You are a young man. May I give you a word of advice?' 'Of course,' I answered. 'Always write', he said, 'about what you know.'

NOTES

Clifford Bax (1886–1962) was a poet and dramatist. His non-fictional writings include *Inland Far: A Book of Thoughts and Impressions* (1925) and *Some I Knew Well* (1951). He also edited *Florence Farr, Bernard Shaw and W. B. Yeats* (1942).
  1. The meeting was at the suggestion of Ernest Rhys.
  2. Duke of Urbino (1458–1501), an Italian nobleman, to whom Yeats referred in poems (see 'To a Wealthy Man who promised a Second Subscription to the Dublin Municipal Gallery if it were proved the People wanted Pictures', *Collected Poems*, p. 119) and prose. See also Corinna Salvadori, *Yeats and Castiglione: Poet and Courtier* (Dublin: Allen Figgis; New York: Barnes and Noble, 1965). Yeats drew his information largely from L. E. Opdycke's translation of Castiglione's *The Courtier* (1903). He also owned a copy of Hoby's translation.
  3. W. B. Yeats, *The Wandering of Oisin* (1889).
  4. Yeats did not write a lyric beginning with this line.
  5. George Frederic Watts (1817–1904) was an English painter and sculptor.

My First Meeting with Yeats*

JOHN MASEFIELD

I was to dine with him at seven o'clock in the evening of November the 5th, 1900.

It was a cold, windy night, with spottings of rain. I did not then know that part of London, and not many people were about in Upper Woburn Place to direct me. I had thought that the turn before me would be Woburn Buildings, but found that it was called Tavistock Place. Seeing a man striding towards me along Upper Woburn Place, I turned to him to ask where Woburn Buildings lay. He was a very tall big man, in the late thirties

* Extracted from *Some Memories of W. B. Yeats* (London: Macmillan, 1940) pp. 8–14.

or early forties; he was pale, and had a fair moustache; he wore a silk hat and a long gray overcoat; he was probably a City man of some wealth; he was walking very swiftly and his mind was giving him no pleasure. I asked, if he could direct me to Woburn Buildings. Usually, an Englishman is beyond most people helpful and courteous when asked such a question. To my very great surprise, this man, without slackening his pace or turning his head, cried, 'I don't know where the hell it is, nor care,' and passed on with a savage gesture of his hand and what Blake calls 'all the fury of a spiritual existence.'

I have often wondered since then what poison, loss, crisis, disaster or quarrel had brought him to that mood.

Almost at once, a burly middle-aged man drew near, of whom I remember these facts, that he was bearded, and spectacled, and that he wore an overcoat of blue woollen stuff known of old to me as 'P-jacket-stuff'. (He was not a sailor.) He told me, that Woburn Buildings was the next turn but one upon the right.

Mrs. Old [1] opened the door to me and led the way upstairs. Yeats received me on the threshold of his sitting-room with the word, 'Delighted.'

We dined on a stewed steak and an apple-pie, cooked and served by Mrs. Old.

During the meal, we talked about the writers then most read by the young men in revolt against the times of their fathers. William Morris, [2] the most gifted and the most practical of the rebels, was the main guide and leader here; we talked of his prose romances, of which Yeats preferred *The Water of the Wondrous Isles*. [3] But the chief literary influences then were French or Belgian, and the greatest of these was Villiers de l'Isle Adam, [4] whose *Axel* [5] was our standard. Yeats praised his *La Révolte*.

We talked of the early plays of Maeterlinck, [6] of which, at that time, he preferred *Les Aveugles*. He said, 'Maeterlinck must be a godsend to the parodist:

> First Princess
> "Ygrono is going to give me a white swan."
> Second Princess
> "I had a white swan, but it flew away."
> Third Princess
> "I had two white swans, but they both died."
> Fourth Princess
> "White swans always fly away or die."'

Verlaine[7] was then much read by the young men. Rimbaud[8] had hardly come into his own; he was talked of only as a part of the Verlaine legend. Yeats spoke of his meeting with Verlaine in Paris, [9] and of the woman who lived with him. 'She was his cook; a woman of the people. Everybody said, "What on earth can he find in her?" The important thing is that she was important to Verlaine.'

He spoke of Verlaine as a dirty, amiable, gentle creature of exquisite sensibilities, who spoke with some pride of having been the victim of a love of Paris. 'I am a moth of Paris . . . Paris have singed her moth.' He had taken down an English dictionary to shew Yeats in print the exact nature of the singeing.

Speaking of Beardsley, Yeats said, 'The thing that impressed me about Beardsley was the power of his mind. He might have been a great soldier or a great financier. The important thing about his art is, that in it he is always sitting in judgment upon himself.' He was delighted, that I read and liked the poems of Ernest Dowson, who had died that February. 'He was in love with a charming child, the daughter of two foreigners who kept a restaurant near Piccadilly Circus. He used to go there frequently in the evenings to play dominoes (some people say cards) with her. She was too young for marriage, but he hoped that at the end of three years he might be allowed to be engaged to her. However, at the end of the three years she married the waiter.'

We talked of *The Yellow Book* and *The Savoy*, so bright with the talent of youth in protest. I thanked him for the intense pleasure his own work had given me.

Like most writers, he was interested only in the work he was doing at the moment. 'One must get all the fruit one can from every mood,' he said, 'for the mood will soon pass and will never return.'

After dinner, Lady Gregory called, to ask about his cold, and to say, that she hoped his throat would be well for some speech which he was to make in London at the end of that week, (I think, to the Irish Literary Society). Yeats said, that not many friends would look in upon him that evening, since so few knew that he was back from Ireland. Later in the evening, a young Irish poet came in with a journalist; then two Irish ladies came; no others. The talk ran upon the Irish poets, especially Lionel Johnson and George Russell (A.E.). Yeats talked with enthusiasm of Russell. 'He has such an extraordinary influence upon the young men in Dublin.'

The young Irish poet said, 'Russell is a strict vegetarian but eats eggs. Somebody said, that a strict vegetarian ought not to eat eggs, since eggs may contain life. Russell said, that he ate only eggs from which the germ had been extracted.'

The degree of blood-guilt in this must be left to casuists.

Lady Gregory, wishing to save Yeats' voice, read aloud some of the poems of Russell and Johnson, including Russell's *Janus* and Johnson's *Te Martyrum Candidatus*. As always, she read very clearly and agreeably, with a just emphasis and a good sense of rhythm. When she had finished, Yeats took a book, saying that there was a magnificent poem in it, which he wanted to read. He then read aloud Dora Sigerson's poem, *Cean Duv Deelish (Dear Black Head)*.

His reading was unlike that of any other man. He stressed the rhythm till it almost became a chant; he went with speed, marking every beat and dwelling on his vowels. That wavering ecstatic song, then heard by me for the first time, was to remain with me for years.

We all came away early, because of his cold. As we parted, he asked me to come in the next Monday after dinner, if I were free.

Some years after this, at another of the Monday evenings, Lady Gregory said to me, 'I was the first friend you had here. On that first Monday, he wanted to send you a telegram, telling you not to come, because of his cold. I told him he had better see you; but he said, "I think I'll put him off." However, he could not do this, because he had lost your address.'

There was a kind of blackguard beauty about Woburn Buildings at night, forty years ago. The houses had come down in the world, and as it were gone on the streets. They seemed to screen discreet vice and secret crime. The court was quiet enough, behind drawn blinds and curtains; but in a street at the eastern end there were nightly rows and singings, and the children seemed never to go to bed.

Yeats was known there as 'the toff what lives in the Buildings'. He was said to be the only man in the street who ever received letters.

He felt the charm of the mystery and vitality of the district, but said that it was incomplete, it had no pawn-shop. He said that the modern poet would remake Dr. Johnson's famous line to,

'Toil, envy, want, the Pawn-shop and the jail.'

NOTES

John Masefield (1878–1967), English poet, playwright, and fiction writer; Poet Laureate (from 1930); member of Order of Merit (1935). Among his notable works are *Salt Water Ballads* (1902), *A Mainsail Haul* (stories of the sea; 1905), *Captain Margaret* (romance; 1908), *The Tragedy of Nan and Other Plays* (1910) and *The Tragedy of Pompey the Great* (1910); the verse narratives *The Everlasting Mercy* (1911), *The Window in the Bye Street* (1912) and *Dauber* (1913); *The Story of a Roundhouse and Other Poems* (1912), *Philip the King* (drama; 1914), *Gallipoli* (prose sketches, 1916) and *Reynard the Fox* (narrative poems; 1919); novels of adventure, as *Sard Harker* (1924), *Odtaa* (1926), *Dead Ned* (1938) and *Live and Kicking Ned* (1939); *Basilissa* (fictional biography of Empress Theodora; 1940); and *Generation Risen* (poems; 1942). Yeats was a close friend of Masefield, of whose departure for a post in the country he once said: 'When he is gone I shall be gloomy enough.' When it appeared that Yeats was not yet certain that he would succeed in realising his Theatre of Beauty in Ireland, he joined with John Masefield, Gordon Bottomley and a few others in London in endeavours to establish the poetic drama as a working theatre form. A pleasant incident of Yeats's convalescence during the winter of 1929–30 was a visit from Masefield, who came from Florence for a day and a night on purpose to see him. To cheer him up Masefield promised him a model boat; the brigantine 'The George and Willie' soon reached Dublin and was thereafter one of the most attractive objects in the poet's study.(Jack B. Yeats, the poet's brother, was also a close friend of Masefield, and they both built and sailed model boats.) Early in November 1930 Yeats took a short English holiday in which the principal event was a day at Boar's Hill with Masefield, who planned a festival in his music-room to celebrate the thirtieth anniversary of his first meeting with the Irish poet. 'Yesterday,' Yeats wrote (8 November) to his wife, 'I . . . had a rather moving experience at Masefield's.' When Yeats died Masefield mingled verse and prose of personal reminiscence in *Some Memories of W. B. Yeats* (1940).

1. Mrs Old, who had been Arthur Symons's charwoman at the Temple, looked in two or three times a week at 18 Woburn Buildings. Later on, she became Yeats's regular and devoted servant.

2. William Morris remained an enduring literary influence on Yeats and was perhaps the only nineteenth-century poet to whose mood he could always adapt himself.

3. *The Water of the Wondrous Isles* (1897).

4. Villiers de l'Isle-Adam (1838–89), French writer and the reputed originator of the Symbolist school in French literature. The only great prose in modern English for Yeats, as for other members of the Rhymers' Club, was Pater's, and *The Secret Rose* (1897) is Pater's style subdued to the matter of Villiers de l'Isle-Adam. See A. M. Killen, 'Some French influences in the Works of W. B. Yeats at the End of the Nineteenth Century', *Comparative Literature Studies*, VIII (1942) 1–8.

5. Yeats saw a production of *Axel*, in Paris, in 1894. The play became his guide and beacon in his theory and practice of a dramatic art where symbol replaces character, events are allegories and words keeps more than half their secrets to themselves.

6. Count Maurice Maeterlinck (1862–1949), Belgian poet, dramatist and essayist who, in 1896, settled in Paris, where he came under the influence of the French Symbolists.

7. Paul Verlaine (1844–96), French poet and leader of the Symbolists. Arthur Symons used to read Yeats selections from Verlaine and Mallarmé.

8. Arthur Rimbaud (1854–91), French poet identified with the Symbolists and associated for a time with Verlaine.

9. In 1894 Yeats made his first visit to Paris, where he visited Verlaine with Arthur Symons. For a description of this visit see V. P. Underwood, *Verlaine et l'Angleterre* (Paris: Librairie Nizet, 1956) pp. 463–4.

Sonnets and Revolutions*

WILLIAM ROTHENSTEIN

Then Yeats: he was greatly admired by poets; but there was too much of what Robert Bridges called Rosicrucianism in his work at this time. Yeats impressed me. True, he had an artificial manner, and when he was surrounded by female admirers his sublimity came near to the ridiculous at times; but he was a true poet, and behind the solemn mask of the mystic there was a rare imagination and, what was less often suspected, shrewd wisdom. Yeats, like Shaw, was a man of great courage, who championed losing causes and men who were unfairly assailed. Moreover, he maintained the dignity of literature, and even in the midst of his lady admirers he was a really fine talker.

Yeats occupied a couple of rooms in Euston[1] Buildings, where every week he held forth on fairies and magic, the cabala, and the philosopher's stone. Sometimes, at these gatherings, Miss Florence Farr would croon to the accompaniment of a single-stringed instrument which Yeats had

* *Men and Memories: Recollections 1872–1900* (London: Faber and Faber; New York: Coward–McCann, 1931) pp. 282–3.

invented. Yeats suspected me of irreverence; but what amused me more than his Rosicrucianism was his friendship with George Moore. He was the Pied Piper who played Moore into Dublin and the Irish mountains.

Stephen Phillips as well was a rising star. I asked Yeats and Phillips to lunch at Glebe Place. Yeats was in one of his best moods, and he and Phillips sat and talked for hour after hour until I, who had a dinner engagement, had to break up the party. In Phillips there was little of Yeats' nonsense, and but little of Yeats' poetic sense; but he had admirers, and his popularity made Yeats curious to meet him. Poor Phillips! there was always something pathetic about him. I suspected that, at heart, he didn't think himself a great poet; but he accepted his luck at being taken for one by Sidney Colvin, [2] and his publishers, and many literary ladies. Max, with his usual prescience, when someone asked him how long Le Gallienne meant to stay in America, remarked 'He is waiting for Stephen Phillips to blow over.' And blow over poor Phillips did; but while he was draped in the mantle of success, we were all a little unkind and ribald. I remember that when Binyon had dedicated a book of poems 'To Joy', I said to Max that Phillips' next volume would be dedicated to 'Hope Brothers'.

Talking to Yeats one day I said: 'Yeats, you must write a poem about a man who was too lazy to make a perfect sonnet, so he raised a revolution instead.' An inconsequent remark, with nothing of prophecy in my mind. But Yeats put me in mind of it many years after when he was staying with us in Gloucestershire, at the time of the Irish Rising of 1915,[3] largely engineered by poets.

NOTES

Sir William Rothenstein (1872–1945) was an English painter. He was an official artist with English and Canadian armies during World War I, and Principal of the Royal College of Art from 1920 to 1935. He also published several series of portrait drawings and wrote interesting reminiscences. It was William Rothenstein who acted as Tagore's cicerone in England, who introduced the Indian poet to Yeats. When the Easter Rising of 1916 broke out, Yeats was staying with the Rothensteins in Gloucestershire. The most curious thing reported of Yeats's attitude on the occasion of the Rising is William Rothenstein's statement that 'he fretted somewhat that he had not been consulted, had been left in ignorance of what was afoot.' During the summer of 1937 Yeats stayed at the Athenaeum. He had been elected a member of the Club earlier but had refused, finding the entrance fee too high. When the entrance fee was later abolished he was re-elected on Rothenstein's suggestion, and gratified 'a childish desire to walk up those steps and under that classical facade'. In the late summer of 1938 Maud Gonne came to see Yeats at Riversdale. Following the visit he wrote to Rothenstein begging him to portray Maud's statuesque old age: 'I wish you would find some way of making a drawing of Maud Gonne. No artist had ever drawn her, and just now she looks magnificent.' See William Rothenstein's reminiscences of Yeats in *Men and Memories* (London: Faber and Faber, 1931–9) and in 'Yeats as a Painter Saw Him', *Scattering Branches*, ed. Stephen Gwynn (London: Macmillan, 1940).

1. Yeats's rooms were in Woburn Buildings, not in Euston Buildings.
2. Sir Sidney Colvin (1845–1927), English literary and art critic.
3. The Easter Rising took place in 1916, not in 1915.

Vacillation*

HENRY W. NEVINSON

In those earlier days Yeats was closely connected with him [Gordon Craig] in mind, and the same love of the drama and beautiful presentation led me to meet Yeats as often as possible, and to attend his lectures and speeches, even on magic. From one lecture on magic (May 4, 1901), though the greater part of it slid over me, I remember that, in answer to some question, he spoke of his own habit of vacillation—how when tortured by this curse he would try to cleanse his mind (I think by fasting and similar means), and when he had reasoned the matter out and made a decision in his best and purest mood, he never allowed any subsequent mood to alter his decision in practice, though his mind would often continue to sway. He also said, 'When two are speaking there is always a third, and in every council there is one for whom no chair is set.' This ever-present spirit he regarded as a real personality, which would go on living long after the council was dissolved, and to a similar spirit he traced the tendency of many people to write or discover the same things at the same time.

On another occasion when I was dining alone with him and Florence Farr, who was then giving exquisite recitations of his poems, I made the following notes:

'I was dull and frozen as so often now, but Yeats was singularly humane and clear-visioned, talking with wonderful insight upon ordinary affairs—politics, Ireland, the drama, and even gossip. He told some grand stories of a find old sailor grandfather in Sligo, who had saved ships, keeping the crews quiet with an oar, and was loved by the whole country in spite of his abusive tongue. Also of his mother's father, or perhaps his own father, who said, when Yeats's poems began to appear, "I have given a tongue to the sea cliffs!" He spoke, too, of a melancholic uncle who used to be a great hunter, but now thought it wicked to ride and yet was chosen judge at all the horse-shows, and whose one and unanswerable complaint at sixty-five was, "My dear boy, in ten years I shall be an old man!" Yeats spoke of the old ideal of "Magnificence," or splendid personality, as was to be found in the *Faerie Queen*. He talked of Milner[1] and Rosebery[2] as being "Heady," meaning that their brains did not work better under excitement as Chamberlain's[3] or Tim Healy's[4] did. The "heady" people have an imagination for the moment, and no real foresight. He gave us a fine

* Extracted from *Fire of Life* (London: James Nisbet, 1935) pp. 122–3.

description of Healy at Louth, and talked much on Irish politics, deeply regretting the gap of ten years when the young men were turning to mere literature, and the old men were cutting themselves off from the generation.'

NOTES

Henry Woodd Nevinson (1856–1941) was an English newspaper correspondent and essayist. He was correspondent of the London *Daily Chronicle* during the Greek and Turkish war (1897) and other wars; writer for the *Nation* (1907–1923); *Manchester Guardian* correspondent at international conferences; and President of the London PEN club (1938). Among his works are *Essays in Freedom* (1909), *Essays in Rebellion* (1913), *Changes and Chances* (1923), *More Changes More Chances* (1925), *Last Changes Last Chances* (1928), *Between the Wars* (1936) and *Films of Time: Twelve Fantasies* (1939). In *A Modern Slavery* (1906) he exposed the Portugese slave trade. His writings on Yeats include 'The Poet of the Sidhe', *Books and Personalities* (London: Lane, 1905) pp. 318–32 and 'W. B. Yeats, the Poet of Vision', *London Mercury*, XXXIX (Mar 1939) 485–91.

    1. Alfred, 1st Viscount Milner (1854–1925), British administrator in South Africa.

    2. Archibald Philip, 5th Earl of Rosebery (1847–1929), British Liberal Prime Minister from 1894–5.

    3. Joseph Chamberlain (1836–1914), British statesman whose eldest son, Sir Austen Chamberlain (1863–1937), was also a statesman.

    4. Timothy Michael Healy (1855–1931), Irish Nationalist leader and statesman who vigorously advocated home rule.

Yeats at the Arts Club*

P. L. DICKINSON

About 1906 a small group of people in Dublin came to a decision that there was room for a club which should bring together those interested in Art—using the word 'art' in a wide sense. In actual fact the main spirits in this venture were not artists.

*   *   *

One night at dinner, when there were present Markievicz,[1] Sparrow,[2] Conor O'Brien,[3] and some one whose name and personality have escaped my memory, the talk turned on one Carrie, then a sculptor, now an actor well known in certain parts in London. Carrie's name cropped up. A hasty verse was written to which, I think, every one contributed. Carrie, it must be mentioned, was a particularly abstemious man:

* Extracted from *The Dublin of Yesterday* (London: Methuen, 1929) pp. 53–5.

> We had to carry Carrie to the ferry;
> The ferry carried Carrie to the shore.
> The reason that we couldn't carry Carrie
> Was—Carrie couldn't carry any more.

Impromptu verse-making was brought to rather a fine art, and after the club dinners amazingly clever verses were often produced on current topics. Every one had their chance; there was no jealousy or no star turn. One entertainment consisted of a song 'Vive la Compagnie', in which the rapid making of rhymes, with no time for reflection, was the point. It depended, of course, for its success on the nimbleness of wit of the people taking part. This song was in full blast one night when Yeats happened to be present. After ten or twelve verses of rather high standard had been reeled off, Yeats turned round and said, 'It's marvellous—wonderful. I never heard such rhyming in my life.' One member of the party was subsequently heard to say that this was the only moment in his career in which he took himself seriously as a poet.

Yeats was, in an intellectual sense, the father of the Arts Club. He attended its dinners and discussions pretty regularly when in Dublin. He was extremely good-natured and kind to folk less gifted than himself, and indeed often cast his pearls before swine in an openhanded and haphazard way.

He was very absent-minded, and I remember one night he came in to dinner rather late, and sat down at the table with Sparrow, myself and one or two more, at the concluding stage of dinner. Yeats was full of some subject or another, I have no recollection what, and started talking, regardless of our conversation. He was in very good form that night, and in a short time we were all absorbed in listening to him. As he talked he ate, and finally caught us up at dessert.

Then came a lull in the flow of his talk and he sat up and took notice—he had reached the climax of his argument. He turned round and said, 'Have I dined, or have I not? I have been so absorbed that I don't know.' For a joke, I said, 'No, you haven't dined; you must be hungry.' He turned to the waitress and asked for dinner, which was duly brought, and he went right through the menu a second time. He was tired, I think, and although he talked well (he always does), the second dinner failed to produce the amazing eloquence of the first. I remember, among many episodes concerning Yeats, another rather amusing one. Sparrow and I were sitting having a drink after the theatre in the Arts Club smoking-room, when Yeats entered. He was obviously dying to talk to some one, and he asked us round to the hotel where he lived (at that time he had no house), and, indeed, insisted on our going. He said, 'I think there is some whisky; and I know there is some wine.' We went, very flattered, and sat in his room till three or four in the morning, while he talked. Such a flow of talk I have never heard before or since. We made an occasional remark, but conversation it was not. It was a series of brilliant lectures on all sorts of abstractions, mainly of a metaphysical nature. I remember no word of what was said, but I do not think I have ever been so enthralled.

Yeats was at his best at such moments, I think. He is (it is rather absurd to say so) a wonderful lecturer and speaker—few men of modern times have such control over ideas and words—but it is when he is in the company of a few congenial people that he reaches his heights. He talked books away that night for the benefit of his own mind and that of two not particularly well-educated young men.

NOTES

Page Lawrence Dickinson (1881–) is the author of *An Outline History of Architecture of the British Isles* (1926), and co-author of *Persia in Revolution* (1910) and *Georgian Mansions in Ireland* (1915). His sister, a masseuse, was a close friend of Yeats.

1. Countess Constance Georgine de Markievicz (1876–1927), Irish politician who joined the Sinn Fein movement and became a noted orator and leader. She was sentenced to death for being involved in the Easter Rising, but the sentence was commuted to life imprisonment. After the Amnesty (1917) she was released. Yeats's 'On a Political Prisoner' (*Michael Robartes and the Dancer*) deals with her. See *Prison Letters of Countess Markievicz*. With a preface by President de Valera (London and New York: Longmans, Green, 1934); A. A. –T. Marreco, *The Rebel Countess* (London: Weidenfeld, 1967); and J. Van Voris, *Constance de Markievicz in The Cause of Ireland* (Amherst Massachusetts: University of Massachusetts Press, 1967).

2. John Sparrow (1906–), author of *Sense and Poetry* (London: Constable, 1934), which makes several references to Yeats, *Half-Lines and Repetitions in Virgil* (Oxford: Clarendon Press, 1931), and *Poems in Latin* (London: Oxford University Press, 1941).

3. Conor Cruise O'Brien (1917–), at present Minister for Posts and Telegraphs in the Irish Government, joined the Department of External Affairs in 1944, became Counsellor to the Irish Embassy in Paris (1955–6), a member of the Irish delegation to the United Nations (1955–60) and an Assistant Secretary of the Department of External Affairs (1960). He was chosen by Dag Hammarskjöld, the Secretary-General of the United Nations (1953–61), as UN representative in Katanga in 1961, at the height of the Congo crisis. After getting involved in the fighting with the Tschombe forces he resigned from the United Nations and from the Irish Civil Service in 1961. He published his account of this episode in *To Katanga & Back* (1962); became Vice-Chancellor of Ghana University under Nkrumah (1962–5) and Albert Schweitzer Professor of Humanities in New York University. O'Brien first achieved notice with *Maria Cross* (1953), a collection of essays on Catholic writers, under the pseudonym Donat O'Donnell. His other works include *Parnell and His Party* (1957) and *Writers and Politics* (1965). See Elisabeth Young Bruehl and Robert Hogan, *Conor Cruise O'Brien: An Appraisal* (Newark, Delaware: Procenium Press, 1974).

Abbey Theatre Scene;
Interview with
Mr W. B. Yeats*

This evening a representative of the *Evening Telegraph* called at the Abbey Theatre in order to get Mr. Synge's views on the opposition on Saturday night and last night to his play *The Playboy of the Western World*. He there found that, with Mr. W. B. Yeats, he had gone to lunch in the Metropole Hotel; and here he had a conversation with the two gentlemen on the extraordinary situation that has arisen.

Mr. Yeats, who is the Managing Director of the National Theatre Company, thinks *The Playboy*

MR. SYNGE'S MASTERPIECE,

and would only discuss it incidentally to what he called the much larger and more important question of the Freedom of the Theatre. His views on this topic are strong, and he expressed them with a good deal of vehemence. Before dealing with this aspect of the business, however, he said that the play had been attacked on the usual grounds of which he thought the people of Dublin had got tired of some years ago, and which had nothing whatever to do with art.

ART, AS A FRENCH WRITER HAD SAID,

is 'exaggeration apropos.' Is Lady Macbeth a type of the Queens of Scotland, or Falstaff of the gentlemen of England? Had these critics read *Bartholomew Fair*, by Ben Johnson [*sic*], the characters in which are all either knaves or fools—are they supposed to be representative of the English people? So far as Mr. Yeats could see

THE PEOPLE WHO FORMED THE OPPOSITION HAD NO
BOOKS IN THEIR HOUSES

All great literature, he added, dealt with exaggerated types, and all tragedy and tragi-comedy with types of sin and folly.

A dramatist is not an historian.

But even, he continued, if the critics were right about the play, that would not make their conduct less than outrageous. A serious issue, said Mr. Yeats, has been rising in Ireland for some time. When

* *Evening Telegraph* (Dublin) 29 Jan 1907, pp. 3–4. Also in *Freeman's Journal* (Dublin) 30 Jan 1907, p. 8.

I WAS A LAD, IRISHMEN OBEYED A FEW LEADERS;

but during the last ten years a change has taken place. For leaders we have now societies, clubs, and leagues. Organised opinion of sections and coteries has been put in place of these leaders, one or two of whom were men of genius. Instead of a Parnell,[1] a Stephens,[2] or a Butt,[3] we must obey the demands of commonplace and ignorant people, who try to take on an appearance of strength by imposing some crude shibboleth on their own and others' necks. They do not persuade, for that is difficult; they do not expound, for that needs knowledge. There are some exceptions, as heretofore, but the mass only understand conversion by

TERROR, THREATS AND ABUSE.

You think the opposition last night represented this school of criticism?

Yes. The forty and odd young men who came down last night, not to judge the play, but to prevent other people from doing so, merely carried out a method which is becoming general in our national affairs. There have been

SEVERAL OF THESE ATTACKS ON THEATRES OF LATE,

and it is nothing to the point that the attacks have not hitherto been on plays of serious purpose. Much they have attacked has been as bad as they thought it, but that is nothing to the issue. When they are in the right they strike at the freedom of their country just as decisively. They have been so long in

MENTAL SERVITUDE

that they cannot understand life if their head is not in some bag. What does it matter whether it is a policeman or a club secretary who holds the string?

Of course we are going on with the play, said Mr. Yeats. We will go on until the play has been heard, and heard sufficiently to be judged on its merits. We had only announced its production for one week. We have now decided to play all next week as well, if the opposition continue, with the exception of one night, when

I SHALL LECTURE ON THE FREEDOM OF THE THEATRE

and invite our opponents to speak on its slavery to the mob if they have a mind to.[4]

Anyone, said Mr. Yeats, who writes that he has not been able to hear shall be sent a free ticket; and we

SHALL GO ON THUS AS LONG AS THERE IS ONE MAN

who has wanted to hear the play and has been prevented by noise.

At this point Mr. Synge remarked that that might mean giving free tickets to the opposition.

That can't be helped, said Mr. Yeats. If our critics wish to make liars of themselves it is not our affair.

In the Abbey Theatre, he added, the artists will always call the tune.
And he made the point that there was

ONE PERSON AT LEAST WHO WOULD COME THE GAINER

out of this tumult—it would, no doubt, sell an extra edition of Mr. Synge's
book.

MR. SYNGE, ASKED ABOUT THE WORD[5] WHICH CAUSED THE UPROAR ON SATURDAY NIGHT

towards the close of the play, said it was an everyday word in the West of
Ireland, which would not be taken offence at there, and might be taken
differently by people in Dublin. It was used without any objection in
Douglas Hyde's 'Songs of Connaught' in the Irish, but what could be
published in Irish perhaps could not be published in English!

On the question of the main point of the play, Mr. Synge repeated Mr.
Yeats's idea about art being exaggerated, and said that as a fact

THE IDEA OF THE PLAY WAS SUGGESTED TO HIM

by the fact that a few years ago a man who committed a murder was kept
hidden by the people on one of the Arran Islands until he could get off to
America, and also by the case of Lynchehaun, who was a most brutal
murderer of a woman, and yet, by the aid of Irish peasant women,
managed to conceal himself from the police for months, and to get away
also.

NOTES

Yeats drew Synge, who had planned to devote his life to writing critical articles on French
writers, into writing about Irish subjects. He urged him, on one of his visits to Paris, to give up
France and 'to go to the Aran Islands and find a life that has never been expressed in
literature'. In "The Municipal Gallery Revisited" he says:

> John Synge, I and Augusta Gregory, thought
> All that we did, all that we said or sang
> Must come from contact with the soil

Synge reached the greatest height of comedy in *The Playboy of the Western World*, the fullest and
most elaborate of all his works. In this play Christy Mahon, a shy youth, becomes a hero when
he reveals that he has slain, as he thinks, his domineering father. He triumphs in the local
sports and wins the spirited Pegeen Mike away from her terrified fiancé. However, when
Christy's father, Old Mahon, arrives, and Christy tries to kill him again, he loses his glamour
as a hero, even with Pegeen. When the play opened on Saturday night, 26 January 1907,
there were riots at the Abbey Theatre. The objections against the play were made on
religious, moral and patriotic grounds. On religious grounds, the audience objected that the
play's references to God, the Catholic Church, and the sacrament of marriage were
blasphemous and profane. On moral grounds, the play's attitude to parricide was found to be
equivocal and morally indefensible. The third line of attack was that the play was unpatriotic
and likely to reflect discredit on Ireland. These objections were raised either by perfectly
sincere Nationalists or by political coteries. See Yeats's description of the events in the *Arrow*
(Dublin) no. 3.

1. Charles Stuart Parnell (1846–1891), Irish Protestant landlord and Nationalist leader. In his youth and early manhood he was comparatively uninterested in politics, but he eventually became a supporter of Isaac Butt, the founder of the Irish home rule movement. As a Member of Parliament he advocated a policy of obstructionism as a means of achieving Irish independence. In 1877 Parnell was elected President of the Home Rule Confederation, and by 1880 he had become the recognised leader of the Nationalist Party. Parnell's influence among the Irish people and among many of his English supporters began to decline in 1889, when William Henry O'Shea, formerly one of his lieutenants, filed a suit for divorce charging that Parnell had committed adultery with his wife. The resulting scandal precipitated a split within the Irish Nationalist Party, with the majority of the members turning against Parnell. 'This Parnell business', Yeats wrote to O'Leary after the divorce case, 'is most exciting. Hope he will hold on, as it is he has driven up into dust & vacuum no end of insincerities. The whole matter of Irish politics will be the better of it.' On Parnell's death in October 1891, Yeats hastily wrote a poem, 'Mourn—and then Onward', declaring that the Nationalist movement should not now turn backwards. He enclosed a copy of it in a letter which he wrote that evening to his sister Lily. The poem was published in *United Ireland* on 10 October 1891. One of Yeats's illnesses in his old age was attributed to a visit from Henry Harrison, who since his youth at Oxford had devoted himself to the defence of Parnell. He spoke to Yeats of a book he had written on Parnell and asked him to write something in praise of the dead political leader. Yeats thought that he should agree that Parnell had nothing to be ashamed of in his love. The result was a vigorous song, 'Come, gather round me, Parnellites' (*Last Poems*) and (as 'a footnote to history') an essay on Parnell.

2. James Stephens (1825–1901), Irish agitator and Fenian leader. After participating in the Young Ireland rising of 1848, he fled to Paris. In 1853 he instituted the foundation of the Irish Republican Brotherhood (founded in New York as the Fenian Brotherhood) on a military basis. He also started the *Irish People* as organ of the party in 1863. After the rising of 1863 he was arrested in Dublin, then escaped to New York, where he was deposed by the Fenians. He was expelled from France in 1885. See Desmond Ryan, *The Fenian Chief* (Oxford, Ohio: University of Miami Press, 1967).

3. Isaac Butt (1813–79), Irish lawyer and nationalist leader. As leader of coalition between Irish Protestants and other nationalists, he inaugurated the home rule movement in 1870. Yeats's grandfather was co-editor, with Butt, of the *Dublin University Magazine*. His father was a friend and admirer of the leader. 'The career of Butt and its disasters', he wrote to his son years later, 'is enough to prove the necessity of the Irish poetical movement.' See Terence de Vere White, *The Road of Excess* (Dublin: Browne and Nolan, [1946].

4. Yeats was absent from Ireland for the debut of the play; he was lecturing in Scotland. While Lady Gregory resolutely kept the play running against organised interruption, Yeats hurried back to Dublin and arranged a debate in the Abbey Theatre on Monday, 4 February 1907, following the week's performances. (The debate was reported in the newspapers of the following day.) Synge's reputation as a playwright largely depended upon Yeats's initial insistence on his merits. Yeats fought the play's case against a hostile audience. The demonstrations convinced him that there could be no appreciation of art or literature in 'this blind bitter land' twisted and strained by the hatreds of politics. In *Hail and Farewell* George Moore paid an unequivocal tribute to Yeats's part in the *Playboy* battle: 'if the play had been altered we should all have been disgraced, and it was Yeats's courage that saved us in Dublin.' Upon the platform was John Butler Yeats, the poet's father, a distinguished artist. (See his account in *Letters to His Son W. B. Yeats and Others* (London: Faber and Faber, 1944) p. 214.) In 'Beautiful Lofty Things' (*Last Poems*) Yeats says:

> My father upon the Abbey stage, before him a raging crowd:
> 'This Land of Saints,' and then as the applause died out,
> 'Of plaster Saints'; his beautiful mischievous head thrown back.

He also wrote in *Estrangement*:

> Those who accuse Synge of some base motive are the great-grandchildren of those Dublin men who accused Smith O'Brien of being paid by the Government to fail. It is of such as these Goethe thought when he said, 'The Irish always seem to me like a pack of hounds dragging down some noble stag'.

5. The word 'shift' (=chemise; slip).

'Abbey' Scenes Sequel: Prosecution in Police Court; Mr Yeats Describes the Disturbance*

To-day, in the Northern Police Court, before Mr. Mahony, Patrick Columb, of 30 Chelmsford road, a clerk, was charged by Police Constables 47 C, 87 C, and 113 D with being guilty of offensive behaviour in the pit of the Abbey Theatre between 10 and 11 p.m. on the previous night on the occasion of the production of a play styled 'The Playboy of the Western World,' by shouting, hissing, and booing, and stamping his feet; and with, when spoken to by a constable, using obscene language, to the annoyance of the audience.

Mr. Tobias and Mr. M'Cune appeared for the prosecution, and Mr. Lidwell defended.

P. C. 47 C deposed that he was on duty in the Abbey Theatre last night when a disturbance occurred, commencing between 10 and 11 o'clock. He saw defendant stamping his feet and booing and hissing. This caused disturbance and annoyance to the audience, some of whom called 'hush.' A number of others

ALSO CAUSED DISTURBANCE.

Defendant said when witness put his hand on his and asked him to stop, 'Who are you, you—?' He refused to stop creating a noise.

Cross-examined by Mr. Lidwell—I went into the theatre at about twenty minutes to 10 o'clock. There was great noise in the place. We were called in to quell the disturbance. Some of the audience wanted to hear the play and some did not.

Did you hear anything offensive on the stage?—I heard one offensive word used. Police-Constable 87 C said he was called to the Abbey Theatre

* *Evening Herald* (Dublin) 30 Jan 1907 pp. 1–2. Examination of Yeats also appears in *Evening Telegraph* (Dublin) 30 Jan 1907, p. 3.

about twenty minutes to 10 o'clock. He heard defendant hissing and booing, and saw him stamp his feet. Some of the audience asked to have defendant put out. Witness and Constable 47 C cautioned the defendant, and defendant used an offensive expression loudly in the hearing of the audience.

Constable 113 D, who was also at the theatre, deposed to there being a great deal of noise. The majority of the people in the pit were

HISSING AND BOOING

whistling and stamping the floor. The people in the stalls were calling for order. Defendant was in the pit. Witness corroborated the statements of the previous witnesses as to the offensive expression used to Constable 47 C.

Cross-examined by Mr. Lidwell—There was a general tumult. I could not hear anything on the stage owing to the noise.

Mr. Wm. B. Yeats, examined, said he was the managing director of the Abbey Theatre, and was there last night when a play called 'The Playboy of the West' [sic] was performed. From the first rising of the curtain there was an obviously organised attempt to prevent the play being heard. That was from a section of the pit. The stalls and balcony were anxious to hear the play. The noise consisted of shouting, booing, and stamping of feet. He did not hear six consecutive lines of the play last night owing to the noise. The section that caused the disturbance was not part of their regular audience. The conduct of this section was riotous and offensive, and disturbed and

ANNOYED THE AUDIENCE.

Cross-examined by Mr. Lidwell—We have a patent for this theatre. I read this play and passed it. The play is no more a caricature of the people of Ireland than 'Macbeth' is a caricature of the people of Scotland, or 'Falstaff' of the gentlemen of England. The play is an example of the exaggeration of art. I have not the slightest doubt that we shall have more of these disturbances.

Mr. Mahony said he was satisfied that the defendant had been guilty of disorderly behaviour. He imposed a fine of 40s and costs or a month, and ordered him to find sureties in £10 for his good behaviour.

Mr. Beaslai was charged by Constable 170 C and 121 C with a similar offence.

Police-constable 170 C deposed that he was on duty in the Abbey Theatre from 20 minutes to 3 p.m. There was booing and shouting and hissing and stamping continuously from about 9 o'clock. It was principally in the pit. The noise prevented

ANYONE HEARING

what went on on the stage. He saw the defendant in the pit. He stamped his feet and then stood up and shouted and booed. Another section shouted, 'Put him out.' He spoke to defendant at twenty minutes to ten, and arrested him. Mr. Yeats was standing beside witness when he made the arrest.

Police-constable 121 C gave similar evidence.

Mr. Wm. B. Yeats deposed that he saw the defendant at the performance in the Abbey Theatre last night. There was an organised disturbance by a section of the pit to prevent the play being heard. Witness saw defendant arrested, and saw him before arrest rise up and yell at the top of his voice.

Mr. Mahony—Did he say anything?

Witness—He addressed some words to me in Irish.

Mr. Mahony—Were they complimentary or the reverse?

Witness—I am sorry to say I

UNDERSTAND NO IRISH.

Mr. Mahony—Well, I know some Irish, and one can say some very scathing things in Irish.

Defendant—If your worship had been present you would have heard nothing unedifying from me.

Mr. Beaslai, in reply to a question from the bench, denied that he was a member of any organised gang who went to the theatre to object. He went with two friends, and did not know the other objectors. Mr. Yeats stood over him and said he would give in charge the next man who booed. Just then a particularly objectionable expression was used on the stage, and he, the defendant, booed in common with others. Mr. Yeats then pointed him out to the constable, and he was arrested. He was

SATISFIED WITH THE RESULT,

and no threats or penalties would deter him from objecting to what he considered an outrage on the Irish people. He had previously been a supporter and admirer of the Abbey Theatre.

Mr. Mahony said this was a different case from the last.

Defendant—I have made my protest. I consider every true Irishman would act in the same way.

Mr. Mahony—You are entitled to indulge in legitimate criticism, and also in a reasonable form of disapproval, but you are not entitled to be guilty of such behaviour as would be offensive to other persons in the play and prevent their performances.

Mr. Mahony, continuing, said he understood the defendant to be an enthusiast with regard to the thing. He did not want to be hard on him, if he would

GIVE AN UNDERTAKING

that he would not take any part in these disturbances in the theatre again.

Mr. Yeats said he would be satisfied with such an undertaking.

Defendant said he would make no appeal to Mr. Yeats, but wished him rather to push the matter to the utmost extremity. They would then have the spectacle of a man brought into the police court for making a protest against an outrage on Irish nationality.

Mr. Mahony—A protest which the law does not permit. Surely you can make a protest without breaking the law.

Defendant—Mr. Yeats pointed me out to the police, and is responsible for his prosecution.

Mr. Mahoney—You were determined

TO STOP THE PLAY.

Defendant—I was not, your worship. I particularly objected to a thing I heard.

Mr. Mahony—I must fine you 40s., or, in default, you must go to prison for a month, and I will take your own sureties for good behaviour.

The Poet is Pleased*

Interviewed after the performance, Mr. Yeats expressed himself pleased with the progress of events. 'Gradually,' he said, 'the audience are beginning to see what the play means. We always had the stalls with us, but to-night for the first time we had the majority of the pit on our side, and any protests that there were were perfectly fair. If members of the audience object to certain parts of the play, of course they have a perfect right to express their dissent in a reasonable way.'

They had to face the same opposition, he said, when 'The Shadow of the Glen' was first produced.[1] The opening performance was hissed, and the hissing at the second performance was still more violent. But now it was played to most appreciative audiences and had two curtains the other day.

Mr. Yeats pointed out that the word which describes a necessary article of female attire[2] and which he said had caused all the row appeared in Longfellow and was a word commonly used in the West of Ireland. No peasant hesitated for a moment about using it. 'It is a good old English word,' he declared.

Further referring to the hostile demonstrations that had taken place, Mr. Yeats said that events were taking the normal course of the work of a man who had a curious, a very new and harsh kind of imagination. There had been a great deal of unreal sentimentalising and idealising of the Irish peasant, and possibly there was now taking place a reaction in the other direction in Irish types of character. That was the way of literature. Ibsen's 'League of Youth' created a most frightful uproar when first produced, but eventually it became the most popular of all the Norwegian's plays.

* Extracted from *Evening Herald* (Dublin) 1 Feb 1907, p. 5. Also in *Irish Independent* (Dublin) 1 Feb 1907, p. 5.

As regards the coming production of G. B. Shaw's 'John Bull's Other Island', in Dublin, he did not think it would give rise to the same display of feeling. 'Shaw's play is merely a debate,' he said, 'and he gives both sides.'

If the play continues during the week to receive the same support that it did last night, Mr. Yeats said, they will have achieved their object and will not continue it next week. In any event, it will not be produced on Monday. That evening will be devoted to a discussion on the play, in which any member of the public may take part.

NOTES

1. The play, by J. M. Synge, opened at the Molesworth Hall, Dublin, on 8 October 1903. Audiences were displeased because the fickleness of the wife in the play might be construed to be an attack on Irish women; Maud Gonne and Dudley Digges walked out of the Hall in protest.
2. 'Shift'.

The Abbey Theatre: Audience Overawed by Police; Interview with Mr Yeats*

On Saturday night the police occupation of the Abbey Theatre was on a far more elaborate scale than theretofore. A semi-circle of constables was ranged around the sides and back of the pit, in which a dozen seats had been allocated to uniformed or plain clothes men. Inspectors from each Division were present, Superintendent Whittaker being in command. Members of the force were also stationed in the gallery and stalls. Throughout the performance crowds were assembled in the vicinity of the building, which was carefully patrolled at several points by police. The house was filled by an audience who entertained divergent opinions. Relatively speaking, 'The Playboy of the Western World' was accorded an attentive hearing. There was nothing even bordering on continuous interruption. Vicious objectionable features evoked hisses, boohs, stamping of feet, and strenuous coughing. These demonstrations of disapprobation were countered by cheers, clapping, and shouts of 'Order!' The so-called comedy has been Bowdlerised not alone by alteration and

---

* *Freeman's Journal* (Dublin) 4 Feb 1907, p. 4.

expurgation, but further by the addition of well-turned epigrams. In a few minutes after the final fall of the curtain the theatre was deserted.

INTERVIEW WITH MR. YEATS

Mr. Yeats again argued the question of the opposition that had been given to plays that had afterwards become popular, like some of Ibsen's. Asked about the attitude taken up by Mr. Boyle, [1] he said that Mr. Boyle evidently did not know the facts about the new play: and, besides, he added, Mr. Boyle's own plays were treated in the same way by the Abbey Theatre audiences when they were first produced. He dwelt especially on 'The Building Fund,' in connection with which, he said, the theatre lost many of its original friends.

Do you think, our representative asked, that Mr. Boyle has finally seceded from the Abbey Theatre?

No, said Mr. Yeats; certainly not. I think he has acted precipitately, and on mere rumour; and I hope he will reconsider his position.

But how could he, if he has a fundamental objection to 'The Playboy of the Western World?'

Well, said Mr. Yeats, he is the last man who should take up such an attitude; for his own admirable plays have by no means been approved of by the class of critics who are so antogonistic to Mr. Synge's.

What evidence, though, Mr. Yeats, have you of that?

Well, in the first place, I know, for instance, that we lost a great many friends in connection with 'The Building Fund,' which was called a libel on Irish character; and, strange to say, he added, today a man gave me a copy of the Christmas number of a certain Dublin weekly which has been about the bitterest opponent of 'The Playboy,' containing an article on our plays, which says that 'The Building Fund,' 'The Eloquent Dempsy,' and 'The Shadow of the Glen,' should be hissed off the stage, and especially the two former, which are both by Mr. Boyle.

Well, do you think, then, that when this particular disturbance has passed over Mr. Boyle may reconsider his attitude?

I hope so, indeed, for I think he has acted

WITHOUT PROPERLY WEIGHING ALL THE FACTS

of the situation. In this connection, too, I think I may refer to the well-balanced letter in this morning's (Saturday) *Freeman* by Mr. Stephen Gwynn. [2]

Well, I said, but what about the remarks of Mr. Wall? [3]

Mr. Wall, said Mr. Yeats, thinks that we are behaving in a high-handed way in face of popular opposition, or rather of the opposition of portion of our audience. A very large number of the great plays of the world have been produced in the face of intense popular opposition. Ibsen's 'League of Youth,' which is now the most popular of all Norwegian plays, had to face an intense opposition from the patriotic party in Norway. It is taken as a satire on the popular side, and now it is most popular with that very party—indeed with all Norway. Every student of drama has read how Moliere was treated when he wrote 'Tartuffe.' He was denounced with extraordinary violence, and was all but denied Christian burial. Fine drama, by its very nature, rouses the most fiery passions. I was told when in Paris, seven years ago, by several young Frenchmen of letters that the earlier performances of the Theatre L'euvre were followed by duels. I have myself seen the two parties shaking their fists at one another. We ourselves are passionate, and will always take things as the French take them, not as the English.

NOTES

1. William Boyle (1853–1922), the Irish dramatist, withdrew his plays from the Abbey. Boyle was among the first playwrights to write for the Abbey Theatre. His plays include *The Building Fund* (1905), one of his best known and most successful plays, *The Eloquent Dempsey* (1906) and *The Mineral Workers* (1906).

2. Stephen Gwynn, 'Mr. Boyle and Mr. Synge', *Freeman's Journal* (Dublin) 2 Feb 1907, p. 2. Gwynn (1864–1950) was an Irish man of letters who served as MP for Galway City and became President of the Irish Literary Society. His many works include *The Masters of English Literature* (1904) and studies or biographies of *Tennyson* (1899), *Thomas Moore* (1904), *Sir Walter Scott* (1930), *Horace Walpole* (1932), *Dean Swift* (1933) and *Goldsmith* (1935). His *Collected Poems* appeared in 1923, and the autobiographical *Experiences of a Literary Man* in 1926.

3. The magistrate.

The Irish Theatre; An Interview with W. B. Yeats*

ROBERT LYND

Mr. W. B. Yeats, who is in London at present in connection with the series of Irish plays being produced at the Court Theatre, sometimes appears in the literary legend of the moment as a typical minor poet with a minor poet's affections—a dreamy, effeminate person in sad velvet. The real Mr. Yeats is the very opposite of this. He is a man of aquiline energy, tall, thin, high-shouldered, keen-faced, a restless and fearless fighter for ideas. He is in his figure nearer Hamlet than Falstaff; but he is a Hamlet of the sword. He may in one aspect be the Hamlet who has seen ghosts and in another

* *Daily News* (London) 6 June 1910, p. 4.

the Hamlet who takes pleasure in riotous and jewelled words. His poetry—the greatest poetry which has been written in Ireland in the English tongue—has come out of some spirit of isolation and luxurious reverie. He is more than a poet, however—more than the Hamlet of the passive reveries and speculations. He has shown himself a pugnacious man of action, too, ever since, at the close of the last century, he set himself to give Ireland a national theatre and to make Dublin a capital of the arts again.

I asked him the other day in his office at the Court Theatre whether he was disappointed or pleased with the results of his efforts in this matter, and he pressed optimism upon me with both hands.

'We have now,' he said, 'a steady popular audience at the Abbey'—the society's theatre in Dublin—'I mean an audience from the people, such as clerks and shop-boys. Our difficulty is to attract the stalls audience—the middle classes.'

'You think, however,' I asked him, 'that the upper classes in Ireland are beginning to take interest in Irish things—the drama, for instance?'

'Undoubtedly,' he said with conviction, 'I think we are at the beginning of a movement in Ireland which will affect people of all classes. I believe we are on the verge, just on the verge, of a great awakening of thought and intellect—a period of ideas and liberation.'

'And the Abbey Theatre is taking a part in this movement? Do you not find that the Abbey plays are too "cultured", too "high-arty", to affect the imagination and thought of the people?'

'No,' repied Mr. Yeats, 'we have taken our plays to Belfast, to Cork, to Galway, to Sligo, and every where the people have come to see them and liked them. Perhaps the transition stage we are passing through explains this. Ireland is waking up to new interests. In some ways Ireland at present is more like Elizabethan England than modern England. In the time of Elizabeth English men and women were passing from the stage where they were absorbed in the beauty of external things and in external events. They were becoming interested in the drama of the soul, in the struggle within a man's self, and as a result the Elizabethan drama is a drama of great souls. Synge in "The Playboy" is an Elizabethan writing about Elizabethans. Compare the people Synge writes about with the people in a modern English play, such as a play of Galsworthy's.[1] Galsworthy's people are people without souls: their only standards, the things they worship and fear, are external to themselves—social conventions, social systems, the British Constitution—all of them as external as the Pyramids of Egypt. What kind of language can you put in the mouths of these poor, pale, shivering creatures obsessed by external things? Synge, on the other hand, gives you the drama of the soul—of his own soul, if you like. And the soul, when it speaks, demands splendour and beauty of language to express itself. Synge did exactly as the Elizabethan dramatists did, in pouring out his soul through his plays in extravagant and joyous words.'

'But do you think,' I interrupted him, 'that the Irish peasant about whom Synge wrote is such an extravagant joyous person as he is sometimes painted?'

'I think he is,' said Mr. Yeats, 'when circumstances permit it. The Irishman, I am sure, had a great deal of the gay, extravagant nature of the Elizabethan Englishman. You remember some traveller described the Englishman of Elizabeth's time as "witty, boastful, and corrupt". The Englishman was more Continental then.'

'You believe, then, that the Irishman, like the Elizabethan Englishman, has a special genius for the drama?'

'I do. Perhaps one reason why we are dramatic in instinct is that we have always had something to fight for. Irish life has been full of stress and danger—an atmosphere which makes for dramatic genius.'

'But the Englishman,' I suggested, 'has been prosperous, and has not had the same struggle, the same insecurity, and yet he has produced more great literature than we have.'

'Literature, perhaps,' admitted Mr. Yeats, 'but not drama, in the last two hundred years. At least the greatest English dramatists for two hundred years have nearly all been Irishmen, or have had Irish blood in their veins. I think, too, Havelock Ellis[2] has made calculations showing what an immense proportion of the actresses on the English stage have had Irish blood. Then our people have, perhaps more than any other people, the gift of fantasy. Go and talk to the Galway peasant and you will find it in him as you will find it in Synge or Lady Gregory, or Oscar Wilde, or Bernard Shaw, or any of the Irish dramatists. It is in all classes of our people. The duellists at the end of the eighteenth century had it. There was fantasy in the man who made the bet that "within a year he would play ball against the walls of Jerusalem". The modern Englishman would say baldly that within such and such a time he would go to Jerusalem and back again. Lever[3] had this gift in some measure, but he was imperfectly educated. Still, we must not underestimate Lever.'

'That reminds me, Mr. Yeats. Sometimes the Abbey dramatists are accused, as Lever was, of not giving us real Irish peasants at all, but a new sort of stage Irishman.'[4]

Mr. Yeats waved his hand in a certain restlessness of scorn. 'Perhaps,' he agreed afterwards, 'our dramatists have selected some types rather than others, as a group of artists always select the types which they find most interesting. You must not think, however, that writers like Lady Gregory and Synge do not know the Irish peasant. Before Synge wrote about the Irish peasants he had gone and lived among them, and Lady Gregory knows the peasant as it could never be said that Kickham,[5] whose peasants were merely amiable fictions, knew them. Still, I think Lady Gregory[6] herself has said that her plays are not merely about Irish life. Someone called "Spreading the News" a satire on an Irish village. It is quite as much a satire on London society. Lady Gregory gives us in her plays her own spiritual version, using the men and women whom she knows best and finds most interesting as to some extent symbolic figures.'

'Still,' I put in, wishing to hear his opinion of the work of the younger men, 'the new Irish dramas—Colum's[7] "Thomas Muskerry" and Robinson's[8] "The Cross Roads", for instance—tend to be realistic rather than symbolic, don't they?'

'Yes, the younger men are undoubtedly becoming realistic.'

'Once when you had seen "Ghosts",' I continued, 'you said that perhaps this sort of realistic drama was needed as the "medicine of great cities". Do you think, as I do, that Ireland requires the medicine of a realistic drama?'

Mr. Yeats drummed his fingers on the arm of the chair, looking as though this were a problem which had troubled him but which he had not yet entirely solved.

'Perhaps,' he said, with apparent regret. 'I sometimes think that the realistic drama will produce the greatest effect in Ireland.'

I rose to leave, but before going away, being a corrupt person, obsessed with politics, I said to him: 'Mr. Yeats, your dislike of political obsessions in the theatre does not mean, I suppose, that you have ceased to be an Irish Nationalist?'

'In our theatre,' he said, 'we have nothing to do with politics. They could only make our art insincere. But, speaking for myself, I cannot see how the Ireland I [illegible] come about without a national Government.'

NOTES

Robert Wilson Lynd (1879–1949) was an Irish journalist who lived in London and was well known as an essayist under the pseudonym Y. Y. His writings include *Home Life in Ireland* (1909) and *Ireland a Nation* (1919), which reflect his strong nationalist sympathies, *The Blue Lion* (1923), *Dr. Johnson & Company* (1927) and many more.

1. John Galsworthy (1867–1933), English novelist and dramatist. *The Man of Property* (1906) was the first part of what was later entitled *The Forsyte Saga*, which was made up of *In Chancery* (1920) and *To Let* (1921), with two additional interludes. His plays include *The Silver Box* (1906), *Strife* (1909), *Justice* (1910), *The Skin Game* (1920), *Loyalties* (1922), *Windows* (1922), *Old English* (1924) and *Escape* (1926). Galsworthy was awarded the Nobel Prize for Literature in 1932.

2. Havelock Ellis (1859–1939), English psychologist. Between 1897 and 1910 he published six volumes of studies in the *Psychology of Sex*, and a seventh was added in 1928. Others of his books on the same subject are *Man and Woman* (1894), *The Erotic Rights of Women* (1918) and *Little Essays of Love and Virtue* (1922, 1931). He also wrote three volumes of essays on art, *Impressions and Comments* (1914, 1921, 1924), and edited the 'Mermaid' series of English dramatists. His autobiography *My Life* appeared posthumously.

3. Charles James Lever (1806–72), Irish novelist, many of whose novels were illustrated by the then famous comic artist Hablot K. Browne, and the illustrations as much as the content of the books infuriated generations of patriotic Irish readers. Lever was accused of helping to create the 'stage Irishman', of distorting the Irish scene and character for profit, and of sneering at his unhappy fellow-countrymen for a cheap popularity among his country's enemies. (It is doubtful if his critics read his later novels which were critical of 'the Castle Establishment' in Dublin). In a book of selections from Irish novelists Maria Edgeworth, Lover, Lever, Gerald Griffin and others published in 1890 in London and in New York, Yeats

closed his introduction with the prophecy of an intellectual movement in Ireland at the first lull in politics.

4. An exaggerated 'Paddy'. Like the stage parson, this caricature was a convention of the Victorian stage.

5. Charles Joseph Kickham (1826–82), Irish novelist and poet. In 1860 he joined the Fenians, and in 1865 was appointed to the supreme executive of the projected Irish republic, but the rising was a failure and he was imprisoned; while in prison he wrote his first novel, *Sally Kavanagh, or, The Untenanted Graves* (1869). His verses and stories are written from the nationalist point of view. Yeats read Kickham's *Knocknagow* (1887) when preparing *Representative Irish Tales,* and included selections from Kickham in this work.

6. Lady Isabella Augusta Gregory (1852–1932), Irish dramatist who, with W. B. Yeats and others, aided in founding the Irish National Theatre Society. For many years she was a supporter of the Abbey Theatre, acting as its Manager; *Our Irish Theatre* (1913) tells of her early work there. For it she wrote many short plays which blend poetry with a gentle irony. Among her best are *Spreading the News* (1904), *Hyacinth Halvey* (1906), *The Rising of the Moon* (1907) and *The Workhouse Ward* (1908). Yeats makes several allusions to her in his *Autobiographies.*

7. Pádraic Colum (1881–1972), Irish poet and playwright who became one of the group of writers, including Yeats, George Russell, Synge and Lady Gregory, who are identified with the Irish Literary Renascence. His play *The Land* (1905) was the Irish Theatre's first success; others were *The Fiddler's House* (1907), *Thomas Muskerry* (1910), *The Desert* (1912) and *Balloon* (1929).

8. Lennox Robinson (1886–1958), Irish dramatist. Among many plays that he wrote for the Abbey Theatre are *The Cross-Roads* (1909), *The Dreamers* (1915), *The Lost Leader* (1918), *The White-Headed Boy* (1920), *Crabbed Youth and Age* (1922), *The White Blackbird* (1925), *The Big House* (1926) and *The Far-Off Hills* (1928). He was at his best in comedies of Irish rural life. In 1947 he edited Lady Gregory's *Journals,* and in 1951 published *Ireland's Abbey Theatre 1899–1950.* He also wrote a study of W. B. Yeats (1939). *Curtain Up* (1942) is a volume of reminiscences. In 1910 Yeats chose Robinson, a newly discovered dramatist, as manager of the Abbey Theatre. He admired Robinson's work, and had sent to Cork for the young man, to whom he had as yet scarcely spoken, and said to him very solemnly. 'I like your face. I believe you have a dramatic future. I am doing what that man did who took Ibsen from behind the counter in the chemist's shop and set him to manage the Norwegian theatre. He was no older than you, and like you was ignorant of the work he was sent to.'

Plymouth Theatre*

The Irish Players will perform J. M. Synge's 'The Well of the Saints,' and Lady Gregory's comedy, 'The Workhouse Ward,' tonight at the Plymouth Theatre. William Butler Yeats was busy yesterday supervising rehearsals.

Discussing tonight's play, Mr. Yeats said: 'The Well of the Saints,'[1] which is our principal piece for Tuesday night, was J. M. Synge's first long play and was produced at the Abbey Theatre, Dublin, for the first time in the spring of 1904.[2] Like almost all of Synge's plays, it met with considerable opposition at first, but gradually came into popularity, and we play it constantly now both in Ireland and England.

* *Boston Evening Record,* 26 Sep 1911, p. 6.

'I am convinced that it was suggested to Synge by a certain story in Lord Lytton's[3] "Pilgrim's [sic] of the Rhine," but when I asked him about it he could not remember any origin for it but an old French farce[4] about a beggar who refused to be cured of some profitable infirmity by some passing saint. The actual origin of the plot, however, is unimportant, for he has made it entirely Irish, dipping deeply into Irish emotions and associations and filling it with his own temperament. Two old blind people who loved their dreams too well to like anything the eye falls upon are Synge's own unconquerable idealism, not the less so because of the violent laughter, the grotesque images and actions, which are the condiment for all his dishes.

'In "The Workhouse Ward"[5] Lady Gregory has gathered a good many folk tales in the walls of a certain workhouse, or infirmary, where she goes frequently to bring tea to the old women and tobacco to the old men. It was after a visit there, if I remember rightly that the idea came to her[6] of this comedy "The Workhouse Ward." The play is one of the most popular in the repertory of the Irish Players.'

NOTES

In 1911 the Abbey Theatre Company, known as the Irish Players, made their first American tour, which was so successful that they were obliged to remain in the United States from September 1911 to March 1912. The tour opened in Boston on 23 September. The critical reaction was generally enthusiastic, but on 4 October an ominous letter by Dr J. T. Gallagher appeared in the *Boston Post*. However, aside from a mild disturbance on the opening night, sporadic hissing at *The Playboy of the Western World*, and an attempt to have the censor ban the plays, the Boston run was successfully concluded with no demonstrations in the theatre. From Boston the company went to Providence, where a deputation of Irish-Americans demanded that another play be substituted for *The Playboy*. Lady Gregory, who accompanied the players throughout, refused. In New Haven, the Chief of Police, acting as the official censor, attended an afternoon rehearsal and demanded that a list of cuts he had noted be made in Synge's play before it could go on in the evening. The company encountered the first organised opposition by the Catholic Church in Washington. Here, the Irish Players were condemned from the altar by priests of Irish descent. In New York, the notoriety given by the riots brought people to the theatre in great numbers. The plays were also a success in Philadelphia, though the entire company were arrested under a law enacted the year previous on the eve of Sarah Bernhardt's visit, forbidding 'immoral or indecent plays'. After Philadelphia, the company went to Pittsburg, Indianapolis and Chicago. The farther west the company went, the less violent the disturbances. In spite of the resolution of Irish-Americans in Chicago that they did not want the play presented there and a threatening letter with a picture of a coffin and pistol which declared that Lady Gregory would 'never see the hills of Connemara again' as she was about to meet her death, *The Playboy* ended its Chicago run in such peace that Lady Gregory 'nearly fell asleep'.

1. *The Well of the Saints* had its premiere at the Abbey Theatre on 4 February 1905. Set in 'some lonely mountainous district in the east of Ireland one or more centuries ago', the story concerns Martin Doul and his wife Mary, blind beggars who have been benevolently deceived by the town's inhabitants into believing they are beautiful. Their sight is temporarily restored by the waters of a miraculous well administered by a saint. The harshness of reality and the realisation of the townfolks' deceit cause Mary and Martin to part, each to find a separate way in the world. But the cure is only temporary, and darkness descends once again. Mary and Martin, having found one another, now refuse the saint's offer

of permanent sight. Thus they reject the spiritual 'blindness' of conventional society in favour of their illusions. Yeats wrote a preface to the play in which he tells of his discovery of Synge in a small upper chamber of house in the Latin Quarter of Paris.

2. Yeats seems to be inaccurate here; the play was only completed in the spring of 1904 but did not open until 4 February 1905. See Gerald Fay, *The Abbey Theatre; Cradle of Genius* (Dublin: Clenmore and Reynolds, 1958) p. 163; Andrew E. Malone, *The Irish Drama* (London: Constable, 1929) p. 343; and Lennox Robinson, *Ireland's Abbey Theatre; A History 1899–1951* (London: Sidgwick and Jackson, 1951) p. 78.

3. Lord Edward Bulmer Lytton (1803–73), English novelist and statesman who for years was the most popular author in England. *The Pilgrims of the Rhine* was published in 1834.

4. On 3 October 1903 Synge made notes of portions of chapters 2 and 3 of the volume *La Comédie et les Moeurs au Moyen-âge* (1886). These chapters include a description of Andrieu de la Vigne's *Moralité de l' Aveugle et du Boiteux* (1456). It is clear that this is the early French farce that *The Well of the Saints* had been inspired by. Actually, one of the versions of *The Well of the Saints* is called *When the Blind See*.

5. *The Workhouse Ward*, a comedy in one act, was first presented at the Abbey Theatre on 20 April 1908. Two doddering old men are involved in an argument when the sister of one appears and suggests that her brother come home with her. The other old man, a long-time friend, asks to be permitted to come too. The sister objects, and whereupon her brother refuses to go with her unless his favourite enemy refuses his request, he accompanies them. She leaves them, and the two men return to their argument with increased vehemence.

6. The genesis of *The Workhouse Ward* is mentioned in the chapter called 'Play-Writing' in Lady Gregory's *Our Irish Theatre* (London: Putnam, 1914). The notion of the two old people kept alive by their joy in a quarrel was given to Lady Gregory by an incident in Gort Workhouse. See also Elizabeth Coxhead, *Lady Gregory: A Literary Portrait* (London: Macmillan, 1961) pp. 116–18.

Yeats Replies to his Critics; Defends Irish Plays Being Produced Here*

The bitter attack upon the Irish plays now being performed at the Plymouth Theatre by the Irish players from the Abbey Theatre, Dublin, contained in the letter from Dr. J. T. Gallagher, Charlestown, printed in the Post yesterday, came as a surprise to William Butler Yeats and the members of the company.

Mr. Yeats carefully read Mr. Gallagher's letter in the Post, and made answer to it to a representative of the Post. Mr. Yeats went into the subject of realism in dramatic art, about which, he said, there seems to be much misunderstanding not only in Boston, but elsewhere. Mr. Yeats said:

'Since my arrival in Boston from Dublin someone in New York has accused the Abbey Theatre dramatists of paganism, and someone in New York and someone in Boston have repeated the charge. The first article gave as its authority Father Hogan[1] of Maymooth [*sic*] College, Dublin,[2] who probably has never seen a play in the Abbey Theatre, for priests do not, as a rule, go to the theatre in their own dioceses in Ireland.

'The accusation is based upon a single sentence in a preface I wrote to one[3] of Lady Gregory's books. "If we but tell these stories to our children," I wrote, "the land will begin again to be a Holy Land, as it was before men gave their hearts to Greece and Rome and Judea!" If I meant that in an anti-Christian sense I might have complained that our interest in Israel geographically has made our own land less sacred, but I should not have brought into the sentence classical Greece and classical Rome. I was writing of the Irish folk mind and it is typical of the folk mind everywhere that it knows nothing but its own country.

'When I wrote that sentence Lady Gregory had just finished a little play called "The Travelling Man" in which Christ (this was long before "The Third Floor Back") comes into a cottage as a wandering tramp. She had got the story in her own Kiltartan, Galway, where they tell of Christ walking the roads of Ireland and doing his miracles there, just as they will point to the golden mountain of the Sileve Ochty range, and tell how the last great battle of the world before the millennium is to be fought at its foot and on its slopes.

'In Ireland every great landmark has its meaning in sacred or heroic legend. I don't think any man is less a good Christian because he believes that Christian persons have lived in his own land and made it sacred, though he may be a worse historian, and I have always wished that Cuchulain[4] and Osgar[5] meant more to the imagination of Irish schoolboys than any hero of Greece or Rome.

'The New York accuser complains that owing to our influence people have begun in Ireland naming their children after pagan goddesses and heroes. None of us has stood godfather to any of them and we are not responsible, and certainly have not advised it. I have no doubt the names of some forgotten Irish saints have been revived amongst the number.

'It is also stated that John M. Synge did not know the people of Ireland! If he didn't, I know not who did, for I know of no man with his mind trained by great literature to judge all human character, who has lived for months in the cottages of the people, speaking their language, sharing their life.

'All these accusations seem to be based upon a single misunderstanding as to the nature of literature. Synge was not photographing life. He was representing it as an artist. His accusers seem to believe that the characters in a work of art must be typical representatives of the people of the place where the scene is laid.

'Don Quixote was typical of something in Cervantes' mind, as Macbeth, or Iago or Shylock were typical of something in Shakespeare's mind. Art deals with the exceptional and it uses local knowledge to express and make vivid to our senses personages who represented states of mind that are in some degree in the minds of all men. An artist brings terrible, august persons and makes them inhabitants of some real or imaginary place. Only the fool takes them for villagers. He may have observed something like them, but he has so expanded and intensified that he has transformed what his eyes have seen out of all recognition.

'By local knowledge the artist creates his illusion; it is merely a fiction that is mixed into his truth. When he represents his country he does so because he has intimately in himself a portion of its mind carried to its highest power and deepened by great knowledge. Even historical plays are not historic, for it was Goethe who said, "We do the persons of history the honor of giving to our own minds their names."

'Synge's mind was Irish, but what he showed (full as it was of incidental truth, or traditional phrases, of profound observation of local character), was too perfect an expression of that mind to represent any one Irish locality. He was as Irish as Cervantes was Spanish. Don Quixote, a work of supreme intensity, is true of all human life, and it is the glory of Spain that one of its writers has been able to express a universal truth while seeming to be expressing a local one. But you cannot make omelets without breaking eggs, and I can imagine a patriotic Spaniard, who thought that it did but poor justice to the gentlemen and peasantry of Spain.

'Only the Irish and Jewish people are at present sensitive in this way, and it is very natural that they should be, considering their history. In Dublin Synge's "Playboy of the Western World," which at first seemed to offend the sensibilities of many, has overcome the hostility that greeted it at first; it has won its fight and now when we produce it it attracts large and enthusiastic audiences. It is not asking too much that what Irish Dublin accepts ought not to be rejected by Irish America without much thought, nor is it, perhaps, saying too much to suggest that Dublin might know its Ireland better than those for whom Ireland is but a memory or a tradition.'

NOTES

1. Edmund Ignatius Hogan (1831–1917), Jesuit, published the famous *Onomasticon Goedelicum* [On Gaelic Place Names], 1910, still the standard reference work.

2. Maynooth College is not in Dublin, but in Maynooth village, Co. Kildare, fifteen miles north-west of Dublin.

3. *Cuchulain of Muirthemne* (1902).

4. Cuchulainn (or Cuchulinn), champion hero of a cycle of Celtic myths who at the age of seventeen defended Ulster single-handed for four months.

5. Most probably Ossian (or Oisin), Gaelic hero and bard, son of Finn, narrator of tales of Finn and his Fianna band. He is the hero of Yeats's *The Wanderings of Oisin* (1889).

A Lively Discussion over the 'Irish Plays'*

The Sunday Post has been able to secure the views—pro and con—of a number of Boston's prominent Irishmen. Interesting in themselves, they are still more interesting in view of the strange diversity of opinion expressed in them.

BY WILLIAM BUTLER YEATS

In a special interview for the *Sunday Post*, Mr. Yeats said:

It is quite true—we have not attempted to give America any of the old-fashioned plays, such as Boucicault[1] produced. It is plays like that, I think, that Irishmen should condemn; it is plays like that which have made it so hard for Irishmen to accept something better.

Those plays were very well for their period; but the world must advance, and we have quite outgrown such things. Yet there are the sentimentalists who still desire the unnatural heroes and the impossible heroines of by-gone days, and who refuse to see that Irishmen are only human beings, after all.

No one has a greater, a deeper, a holier love for Ireland, its people, its tradition, and its honor than have I: yet, I do really believe that there actually exist in Ireland, cowards, villains, brutes, and all sorts of vicious types—just as they have existed among every people that ever trod the earth. To try to eliminate all that is evil from our plays would be to falsify life itself. Would we be any nearer to actuality if we deliberately glossed over the realities of life?

Our critics complain that our characters are all vicious. Let anyone read 'Birthright'[2]—let him find a line, a word, an action, in the role of Maura, the mother, that is not typical of a woman of the finest, kindliest, most God-fearing instincts and sentiments. No mother would be disgraced by being patterned after that wonderfully pathetic figure of the noble, honest, pious and saddened mother.

And what is so vicious in Hugh, the son? Is he not the type of outspoken man, who simply says what he thinks, even though he may be mistaken? Is he not a champion for his mother? Is he not courteous to his father? Is he not a loving son to her? Is he not of the athelic type that has won for Ireland so many honors at home and abroad?

* *Sunday Post* (Boston) 8 Oct 1911, p. 37.

And is Pat, the father, so horrible, except that he inclines to favor one son? It is a human trait, not especially Irish nor peculiar to any race, but only, simply, human. And Shane, the younger son, is only the type of younger son that poets, play authors and tale tellers of every nation and clime have portrayed, without offending anyone.

Is Nora so bad in 'The Shadow of the Glen?'[3] Is she not the type of woman that is starved for a bit of love, who is desperately sick of the monotony of her lonely life, who simply must do something to get away from it?

Is not the tramp, with his love of nature, his enjoyment of God's own skies and his own world-garden, more alluring, more attractive than the rather covetous young herdsman, who would lead her a life little better than that one she is leaving?

And is the rather covetous young herdsman so bad, after all? Is it not rather the inborn thrift of his calling that makes him figure on the ways and means of existence in case of his marriage to Nora?

Our critics contend that Michael is a coward. No, he is not necessarily that. Is it not natural for a man to shrink from seeing a corpse rising from the dead? Would it not be natural, in a simple peasant lad, to be more or less 'afraid' of a man who was dead, and who came to life on a sudden? And is not the righteous indignation of a husband, perhaps, always conducive to that respect and awe that may be easily mistaken for fear?

Again, humor is a matter of temperament. What is humorous to one is not so to another. The fact that Lady Gregory's piece[4] has met with immense success everywhere must prove that some like it. Surely, we would not continue to keep a play in our repertoire that, being a comedy, is sad.

I fear that our critics greatly misunderstand us. We have had the same uphill fight in Dublin. The sentimentalists opposed us for a long time; they didn't exactly want the old Boucicault type of play, but they didn't want what we offered. They didn't know just what they did want, it seemed.

But we finally showed the nationalists—our first great opponents—what our aim is; and today they flock to our theatre time and again to see the plays performed. Our great support comes from the Nationalist ranks, from the people who represent the 'common people'—from the great Irish population. Later, we began to appeal to others; and soon gained the patronage and regard of all Dublin Irishmen—no matter of what political opinions.

It is said that we tend to show the unfitness of the Irish for Home Rule. I am a worker for Home Rule[5]—I believe in it—I want it, pray for it—and feel assured that Ireland must and will get it, not in the dim future, but soon.

As for the 'evil' element in our plays, it must be known to all men who have studied the drama, that without the moving power of evil, all will fall flat. That is, the evil is ever the great power for ultimate good.

In 'Macbeth,' there is evil a-plenty; nor are the Scotch made particularly noble and upright: yet the Scotch do not complain.

'King Lear' does not teem with 'good' characters; yet the British people do not rise in their wrath and object.

One could cite many instances—instances without limit—where the really great plays have centred about evil actions; necessarily so. And to have made our Irish men and women all 'good', would have been to condemn them as literature, and would have made us untrue to our principles; and it is the literature of Ireland we have at our hearts.

NOTES

This interview was given following the opening of the Irish Players' first American tour in Boston on 23 September 1911. The plays selected for the occasion were T. C. Murray's *Birthright*, Synge's *The Shadow of the Glen* and Lady Gregory's *Hyacinth Halvey*. Other participants in the 'discussion' were T. J. Dillon, Mary Boyle O'Reilly, Michael Maynes, Katherine R. Walsh, Margaret Foley, Felix W. McGetrick, Edward F. Timmins, Mary A. Cavanagh, Lady Gregory, Congressman O'Connel, Mayor Fitzgerald, William A. Leahy, Kark H. Crehan, W. T. A. Fitzgerald, and J. F. Gallagher.

  1. Dion Boucicault (1822–90), Irish actor and dramatist who wrote and produced more than 140 plays in London, Dublin and America. Among his many successes are *London Assurance* (1841), *The Corsican Brothers* (1848) and *The Shaughraun* (1875). More than any other dramatist of the day he had 'the trick of the theatre', and his material, whatever its source, was always shaped to the taste of the time.

  2. Murray made his name in *Birthright*, produced at the Abbey Theatre in 1910. It is a play of rivalry and family jealousy.

  3. J. M. Synge's first play, *In the Shadow of the Glen* (1903), begins the series of grave, original studies of Irish character and thought which from time to time drew upon Synge the hostility of his audiences, but are now appreciated wherever Irish drama is played. It is a one-act comedy based on a folk tale Synge heard on the Aran Islands.

  4. *Hyacinth Halvey.*

  5. Yeats's nationalist views were largely shaped by John O'Leary, who returned late in 1884 from five years of imprisonment in England and long exile in France. Yeats decided that Ireland and her heroic past must be the subject of his poetry. After 1898, however, he gradually dropped out of active politics and his nationalism became more purely literary. Suspected by Dublin Castle as a revolutionary influence, and by many Anglo-Irish friends as a traitor to his class, he in fact kept himself deliberately clear of all real political involvement. His close friend and ideal of beauty, Maud Gonne, lost patience with his attitude. She was more actively involved in the revolutionary movement until the breakdown of her marriage in 1905 when she virtually retired from public life.

Yeats Defends 'The Playboy'

Irish Poet and Playwright in New York Points to Success in Dublin*

[Special Dispatch to *The Herald*]

NEW YORK, Oct. 11—William Butler Yeats, the Irish poet and playwright, came to New York from Boston today to make arrangements for the appearance here of the Irish Players. At the Waldorf-Astoria he had something to say about the adverse criticism the Irish Players, and more especially their Irish plays, have received. In Boston there seems to have been a division of opinion among the Irish people, and in New York last Sunday night the United Irish-American societies passed resolutions condemning Synge's play, 'The Playboy of the Western World', as being immoral and untrue to Irish life, because it made a parricide a hero.

'When we produced "The Playboy of the Western World" in Dublin,' said Mr. Yeats, 'there were riots in the theatre, not against the play, but made by agents of an organisation that was trying to silence us. The question of the artistic merit of the play did not enter into the controversy. We then took the play to London in order to get an unbiased opinion of its merits. We presented it for a few performances at the Queen Street Theatre and were asked to keep it on for a run. But that was not our object. We wished it to have an honest hearing in Ireland.

'After some delays, caused by the illness of Synge and his death, we put it on again in Dublin[1] and it met with unqualified success. We took it on tour through Ireland, England and Scotland, and it was well received everywhere, especially in Belfast and Cork. Critics said it was the greatest imaginative comedy of the last century.

'The Irish-Americans,' emphasized Mr. Yeats, 'should be very careful how they criticise the drama of the Irish Players. Not that they should not criticise if they find reason, for the right to think independently is theirs, but they should not form hasty judgments about things upon which the Irish of Ireland had already given a favourable opinion.

'As to the opposition in Boston,' he explained, 'it is the opposition of individuals and not of organizations. Lady Gregory is to be entertained next Sunday night at a branch of the Gaelic Society in Boston, and we have been in receipt of many congratulatory letters from prominent Irishmen of that city. I would not say that we are supported by any of the prominent organizations in Ireland, but one[2] of our vice-presidents is a Nationalist,

* *Boston Herald*, 12 Oct 1911, p. 8.

another belongs to the opposition, and Miss Redmond, daughter of the Nationalist leader,[3] has written a play for us. We are neither supported nor opposed by either party or by the church. We have friends and opponents among individuals in all parties.'

Mr. Yeats said that 'The Playboy of the Western World' would have its first presentation in this country at the Plymouth Theatre, Boston, next Monday night. When the Irish players would come to New York was uncertain, but it would not be for six weeks or two months perhaps.[4]

NOTES

1. *The Playboy of the Western World* was revived at the Abbey Theatre in May 1909.

2. Lennox Robinson (1886–1958), who joined the Volunteers in 1914.

3. John Redmond (1856–1918), who was leader of Parnellite group on Parnell's death (1891); adopted conciliatory attitude towards government and anti-Parnellites; and brought about amalgamation of the two Irish Nationalist parties (1900), aiming at a free Ireland within the British Empire.

4. The Irish Players performed at Maxine Elliott Theatre, New York, from 20 November to 30 December 1911.

Mr Yeats Explains*

Mr. Yeats spent Wednesday in New York to prepare the way for the Irish Players there. Happily they will stay here at the Plymouth for another fortnight and then they are likely to appear in other cities before they act in New York. Already, it seems, objection is brewing there to some of their plays, especially to those of Synge, and Mr. Yeats repeated to the reporters much that he has already said here in refutation of it. Newly, however, he touched on the alleged hostility of the Roman Church in Ireland—and maybe elsewhere—to the Irish National Theatre. 'We were often told at the start,' he said, 'that we would find the priests opposed to us, but, on the contrary, I have frequently seen priests among our audiences, and we have given performances in the Irish provinces where priests were found in the audiences. . . . When we went to Sligo and played in the Town Hall our audience was organized by a priest. The Catholic Church in Ireland is not opposing "The Playboy". Of course, I do not claim it is supporting it.'

Incidentally, too, Mr. Yeats answered the reiterated assertion that Synge was influenced by the so-called 'decadent'[1] poets of Paris. 'When I first met him in 1897 I found that he wanted to write about French literature. He had been studying Molière, Corneille and Racine. I told him that if he was to write for the English papers he would find that they demanded something about modern French literature. Of the latter he

---

* *Boston Evening Transcript*, 13 Oct 1911, p. 14.

knew nothing. If he was influenced by French writers they were of the pre-Molière period, and about them there was certainly nothing decadent.' Synge as a 'decadent' is beyond the range of any but very heated or purblind imaginations. He was, he is, manhood itself.

NOTES

1. The Decadents were a group of late nineteenth-and early twentieth-century writers who held that art was superior to nature, that the finest beauty was that of dying or decaying things, and who, both in their lives and their art, attacked the accepted moral, ethical and social standards of their time. The precepts of the Decadents were summarised by Gautier in the 'Notice' he prefixed to an edition of Baudelaire's poems, *Les fleurs du mal* (1868). See R. L. Peters, 'Toward an "Un-Definition" of Decadent', *Journal of Aesthetics and Art Criticism*, XVIII (Dec 1959) 258–64.

Abbey Theatre: Pupils' Performance; Address by Mr W. B. Yeats*

Last evening a large number of people were present at the Abbey Theatre to witness the beginning of a new epoch in the history of the Abbey Company, which has won praise everywhere for the excellence of its acting. The success of the actors and actresses who compose it have led the directors to start a School of Acting, which will follow the style of the principal body, at present in America. It appears to be the intention of those responsible for the existence of the theatre to continue the usual winter Abbey season, while the original company is away on tour, with performances of the school, and, to judge by the marked appreciation shown at the initial venture, there is no reason to doubt that the project will be successful. The 'No. 2' Company, though it had to go through the severest of tests—performing plays which had never been produced before—showed but few signs of amateurishness, and after a few further evenings these will probably be effaced. A morality play is an unfamiliar thing to Dublin play-goers, and after the success of 'The Interlude of Youth'[1] it is to be hoped that more of its kind will be given at the Abbey Theatre.

The second play was 'The Marriage,' by Dr. Douglas Hyde, translated by Lady Gregory, and in it the players were equally successful.

* *Evening Telegraph* (Dublin) 17 Nov 1911, p. 5.

The last piece was 'The Shadow of the Glen,'[2] and, though it must have been familiar to everyone present, it was received with enthusiasm.

ADDRESS BY MR. YEATS

At an interval Mr. Yeats delivered a brief address concerning the purpose of the school. Incidentally he stated that the regular Abbey Theatre Company was having a tremendous success in America—an announcement hailed with loud applause. He urged the audience not to believe one solitary word of what they saw in the newspapers about the reception they were supposed to be getting. There had been great enthusiasm every where. They would find in the newspapers here every hostile criticism selected. These hostile criticisms were not one to fifty in proportion to the enthusiasm. The other day, for instance, at Providence, Rhode Island, they had produced 'The Playboy.' Providence, they had been told, was the stronghold of their enemies. Some of their own countrymen went down to the police convinced no doubt that the play was as wicked in the eyes of others as in their own. The police sent down a censor of their own, and the censor said he had greatly enjoyed his experience (laughter). There was not one hiss in the place; on the contrary, there was great enthusiasm. Coming back to home affairs, Mr. Yeats said that it was possible that in the future the main company of the Abbey would tour for several months each year. They therefore hoped to have another company to play at the theatre in Dublin, and that other companies taught in that school would be spread over the country. A great academy of dramatic art would arise in that way. They had selected for their plays several moralities, one of which they had just witnessed, and they had done so because the ordinary amateur was accustomed to learn Shakespeare, and was inclined to imitate other actors. Good art could not exist where there was imitation, and they must have plays where imitation was impossible. None of their players had ever seen Sir H. Tree play 'The Interlude of Youth,' and that fact helped them to do something very charming and fresh. Before the Shakespearean drama arose there were three great types of play in England; there were the mysteries founded on the stories of the Bible, the miracle plays founded upon the histories of the saints, and then there were moralities, dramatic sermons of the kind they had witnessed. In their new Irish plays they had those three types—the miracle play in Dr. Hyde's 'Nativity,' and the morality in his (Mr. Yeats') 'Hour Glass.' They must not think of those types of play as having merely preceded Shakespeare. They went side by side with him, and he must have seen them performed. They would find the influence of the morality play in Marlowe's 'Dr. Faustus,' which was evidently shaped by a man familiar with the morality plays. A mystery play would be given by the school in a week or two. They were not, of course, going to confine themselves to those plays; they were not going to neglect the dialect work. On the contrary, they were going to play such work as the amateur did not see Sir H. Tree perform (applause).

NOTES

1. Author anononymous; first printed in 1554.
2. By J. M. Synge

The Playboy:
Another American Surprise.
Players Arrested; Interview
with Mr W. B. Yeats*

A telegram from Philadelphia, published in the London evening papers, says:—The Company of Irish players who are playing John Synge's 'The Playboy of the Western World' have again got into trouble, all the players being arrested here yesterday on the ground that the 'Playboy' is an immoral production. Later they were held in 5,000 dollars to appear before the magistrate on to-day (Friday).

When the play was produced in New York in Maxine Elliott's Theatre the actors were howled down by an organised opposition.

Interviewed to-day in reference to the reported arrest of the Abbey Theatre players in Philadelphia, Mr. W. B. Yeats, co-ordinator of the Abbey Theatre with Lady Gregory, said his latest letters from America stated that everything was going well with the company. They had been playing in a number of small towns and getting sometimes good and sometimes small audiences, but always having cordial local appreciation and a great many complimentary references in the newspapers. 'The only

EFFECT OF THIS OBJECTION

to the "Playboy of the Western World" will be to give a tremendous advertisement to the play,' said Mr. Yeats. 'That was the effect of the tumult in New York. The play got such an advertisement that the local managements have been most anxious for it; in fact we had to refuse to play it as often as they wished. It would pay us better to run that play alone if our object was to make money, but our object is to represent different phases if [sic] the Irish Literary and dramatic movement, and we endeavour to give an equal share to each of the eighteen plays in our repertoire. We do not care to represent Ireland solely by this play. Our

* *Evening Telegraph* (Dublin) 19 Jan 1912 p. 3.

plays include representations of idealism, such as "Kathleen Ni Houlihan"[1] and "The Rising of the Moon,"[2] and satire and extravagant
phantasy, such as Synge's works. We consider "The Playboy" a work of
genius, but we don't think it would be right to put it forward as the
exclusive representation of the Irish dramatic movement.

This objection to the play in Philadelphia

WILL NOT INTERFERE WITH THE CONTINUATION OF THE TOUR.

It cannot. It can have nothing to do with the continuation of the tour.
There is no such thing in America as a Censor, whose word runs through
America.

'Organised America,' added Mr. Yeats, 'is in the state of opinion of the
Ireland of twenty years ago. It is living in the epoch of Boucicault, who, in
spite of his later birth, was the latest of the Young Irelanders. Up to the rise
of this movement there was

NO EDUCATED NATIONAL IRELAND

—no national Ireland interested in literature or the arts. Now there is an
educated national Ireland interested in Ireland and in literature and the
arts, and insisting upon having its own standards recognised. In America
you have the old state of things unchanged so far as the organisations are
concerned. In America educated young Irishmen and women are the
descendants of Irishmen who find nothing to attract them in the Irish
influences and get merged in the general stream of American life. Our
plays have awakened the consciousness of their Irish origin in thousands of
educated Irish people in America, and has got them interested in Ireland.

THE AGITATION AGAINST THE 'PLAYBOY,'

Mr. Yeats went on to say, was raised by organised Irish-American, and
had been very vicious and very untruthful. 'For instance,' said he, 'The
Aloysius Society[3] had distributed pamphlets at the chapel doors all over
America containing this sentence:—'The "Pall Mall Gazette" attacks
these so-called Irish plays, and says they are photographs of bestial
depravity and stupidity.' Last evening the 'Pall Mall Gazette' repeated its
repudiation of that quotation. Again a certain Father Kenny, of the Jesuit
Order, has quoted Mr. Stephen Gwynn, M. P., as saying something of the
same kind, and Mr. Stephen Gywnn has written to me to say that he has no
sympathy with the agitation against the 'Playboy,' which he greatly
admires. There are other quotations equally fraudulent. They are quoted
from paper to paper, from society to society, from speech to speech, and so
a hysterical agitation founded on nothing is raised. Truth can never
overtake such lies. One has to leave them to time.

'WE IRISH ARE ALWAYS AFRAID OF THINGS,'

said a celebrated theatrical manager to me, added Mr. Yeats, and there is some truth in the remark. Ireland used to be a nation of soldiers; to-day it trembles before a play or a newspaper article or the report of a divorce case. Our nationality and our purity seem such fragile things when they can perish at a shadow. It is only a passing fit of panic. Ireland will recover its courage and remember its past.

NOTES

1. By W. B. Yeats.
2. By Lady Gregory.
3. Named after Saint Aloysius Gonzaga (1568–91), the Italian Jesuit priest.

The Playboy: A Stay in the Court Proceedings; Mr Yeats Interviewed*

(From Our Own Correspondent.)

New York, Friday.

To-day's proceedings against the members of the Abbey Theatre Co., charged, on the complaint of a wine and spirit merchant[1] named Garrity, with producing an 'immoral play'—'The Playboy of the Western World'—were awaited with considerable interest in Philadelphia, but it was early announced that the action could not be proceeded with on its merits until a decision had been given by another Court.

The Irish Players, who were arrested on Wednesday and admitted to bail, were advised by their lawyer to apply for writs of habeas corpus against the Judge who granted the warrants, and to contest the constitutionality of the law under which they were arrested.

The application was made in another Court, and until the second Judge's decision is given the first Court cannot go on with the case.

The public feeling is that the Irish Players would have had no difficulty in winning their case in the first Court, but as their performances were

* *Irish Independent* (Dublin) 20 Jan 1912, p. 5.

liable to be stopped by a Court order, doubtless they acted under good legal advice in contesting the legality of the first proceedings.

MEANING OF THE PLAYBOY

Mr. W. B. Yeats Interviewed

The ethics and objects of Abbey Theatre plays in general, with special consideration of 'The Playboy,' which is causing such commotion in the Western World, were the subject of an interesting interview by an 'Irish Independent' representative with Mr. W. B. Yeats yesterday. In Mr. Yeats' opinion—and this was also, he says the author's intention—'The Playboy of the Western World' is a comedy or 'satiric phantasy.' 'It satirises everything that exists in all parts of the world, not the people of the West of Ireland alone, but also the people who sit in the stalls of the theatre. Every satiric artist does the same.'

Except for the newspaper reports, Mr. Yeats said he had no confirmation of the Philadelphia arrests. The arrests, if true, were absurd, he said, and the players, he expected, would be discharged.

'The only conceivable effect,' he added, 'will be to give "The Playboy" another advertisement. Since the New York riot we've had a good deal of pressure from local managers to put it on continually, but we refused, as we want to show the whole repertory of our plays. This opposition will not cause us to withdraw the play. It will mean more pressure from local theatres to have it more often, but Lady Gregory will not allow it oftener than three times a week.'

SYNGE'S IMAGINATION

'I see in the play the noble, fantastic imagination of Mr. Synge. Irish-Americans see it as they do because they are accustomed to Boucicault. They can only understand literature as something which gives what they consider a pleasing representation of Irish life. I found in America that Irish men and women who passed through the Universities—the type most valuable to a nation—had fallen under the enchantment of Synge, Lady Gregory, and our other players, and were turning their eyes to Ireland again. We played "The Playboy" in Oxford to an enthusiastic audience of undergraduates, and I believe their enthusiasm had something to do with the all-but-unanimous vote of Home Rule passed next day by the Oxford Union.

'This American agitation is an artificial thing, created by half-educated men, who are bewildered at the old alleged photography professing to resemble nature, but not doing so, of Boucicault and the worst of the

Young Irelanders,[2] which is giving way to the impressionistic painting of Synge, Lady Gregory, S. L. Robinson, and T. C. Murray.

FANTASTIC COMEDY

' "The Playboy" was the last complete[3] play by Mr. Synge. He meant it as a fantastic comedy, and said so at the time. He didn't intend it to be taken literally, and never to my knowledge suggested or said anything as to its being anything else but a fantastic or satiric comedy. He certainly did not mean it to be taken as characteristic literally of Irish life.

'It is absurd to suppose that the play, whether a slander or not, does any harm to the reputation of Ireland. One man who throws an egg or red pepper on a stage does more harm than such a play, and there is no man of genius behind the red pepper.'

The Abbey Players will next visit Chicago, where they will conclude the tour and leave for Dublin on the 28 February. They are at present rehearsing new plays[4] by Messrs. T. C. Murray and S. L. Robinson and others, and will open their Dublin season with a new play[5] by Mr. Wm. Boyle. In future, Mr. Yeats said, they will play continuously the whole week, and not at week-ends, as heretofore.

NOTES

1. 'The liquor-seller, our prosecutor, was the first witness'—Lady Gregory, *Our Irish Theatre* (London and New York: G. P. Putnam, 1913) p. 227. See the chapter entitled ' "The Playboy" in America'.

2. 'Young Ireland' was the name given to the revolutionary party in Ireland in 1848 comprising W. Smith O'Brien, Gavan Duffy, Thomas Osborne Davis and Thomas Davies. Their propaganda and actions led to several state trials for sedition and treason. On the formation of the Young Ireland Society Yeats says (*Autobiographies*, p. 99): 'A Young Ireland Society met in the lecture-hall of a workmen's club in York Street with O'Leary for president, and there four or five university students and myself and occasionally Taylor spoke on Irish history or literature.'

3. Synge left an unfinished play, *Deirdre of the Sorrows*.

4. *Maurice Harte*, by T. C. Murray (1873–1959), was first produced on 20 June 1912. *Patriots*, by Lennox Robinson (1886–1958) opened on 11 April 1912.

5. *Family Failing*, by William Boyle (1853–1922), was first presented on 28 March 1912.

What We Try To Do[*]

W. B. YEATS

When the idea of giving expression on the stage to the dramatic literature of Ireland was about to be carried out in 1899 it was found that no Irish actors were to be had. So we brought an English company to Dublin and Irish plays were presented by them for a short period. This method, however, did not produce the results we had hoped for; the English actors lacked the proper feeling for the Irish spirit. In 1902 there was a nearer approach to a realization of a truly national Irish theater, for a company of amateurs produced Irish plays in small halls in Dublin. The players received nothing, nor did they ask remuneration. Since they had to gain a living by another work to carry on the work they were interested in the double burden told heavily on them.

When it looked as if all might have to be given up my friend Miss Horniman[1] arranged for a little theatre in connection with the Mechanics' Institute[2] and after a struggle the idea of a national Irish theater became an assured fact. The National Theater Society now has the Abbey Theater in Dublin and it is entirely independent and paying its way. But this does not mean that we did not have a hard fight. Our great difficulty was that in our first years our income was mostly from sixpenny and one shilling seats in the gallery and pit. Clerks, shop boys, shop girls and work-men—audiences of much enthusiasm but little money—came to see our plays, which appealed to them. Our theater had its beginnings not among the rich, as did the New Theater[3] in New York, but right in the masses of the people. The working people showed the way and now that all classes come to us we constantly fill the Abbey Theater.

THE PREDOMINANT PEASANT

With us the Irish peasant is predominant for the moment, as was the peasant in the Norwegian movement. During the youth of Ibsen[4] and Bjornson[5] their phrase was 'To understand the peasant by the saga and the saga by the peasant.' Our whole movement could apply to itself the same phrase.[6] Lady Gregory, the author of our most amusing comedies, is also the author of the standard translation of the Irish epic stories, which she has translated into the speech of the Irish peasant. Synge, too, when he put an old heroic tale into dramatic play made use of dialect.[7]

---

[*] *Sunday Record-Herald* (Chicago) 4 Feb 1912, pt. 7, p. 1.

Speaking of Synge, we have two opposite types of characters in Ireland that both seem peculiarly national. One is the gentle, harmless—you might call saintly—type, that knows no wrong, and goes through life happy and untroubled, without any evil or sadness. Goldsmith[8] was an Irishman of that type, a man without any real knowledge apparently of sadness or evil. And that kind of Irishman is common in Ireland, chiefly among the better-off people, but among the country people you find it too. There are a surprising number of constitutionally happy people in Ireland.

The other type that is also so characteristically Irish is represented by Swift.[9] It is true he had little or no Irish blood, but in bringing up he was an Irish product. And that type is terribly bitter, hostile, sarcastic.

Now Synge belonged to this bitter, sarcastic type in so far as he was a satirist. He was no reincarnation of Goldsmith, but rather the opposite. Yet his personality, his emotions were remarkably sane and healthy, even though they were not placid. Only the other day I heard a paper read in which he was described as the embodiment of a healthy mentality.

That was the truth, and I agreed with it. But the strange part was that Synge gained his healthiness from living for years facing death.[10] He faced death in his own body, for he was constitutionally weak. And in going to the Aran Islands he found a people that faced death, and he lived with them. The islanders are all the time being picked off by the sea, from which they make their livelihood, yet they are a strong, healthy people. And so, in his life facing death, Synge in the end gained a wonderful mental healthiness, though only after a struggle.

FIRST MEETING WITH SYNGE

When I first met Synge in 1897 I found that he wanted to write about French literature. He had been studying Molière, Corneille and Racine. I told him that if he was to write for the English papers he would find that they demanded something about modern French literature. Of the latter he knew nothing. If he was influenced by French writers they were of the pre-Molière period, and about them there was certainly nothing decadent.

He was a nationalist, but he never spoke of politics. Nothing interested him but the individual mind. It was no malice, no love of mischief, that made him imagine, instead of colleens of the old sort and the good young men of Boucicault, blind Martin and his wife, in 'The Well of the Saints,' the erring wife in 'The Shadow of the Glen,' the fantastic mistaken hero-worship of the people in his 'Playboy of the Western World.' Dublin for a time saw but one-half his meaning and rejected him, rioting for a week after the first performance of his greatest play, rejecting him as most countries have rejected their greatest poets. But Dublin has repented sooner than most countries have repented and today 'The Playboy' is played constantly in Dublin to good houses, drawn from all political and social sections.

NOTES

This is part of a discussion entitled 'The Story of the Irish Players'. Other contributors are George Moore, Sara Allgood, T. W. Rolleston, and Lady Gregory.

1. Annie Elizabeth Fredericka Horniman (1860–1937), wealthy English theatre manager and patron, one of the first to organise and encourage the modern repertory theatre movement, and a seminal influence in the Irish and English theatres at the beginning of the twentieth century. She was interested in the Irish theatre movement and acted for some time as unpaid secretary to Yeats. In 1903 she went to Dublin and there built and equipped the Abbey Theatre, with which she remained connected until 1910, when she disposed of it to a board of trustees. In the meantime she had bought and refurbished the Gaiety Theatre, Manchester, where from 1908 to 1917 she maintained an excellent repertory company. See James W. Flannery, *Miss Annie F. Horniman and the Abbey Theatre* (Dublin: The Dolmen Press, 1970).

2. Miss Horniman bought the hall of the Mechanics' Institute in Abbey Street (built on the site of the old Theatre Royal, burnt down in 1880) and an adjoining building, and there erected the Abbey Theatre. The licence was issued in Lady Gregory's name (as Miss Horniman was not resident in Ireland), and she and Yeats were the only directors. The theatre opened on 27 December 1904 with Yeats's *On Baile's Strand* and Lady Gregory's *Spreading the News*.

3. The New Theatre opened on 6 November 1909 and was intended as a home of modern repertory. In spite of a large and expensive company and the reputation and experience of those connected with the enterprise the venture was not a success; the general public felt that it was a theatre for the few and stayed away. It closed, and reopened as an ordinary playhouse under the name of the Century on 15 September 1911. In 1929, however, it closed and was pulled down a year later.

4. Henrik Ibsen (1828–1906), leading Norwegian dramatist who had great impact on modern drama. 'As time passed,' says Yeats in his *Autobiographies* (p. 279) 'Ibsen became in my eyes the chosen author of very clever young journalists, who, condemned to their treadmill of abstraction, hated music and style; and yet neither I nor my generation could escape him because, though we and he had not the same friends, we had the same enemies. I bought his collected works in Mr. [William] Archer's translation out of my thirty shillings a week and carried them to and fro upon my journeys to Ireland. . . .'

5. Björnstjerne Björnson (1832–1910), Norwegian poet, dramatist, novelist and political and social leader; winner of 1903 Nobel prize in literature.

6. See John Hofstad Kelson, 'Nationalism in the Theater: The Ole Bull Theater in Norway and the Abbey Theater in Ireland: A Comparative Study', Ph.D. dissertation (University of Kansas, 1964).

7. The Anglo-Irish idiom was not discovered, much less invented by Synge—Dr Douglas Hyde and Lady Gregory had used it before him in their renderings of old Irish literature—and in its main peculiarities it is a genuine folk speech in which Gaelic locutions are substituted for current English, and some older English words and usages, gone out of fashion in modern English, are retained; as Yeats put it, it is 'the beautiful English which has grown up in Irish-speaking districts, and takes its vocabulary from the time of Malory and the translators of the Bible, but its idiom and its vivid metaphor from Irish.' Synge, however, writing of a life that in its external relations is limited to a little known locality in a language equally limited, was the first to rise above the essential narrowness implicit in these limitations and construct a drama of universal interest.

8. Oliver Goldsmith (1728–74), Irish poet, playwright, essayist and novelist who became acquainted with Dr Samuel Johnson (1761) and a member of the famous club centred around Johnson. His works include *The Citizen of the World* (1762), *The Traveller* (1764), *The Vicar of Wakefield* (1766), *The Good-Natured Man* (1768), *The Deserted Village* (1770) and *She Stoops to Conquer* (1773).

9. Jonathan Swift (1667–1754), Irish satirist. His writings include *The Battle of the Books* (1704), *A Tale of a Tub* (1704), *Gulliver's Travels* (1726) and *A Modest Proposal* (1729).

10. In 1908 exploratory surgery revealed that the growth in Synge's side was inoperable. In early 1909 he entered a nursing home in Dublin, where he died soon after on 24 March 1909.

An Interview with
Mr. W. B. Yeats*

HUGH LUNN

Many artists to-day try to look like business men, and succeed in thinking like them. But Mr. Yeats resembles, in appearance and in manner, the popular idea of a poet; dreamy, abstracted, bringing himself only with an effort into touch with the humdrum details of life. To give an example: I had written asking for an interview, and getting no answer I called on him at 18, Upper Woburn Buildings.[1] He opened the door himself, and I reminded him of my letter. 'Yes,' he murmured, 'I remember dimly, dimly.' I felt vulgar and mundane, but as soon as Mr. Yeats realised why I had come, he welcomed me very courteously, and took the greatest pains to make every remark clear to the meanest intelligence. (I gathered from a chance remark that he had given many interviews to American reporters.)

'At present,' he said, 'we are busy producing the *Hour-Glass*[2] at the Abbey Theatre, Dublin. I have had great trouble with this play, for in its original form the treatment made it seem platitudinous. A music-hall singer who saw it was converted; that was very distressing. Had it not been for Gordon Craig's[3] designs, I should not have troubled to rewrite it. But they helped me wonderfully, and I think I have banished platitude from the *Hour-Glass* in its present form. Gordon Craig is the greatest producer living, greater than Reinhardt,[4] or any other.'

'Do you think,' I asked, 'that Bernard Shaw is typically Irish?'

'Yes,' answered Mr. Yeats, in the slow, measured voice he always used when speaking on any subject to which he had given especial thought, 'Shaw is irreverent, headlong, fantastic; and those are the typical Irish qualities, though the English like to credit Irishmen with all the virtues that England despises. Shaw has, also, the feminine logic, which is led in Ireland by scholastic philosophy. It may amuse him to argue, as women do, from absurd premises, but, like women, he is always flawlessly logical. During Shaw's childhood, the Ireland created by English politics reached its climax, and its products were men like Shaw, Wilde, and George Moore. Shaw, of course, must not be confused with the other two, for he has an extraordinary sense of moral responsibility; but he shares with them

* *Hearth and Home* (London) 28 Nov 1912 p. 229.

a certain harsh, unsympathetic quality. They had no home in Ireland, and England was always a foreign country. The effect of this on Wilde and Moore was to make them personally irresponsible. Deprived of a resting-place for the soul, they became spiritual adventurers. And England drew them with the attraction of strangeness. That explains for me what some people call Wilde's snobbishness. It was not snobbishness; it was the wonder of a traveller. The English aristocrats were as marvellous to Wilde as nobles of Baghdad.'

I asked Mr. Yeats in what relation he himself and his fellow-workers stood to Ireland.

'We feel ourselves responsible to Ireland. Our task has been to create a public that will feel joy and pride in its own country; and we realise that we can only get to Ireland through England. Synge took no pleasure in the performance of his plays in England, but he felt the importance of gaining the appreciation of the English. I remember once saying to him: "Synge, do you and I write out of hate or love of Ireland?" And he replied, "I have often asked myself that question but I have never found an answer."'

'Synge's interest in Ireland developed rather late in his life, didn't it?' I asked, with perhaps too abrupt a return to the matter-of-fact.

'Hardly. He studied Irish when at college. His enemies in Ireland assert that he was devoted to decadent French literature. A Catholic Evangelist accused him in one newspaper of translating the infamous poetry of "Bandolier"; but the truth is that he cared very little for Baudelaire or any other modern Frenchman. Indeed, I remember telling him that if he wished to live by writing about French literature, he must write about later poets than Racine. His interest was never in literary or artistic people. He always cared more for peasants and the poor, and he lived among them in many of the countries of Europe.'

'You don't think much of Thos. Davis,[5] and the other Irish writers of the 'fifties, do you?'

'I think they did good work in their time, but Ireland's need is different to-day. We are trying to discipline the Irishman's imagination, to refine his emotions, and to make the educated feel Ireland's past. Many of the younger generation are on our side. Even in Trinity College the difference in the last ten years is enormous. Trinity has been like a ship at sea, and the students like a foreign garrison. But recently when the Governing Board asked that Trinity might be put outside the Home Rule Bill, a protest was drawn up, signed by two hundred students and ten junior Fellows. The aim of the Board was to prevent legal persecution by the Catholics. But the decision of the Board substituted a certain evil for a remote possibility. I earnestly hope that the proposal will be withdrawn, for it may mean the ruin of Trinity. Home Rule is essential because all the characterstic Irish public faults come from the absorption of the nation in one subject of political discussion. No Irish movement can succeed till the intellect of Ireland has been liberated from national obsession. No country can prosper till the greater part of its intellect is occupied with itself. With Home Rule a governing mind would grow up in Ireland; our ambitious men would no longer invariably seek an education to fit them for alien service, and so no longer set the tone for all. At present we educate for export, for India, not for Connaught.[6] We will only know what Ireland's capacity is when we have freed its mind from the great obsession, and formed its mind for the country's service.

'Pitt[7] decapitated Ireland. It is like a turkey-cock running headless round a yard; no wonder its movements are spasmodic and unmeaning.

'I hope that image isn't too wild,' added Mr. Yeats with a smile.

Wishing to find out Mr. Yeats's attitude towards the English writers of to-day, I asked him whether he preferred contemporary literature to the literature of the 'nineties.

'No; I cannot say I do. In the 'nineties a man set out to write well. He wrote to please himself, and did not keep his eye on the reader.'

'But don't you think the writers of that period kept themselves too aloof from real life?'

'Certainly they were removed from the questions of the hour. But Dowson,[8] for instance, wrote of wine and women, and both these are much nearer to our hearts than the subtlest politics of Mr. H. G. Wells.[9]

'The truth is, I don't know much about contemporary writers, except the poets. Till a few generations ago, writers founded themselves on the classics, and so saw their own age at a distance, and more clearly. But a modern writer, if, like so many of us, he has not the classics, must get his place apart from life by avoiding his contemporaries. I always advise young writers to read the English authors of the seventeenth century. Even Wordsworth, even Keats and Shelley, have the same illusions as us. We are too near to see what is worthless in them. Now, Donne, whom, as you see, I am just reading—well, really I can't find anything bad in Donne. But you see what I mean . . .'

And so I left Mr. Yeats, after running across to a shop to fetch him a morning paper (no doubt Mr. Yeats felt that even a contemporary can discern what is worthless in a newspaper).

Mr. Yeats will be remembered as a wonderful lyric poet; at his best as magical as Shakespeare or Keats in such lines as:—

'Beauty grown sad with its eternity.'

But he is too Ariel-like to be among the great dramatic poets. His feet never touch the earth, except in Ireland, and even in Ireland he has not the dramatist's preoccupation with individual characteristics. It may even be that he will be remembered less as a singer than as the supreme influence in a great spiritual revival. As usual, it is the music-maker and the dreamer of dreams who leaves behind him a solid and lasting achievement to the confusion of the so-called practical man.

NOTES

1. In the summer of 1895 Yeats moved away from the family and took rooms with Arthur Symons in Fountain Court; then a few months later, he moved into rooms of his own in Woburn Buildings.

2. Yeats's play *The Hour-Glass*, was first produced by the Irish National Theatre Society at the Molesworth Hall, Dublin on 14 March 1903.

3. Edward Gordon Craig (1872–1966), English actor, stage designer, and producer; son of Ellen Terry; and author of *The Art of the Theatre* (1905). Yeats thought that scenery should be simple; in this he was influenced by Craig. In a letter to Frank Fay dated 21 April 1902 he says: 'I have . . . learnt a great deal from Gordon Craig.'

4. Max Reinhardt (1873–1943), Austrian theatrical director and stage manager; specialist in impressionistic mass effects.

5. Thomas Davis (1814–45), Irish writer and poet; founded the *Nation* with Charles Gavan Duffy and J. B. Dillon; swiftly came to be regarded as *the* national poet, and was the inspiration of the Young Ireland movement. Under O'Leary's influence Yeats half intended to start up some day a new Young Ireland movement like that of Davis; it would produce nationalist literature, too, but of better quality, and would play a less active role than Davis's group in practical politics, in which Yeats had no interest. In 1914 Yeats consented to speak at a commemoration of Thomas Davis's centenary organised by the Gaelic Society of Trinity College.

6. A north-western province of Eire.

7. William Pitt (1759–1806), English statesman, probably England's greatest prime minister; compelled by George III to withdraw proposal of Catholic emancipation introduced for quieting Irish rebellion of 1798, temporarily allayed by union with Ireland (1800–1) secured through political corruption.

8. Ernest Dowson (1867–1900), English poet.

9. Herbert George Wells (1866–1946), English novelist who turned first to what is now termed science fiction, and in his final period became a political and sociological writer pure and simple. His many writings include *The Time Machine* (1895), *The Invisible Man* (1897) and *Outline of History* (1920).

Mr W. B. Yeats: Poet and Mystic*

SYBIL BRISTOWE

When one already holds one's preconceived notions of a man and his personality, one is apt to form an imaginary picture of his surroundings and to fear that stern fact will dispel this pleasant little fancy. It was, therefore, with a somewhat perturbed feeling that I sought an interview with Mr. Yeats at his own rooms in 18, Woburn Buildings. But my fears were unnecessary. I had dreamed of a subdued atmosphere, free from the disillusioning effects of electric light and all the latest improvements—and I found it. The house was reticent; the poet himself opened the door and

* *T.P.'s Weekly* (London) 4 Apr 1913 421.

led me up the narrow, dark staircase till we reached his own bachelor room, dimly lighted by the red-hot coals cuddled together in the grate, and two candles in tall green candlesticks set upon a table. The pictures on the walls looked sleepily through the shadows, and, as I sank down in a low armchair in front of the fire, I felt with relief that this was a fitting house for a poet and a mystic, the avowed follower of William Blake and Jacob Boehme. Mr. Yeats seated himself upon an old wooden settle opposite me, a tall dark man, with an almost Spanish type of face, and a quiet modulated voice, as unlike the caw of a rook, so picturesquely described by Mr. George Moore, as it is possible for a voice to be.

Celtic or Irish?

I explained that I had come to find out what I could about Mr. Yeats' connection with, and interest in, the Celtic movement,[1] but he interrupted me. 'The word is not mine,' he said. 'I prefer to call it the Irish movement.' He then told me of his early ambitions to found an Irish National Theatre in Dublin, where Irish plays written by Irish authors might be acted, and where he and others could carry out their own ideas of stage management with Irish actors, all unversed in the art of the English school of acting, under their direction. Lady Gregory financed them. Their actors they drew from the Boys' Patriotic Club, boys who had never heard of Sir George Alexander[2] and who were plastic material in their hands; and Mr. William Fay,[3] a man who originally started life as an electric light organiser, and who had always been fond of acting farces, became their stage manager, so that between Mr. Fay's practical experience and Mr. Yeats' theories these plays were eventually started.

Speech and Ear

The first productions,[4] under the régime of the Coffee Club Players, were a play[5] by Mr. Russell and 'Cathleen ni Hoolihan,' the first prose play written by Mr. Yeats. The managers had set before themselves three ideals:—

1. The reduction of all unnecessary movement.
2. Immense care of speech.
3. The decorative details of the stage.

Lady Gregory and Mr. Synge, whose beautiful plays are such a feature of the movement, went further than Mr. Yeats in their appreciation of speech and ear. They looked upon speech as the primary object in dramatic performance. Voice and hearer, not sight and seer, showed the most intellectual insight into the stage, and Mr. Synge gave the greater portion of his time to the consideration of cadences.

Stage Decoration and Synge

Mr. Yeats, on his part, desired to sweep away the Victorian type of scenery as presented by the late Sir Henry Irving[6] and Sir Herbert Tree,[7] and introduce a new decorative style of art upon the stage. In this he found a valuable ally in Mr. Craig, the greatest manager, he averred, of modern times. He picked up a small drawing of a masked man by Mr. Craig and passed it to me to look at; then, taking a candle, he led me to a picture painted in the decorative style, a design for a stage effect by Mr. Gregory. 'This will show you a little what we are striving after,' he said, as I gazed up at the faintly lighted picture. 'And can you tell me anything about Mr. Synge?' I asked, as I sat down again before the fire and Mr. Yeats walked up and down the room. 'There is little to say,' was the reply. 'Silent, charming, absorbed in his work, always ailing but physically strong, he kept himself a sketch, with little to say, for his own work completely absorbed him. He belonged to an old Irish family, which had seven bishops[8] in it, and he lived in one of the show places of Dublin—an old Georgian house, built by an ancestor. He had few friends, he was simply an artist who only cared for the poor—not because he had any philanthropic interest in them, not because he possessed any democratic fervour, but because he liked a poor man by reason of certain qualities a hard life produced. He discovered his genius by living in the Isle of Arran,[9] where people live literally through necessity and the pressure of great realities.'

Oscar Wilde

'As for Oscar Wilde,' he continued, prompted by another question from me, 'I knew him in his early prosperous days, when I was about twenty-one or twenty-two. I remember he asked me to dinner one Christmas Day and read to me, and to his charming wife (who died before him, overwhelmed by his great tragedy),[10] his then unpublished "Defence [sic] of Lying," the most brilliant of his essays. After that I saw him from time to time. He was incomparably the finest talker of his epoch. It was, perhaps, because I admired his conversation so much that I never fully appreciate his books. They remind me of something else, incomparably more spontaneous. In literature I am for the "Meek in spirit." In those days there was a story (fabulous, perhaps) that he filled notebooks with the casual inspirations of his own conversation and made his plays out of these notebooks. Both he and George Moore seemed to me like Tennyson's Launcelot, who, by sheer vehemence of nature, all but saw the Grail . . . but the full vision was only for the meek Galahad.'

George Moore

'I think that I met the greater men of that epoch in the evenings at "The Cheshire Cheese,"[11] men whose names were still all but obscure, untranslatable spirits, who will cross no frontiers in our time. All our judgments are perverted at present by the great fame of the translatable authors. It means that the style of the more spiritual quality exists less than in an age when the translator was slower at his work. Every country is affected by it. Its standards are altered. No country gives another of its best.' Here I interrupted him. 'Is Byron an example of your meaning?' 'A perfect example. Except as a master of satire he has ceased to have any influence in England, because he has no style, no delicacy of rhythm, no minute sincerity.' 'And . . . will you tell me something about your connection with Mr. George Moore?'

'But why should we speak of him?—he is so eloquent about himself! He creates better than Zola, though he thinks like a child. When he came to Ireland he tried to get Archbishop Walsh to establish a censorship of the Irish stage. He wrote vehement letters to the "Freeman's Journal" on the subject. He was indignant with me because I repudiated him. Now he has discovered that Catholicism and literature are incompatible. If I were to remind him of the Odes of Coventry Patmore, which I think great lyric poetry, he would be indignant with me again. The child has barked his shins over a stool. I do not greatly like the shape of the stool, but there it is, and there it is likely to remain. But what courage he has! He will bark his shins over another stool to-morrow and not abate his headlong pace.'

Debt to William Blake

The conversation then trailed off into the consideration of more intimate things; of religion and mysticism, and of the debt that Mr. Yeats owed to William Blake[12] and the European gnostics.[13] He told me that he worked every day till four o'clock, after which he dressed and was able to see visitors. In the evening he frequently attended a night class, and at present he was studying French. Time slipped away so quickly under the spell of Mr. Yeats' conversation that I did not realise how long I had been sitting there before the fire till the chiming of a distant clock reminded me that it was time to go. I took my leave regretfully, and as I passed out of the quiet house into the busy streets I felt that even then I had not learned one half of what I really wished to know.

NOTES

1. The Celtic Renaissance, also known as the Irish Literary Revival, identifies the creative period in Irish literature from about 1885 to the death of Yeats in 1939. Some of this literature was written in Gaelic (Irish), a Celtic language, but the major authors wrote in English. The movement was stimulated by the works of Yeats, who, with others, sought to dignify Irish culture by producing art related to Irish life and tradition. Yeats called one of his books *The Celtic Twilight* (1893). James Joyce ridiculed the phenomenon in his phrase 'cultic twalette'. Yeats later renounced the whole early Celtic twilight movement and its trappings, and he made it quite clear that this was so in his poem 'A Coat' (in *Responsibilities*). See Ernest A. Boyd, *Ireland's Literary Renaissance* (Dublin: Talbot Press, 1916).

2. Sir George Alexander (1858–1918), English actor – manager who managed St James's Theatre, London from 1891 until his death.

3. Frank J. (1870–1931) and William George (1872–1947) Fay, Irish actors who were important in the early history of the Abbey Theatre. They began their careers at the Dublin Dramatic School, run by Mrs Lacy, wife of a touring manager. In 1898 they formed the Ormonde Dramatic Society. In 1902 the Irish National Dramatic Society included the two Irish actors. Stephen Gwynn, in *Irish Literature and Drama*, says: 'The style of acting identified with the Abbey Theatre is due to the genius of the Fays—and of W. G. Fay especially.' William Fay left the Abbey and went to America in 1908. Yeats's ideas on acting were partly due to the technique of the Fays, who allowed but small movement and gesture. See William

George Fay and Catherine Carswell, *The Fays of the Abbey Theatre* (London: Rich and Cowan, 1935).

4. The plays were presented by W. G. Fay's Irish National Dramatic Company at St Teresa's Hall, Clarendon Street, Dublin.

5. *Deirdre*, by George Russell (AE).

6. Sir Henry Irving (1838–1905), English actor; lessee and manager of Lyceum Theatre, London; professionally associated with Ellen Terry; and first actor to be knighted. Irving dominated the London stage for the last thirty years of Queen Victoria's reign. At the height of his renown there were people who found his mannerisms unsympathetic and even slightly ludicrous. To Irving acting was movement. As a manager he was not content until he had enlisted in the service of his theatre some of the finest archaeologists, painters and musicians of the day.

7. Sir Herbert Beerbohm Tree (1853–1917), English actor–manager; half brother of Max Beerbohm; lessee and manager of Haymarket Theatre, London from 1887 to 1897; and manager of Her Majesty's Theatre from 1897. Tree played a wide range of parts, attempted to revive poetic drama with Stephen Phillips's plays, and staged over-elaborate productions of Shakespeare.

8. The Synges produced only five bishops and a quantity of other clergy and missionaries over the years since the first Synge came to Ireland in the seventeenth century. David H. Greene and Edward M. Stephens in their authoritative biography, *J. M. Synge 1871–1909* (New York: Macmillan, 1959) p. 13 say: 'The Irish branch of the family produced five bishops, beginning with the first Synge who came to Ireland in the seventeenth century.' See also Robin Skelton, *Synge and His World* (London: Thames and Hudson, 1971) p. 7 and Edward M. Stephens, *My Uncle John*, ed. Andrew Carpenter (London and New York: Oxford University Press, 1974).

9. One of the Aran Islands, off the west coast of Ireland. Yeats had advised Synge to visit the Aran Islands and 'express a life that has never found expression'.

10. Oscar Wilde (1854–1900) was tried on a charge of sodomy, convicted and imprisoned for two years (1895–7), during which time he wrote a prose apologia, *De Profundis*. After his release he wrote anonymously *The Ballad of Reading Gaol*, reflecting his tragic experiences. Constance Wilde died in Genoa on 7 April 1898.

11. Yeats discussed with Ernest Rhys the need for the poets to know one another lest they become jealous at one another's success. From this conversation came the Rhymers' Club, formed by the efforts of Yeats, Rhys, and T. W. Rolleston. It met in the Cheshire Cheese, London, and its members soon included Lionel Johnson, Ernest Dowson, Arthur Symons, Richard Le Gallienne, John Davidson, Selvyn Image, Edwin Ellis, John Todhunter and Herbert Horne. See Ernest Rhys, 'W. B. Yeats: Early Recollections', *Fortnightly Review* (July 1935) pp. 52–7 and W. B. Yeats, *Autobiographies* (London: Macmillan, 1955) pp. 204–6.

12. When Yeats was fifteen or sixteen his father had talked to him of Blake and Rosetti, given him their works to read, and told him of his own essentially pre-Raphaelite literary principles. An edition of Blake undertaken by Yeats in collaboration with Edwin Ellis appeared in 1893 and was followed by a selection of Blake's poems edited by Yeats with an enthusiastic introduction.

13. Adherents of Gnosticism, the thought and practice of various cults of late pre-Christian and early Christian centuries distinguished by the conviction that matter is evil and that emancipation comes through gnosis.

The Early Days of the Irish National Theatre*

P. J. KELLY

'I was just nineteen when I became a member of the Irish National Dramatic Company. Our first production was "Deirdre," a play by George Russell, the mystic poet and painter. A little later W. B. Yeats gave us his "Kathleen Ni Houlihan," a peasant play in one act. These plays were presented for the first time on April 2, 1902, at St. Teresa's Hall, Clarendon Street, Dublin. Both plays were rehearsed by W. G. Fay; the scenery was painted by Mr. Russell and Mr. Fay, and the dresses for "Deirdre" were designed by Mr. Russell and made in Dublin by some of his friends.

'Among those in the cast presenting these two plays were Dudley Digges,[1] (now playing here in "John Ferguson,")[2] Mrs. Digges, (Maud Gonne,)[3] a lady of great beauty and talent; Padraic Colum,[4] and myself.[5] The success of these two plays was such that those engaged in presenting them felt it would be a great pity to let the work so enthusiastically begun drop at this point. There being no money, however, to go on with the project, we took up a collection among ourselves and rented a little hall at 34 Lower Camden Street, where we stored the scenery and properties we possessed and began rehearsal again under the direction of W. G. Fay. Our repertoire this time included, besides "Kathleen Ni Houlihan" and "Deirdre," a farce by Mr. Yeats entitled "A Pot of Broth."[6] This is the bill which formed the program of the Samhain[7] Festival, the company presenting them having been known up to that time as W. G. Fay's Irish National Dramatic Company. After this the title was changed to the Irish National Theatre Society. It was hoped to make Mr. Russell, who had given them their first play, the first President, but he insisted that this honor should go to W. B. Yeats.

'In the modest beginning of the Irish National Theatre Society, which is now directed by Mr. Yeats and Lady Gregory, and which owns the Abbey Theatre, Dublin, we all worked gratis,[8] and worked with all the love of the art there was in us as inspiration. No task was considered too menial to undertake by any member of that first little company of players and producers. Playwrights, actors, and producers combined in building

* Extracted from *New York Times*, 1 June 1919, section 4, p. 2.

props, painting scenery, constructing with our own hands everything that was necessary, even down to building the chairs upon which the audience sat. A new member of the company was usually handed either a paintbrush or a hammer and bag of nails.

'Of our first performance Mr. Fay wrote to a friend: "We took in four pounds, fifteen shillings, on our opening night, so we saw no reason to complain financially."

'In addition to Mr. Yeats the roster of the Irish National Theater Society included such distinguished names as George Moore, Edward Martyn, and John Millington Synge, with many other equally brilliant men and women. The society, and my association in it with these great artists, was a veritable wonderland to me. I confess that it is so yet. I often turn in thought from these more commercial days in the theatre to my work in this splendid literary movement of Ireland, and remember with a never dying interest the many amusing incidents along the way of its growth, particularly those pertaining to the brilliant folk associated with it.

'Probably the most interesting figure in the Irish literary renaissance is W. B. Yeats. Mr. Yeats is a man of lofty idealism, as his writings all show. It was sometimes extremely difficult, however, to follow his thought. I remember one instance in particular. Mr. Yeats was collaborating with George Moore in writing a three-act play called "Diarmid [sic] and Grania,"[9] which was produced in Dublin by the Benson[10] Shakespearean Company prior to the formation of the Irish National Theatre Society. During the collaborations[11] Yeats explained to Moore that the first act must be horizontal, the second act perpendicular, and the third act circular.

'"When is an act perpendicular, horizontal, or circular?" George Moore demanded to know, whereupon Yeats gave him a look of disgust and made no further effort to explain. In his own mind his meaning was evidently clear enough, but no one else ever found out what he meant by the application of such terms to a play.

'Yeats is also an extremely absentminded man: At a social gathering I once saw him pour a jug of milk into a teapot instead of the hot water necessary to make the tea. This incident is typical of the man, whose thought was so occupied with the creation of literature that he was quite liable to forget to go to bed.'

NOTES

Patrick J. Kelly was one of the signatories to the book of rules of the Irish National Theatre Society who were to constitute the society in 1903 until a general meeting had been held to appoint a president and admit other members. There were seven of them, the first official founders of the Society: William G. Fay, Patrick J. Kelly, Frederick Ryan, Helen S. Laird, Maire Walker (Maire Nic Shiubhlaigh), James Starkey and Frank J. Fay with George Roberts as Secretary. The society was the result of the amalgamation of the Irish Literary Theatre with W. G. Fay's Irish National Dramatic Company, of which P. J. Kelly was a leading member. 'One of our people', wrote Frank Fay, 'suggested the formation of what he calls an Irish National Theatre Society, but he has not worked out his idea and personally as I said before I dislike asking for people's money. It is certain that one of these days Mr. Digges and Mr. Kelly will have to be paid if we want to retain them.' This letter was in reply to one from Yeats dated 21 April 1902. In 1904 Miss A. E. F. Horniman made her official offer to buy the hall of the Mechanics' Institute, Abbey Street, and a building next door, in Marlborough Street, and turn them into a small theatre. Her letter and the reply to it (both quoted in full in Lennox Robinson's *Ireland's Abbey Theatre*) are the birth certificate of the Abbey Theatre. The acceptance of Miss Horniman's offer is dated 11 May 1904 and it was signed by all the founder members except P. J. Kelly, who did not remain long in Dublin. The organisers of the Irish Section of the St Louis Exposition invited the company to visit the United States and give performances of Irish plays at the exposition and elsewhere. The company as a whole, or as an Irish organisation, found itself unable to accept the invitation, because it was 'thought that our work should be in Ireland for the present'. Some members of the company, including P. J. Kelly, Dudley Digges and Maire T. Quinn, accepted the invitation, and never returned to Ireland.

1. As Naisi in *Deirdre* and as Michael Gillan in *Cathleen ni Houlihan*.

2. By St John Ervine. The play was first produced at the Abbey Theatre in November 1915.

3. At that time there were several theatrical bodies using the drama as a vehicle for political propagandist purposes, and it was one of these bodies, Inghinnide na h. Eireann [the Daughters of Ireland], which first produced Yeats's *Cathleen ni Houlihan*, with Maud Gonne in the title role. Maud Gonne was then a very prominent leader in the militant political movement and she brought to her acting all the intensity of her political beliefs. 'It was a very fine thing', wrote Yeats, 'for so beautiful a woman to consent to play my poor old Cathleen, and she played with nobility and tragic power.' The play represented the height of Yeats's nationalism and love. Written in 1902 for Maud Gonne to act, the play is a powerful rewriting of the theme of *The Land of Heart's Desire* in terms of nationalism.

4. As Buinne, son of Fergus, in *Deirdre*. At that time, playwrights such as George Russell and Padraic Colum took part in their own or their fellows' plays in the lesser roles.

5. As Fergus in *Deirdre*.

6. First produced by the Irish National Dramatic Company at Antient Concert Rooms on 30 October 1902.

7. 'Summer's End'. Originally the Druid festival of harvest fire.

8. 'Up to this time the actors had received no pay, giving their services for love of country and of art, but with the more frequent performances and their attendant rehearsals it became necessary to take a large part of the time of the leading men and women, and then, of course, they had to be paid.'—Cornelius Weygandt, *Irish Plays and Playwrights* (London: Constable, 1913) pp. 21–2.

9. The play was presented by the Irish Literary Theatre at the Gaiety Theatre, Dublin on 21 October 1901. The task of producing the play was undertaken by the Benson Shakespearean Company.

10. F. R. Benson played the part of Diarmuid, and Mrs F. R. Benson that of Grania, the King's daughter.

11. For two years Yeats collaborated with George Moore, helping him first with a revision of a play by Edward Martyn (*The Tale of a Town*), and then writing in full-scale collaboration an Irish heroic drama, *Diarmuid and Grania*. Though Yeats hated Moore's style, he respected his skill in construction. 'I saw Moore daily,' says Yeats, 'we were at work on *Diarmuid and Grania*. Lady Gregory thought such collaboration would injure my own art, and was perhaps right.' A heated correspondence passed between them on the subject. Inevitably they quarrelled and broke apart. Yeats kept a copy of the manuscript, but neither he nor Moore ever wanted to print the play. See Yeats's account of the collaboration in his *Dramatis Personae*; and that of Moore in *Ave* in (*Hail and Farewell*).

Some Impressions
of My Elders:
William Butler Yeats*

ST JOHN ERVINE

I

I HAVE been acquainted with Mr. Yeats for a longer time than I have with any other man named in this book, but I seem to myself to know very little about him, for he is extraordinarily aloof from life. His aloofness is different from that of Mr. Galsworthy who is perturbed about mankind. Mr. Yeats is totally unconcerned about problems of any sort. He is more interested in the things men do than in men themselves. He prefers the symbol to the thing symbolized. The harshest condemnation I ever heard him utter was delivered on 'A.E.,' of whom he said that he had ceased to be a poet in order to become a philanthropist! I met him last in Chicago, and I felt when we parted that I knew no more of him then than I knew when I first met him ten years earlier. Our meeting followed on the fact that I had sent a one-act play, entitled *The Magnanimous Lover*,[1] to him. It seems to me now to be a crudely-contrived, ill-written and violent piece, but when I sent it to Mr. Yeats I thought it was a remarkable work. It was performed after the production of Stanley Houghton's *Hindle Wakes* and Mr. Galsworthy's *The Eldest Son,* which have similar themes, but was written several years before they were performed. One evening, a few weeks after I had sent the manuscript of *The Magnanimous Lover* to him, I received a letter from Mr. Yeats, written in that queer, illegible, thick style which is so difficult to read. Many of the words were incomplete: all of them were badly-formed. The contrast between the handwriting of Mr. Shaw and Mr. Yeats is remarkable. Mr. Shaw's is very clear and neat and most beautifully-shaped, as delicate as a spider's web, but Mr. Yeats's writing is obscure, untidy, sprawling and hard to decipher, looking as if it had been done with a blunt pen. Mr. Wells writes in a small, clean, but not very clear hand, a deceptive fist, for it seems easier to read than it is. There is some oddness in

* *North American Review* (New York) CCXI (Feb 1920) 225–37; (March 1920) 402–10. Reprinted in *Some Impressions of My Elders* (London: George Allen and Unwin, 1923) pp. 248–86.

the fact that the handwriting of the poet should be so coarse and ungainly, while the handwriting of the dramatist, with so little of poetic emotion in him, is fine and shapely. The letter[2] from Mr. Yeats was to say that he liked my play, but could not make a definite decision about it until he had consulted his co-director at the Abbey Theatre, Lady Gregory. It had the formal, distant tone which is characteristic of his speech and writing, but it had a postscript which gave me great pleasure. In this postscript, he said that my play was the only example of 'wayward realism' that he had ever read. I did not quite understand what he meant by the phrase, but it was a compliment from a distinguished man, and compliments from distinguished men had never come my way before. I have had many praising letters from him since then about my work, but none that ever raised me to such a state of dizzy delight as that first letter did. He told me, in another postscript, that he found in my 'dialogue a quality of temperament, as distinguished from the usual impersonal logic. You have more than construction, and it is growing rare to have more.' He thought highly of *John Ferguson*[3]—so did Mr. Shaw and 'A.E.'—and when I was attacked in Dublin because of this play, I comforted myself with the thought that my betters liked what was denounced by my inferiors. Mr. Yeats wrote to me that *John Ferguson* was 'a fragment of life, fully expounded and without conventionality or confusion. I think it is the best play you have done, though not likely to be the most popular.' His criticism is especially valuable when it is adverse. I had written a play called *Mrs. Martin's Man* which I now know to have been a dreadful mess of motives. I sent it to Mr. Yeats in the hope that he would permit it to be done at the Abbey. He wrote lengthily to me about it, and when I had read his letter[4] I put my play in the fire, though afterwards I used the theme, purged of the faults he had found in it, for a novel with the same title. 'I believe,' he wrote,

> I believe that the play is an error. I am very sorry indeed to say this, for I know what a blow it is to any dramatist to be told that about work which must have taken many weeks. Shaw has driven you off your balance, and instead of giving a vision of life, which is your gift and a most remarkable gift to have, you have begun to be topical, to play with ideas, to construct outside of life. Shaw has a very unique mind, a mind that is a part of a logical process going on all over Europe but which has found in him alone its efficient expression in English. He has no vision of life. He is a figure of international argument. There is an old saying, 'No angel can carry two messages.' You have the greater gift of seeing life itself. . . .

I print that extract from his letter, partly as a corrective to my own pride, but chiefly because of its commentary on Mr. Shaw. Later, in this chapter I will make specific reference to Mr. Yeats's relationship to Mr. Shaw's work, but here I may say that, in spite of his sincere regard and admiration for Mr. Shaw, Mr. Yeats seems to be totally incapable of comprehending his work.[5] He is able to communicate with ghosts, but he cannot communicate with Mr. Shaw. He can understand astrologers and necromancers and spiritualists and thimble-riggers of all sorts and conditions, but he cannot understand Mr. Shaw. He told me on one occasion of an experience he had with a medium, a young girl who differed from all other mediums known to him in being a member of the upper class. The spirits, seemingly, prefer to communicate their messages through the lower orders. This girl's family were ashamed of her cataleptic powers and tried to conceal them from their neighbours, but they were persuaded to permit Mr. Yeats to see her in a trance. 'While she was in the trance,' he said to me, 'her fingers closed on her palm. Then they opened again, and I saw a small green pebble in the centre of her hand!' That was all! Immortal souls had disturbed the harmony of the universe and thrown a young girl of the upper class into a trance in order that they might place a small green pebble in the centre of her palm! And Mr. Yeats saw something wonderful and significant in that performance, but is unable to see anything significant in the work of Mr. Shaw. That to me is a thing so incomprehensible that I have abandoned all attempts to understand it. But all of this is digression and anticipation. Soon after I had received the letter in which he praised my 'wayward realism,' I heard from Mr. Yeats again. He invited me to call on him on the following Sunday evening at his rooms in Woburn Buildings, behind the Euston Road, in London; and thither, in a state of some excitement, I repaired. I had no trouble in finding the house, for Mr. Yeats, who, in some ways, is much more precise and clear-minded than people imagine or his handwriting indicates, had given me very explicit directions how to get to it, and had even drawn a rough sketch of the neighbourhood so that I should not fail to find him. Woburn Buildings consists of a number of tall houses in a narrow passage off Southampton Row, and running parallel with the Euston Road. It is a dingy, dark place, with an air of furtive poverty about it, and on Sunday nights it is depressing enough to fill a man's mind with plots for drab dramas. I have heard that Mr. H. G. Wells thought of the plot of that clever, devilish story of his, *The Island of Dr. Moreau*, in the Tottenham Court Road on a Bank Holiday when he was in a mood of discontent. I believe that the whole of the 'drab drama' was first conceived on Mr. Yeats's doorstep!

Shops form the ground floor of these houses, little, huckstering shops that just contrive to support their proprietors, and Mr. Yeats's rooms were on the third and fourth floors of a house which had a cobbler's shop on the ground floor. The cobbler was a pleasant, bearded man, wearing spectacles, who had some share in the management of his affairs; for when one, unable to obtain admission to the poet's rooms, required information about him, the cobbler invariably supplied it. He could tell whether Mr. Yeats had gone to Ireland or was merely taking the air, and when he was likely to return, and he would offer, with great courtesy, to take a message from you to be faithfully delivered to him on his arrival.

Mr. Yeats has poor and failing sight, and in the dusk of the Sunday evening on which I called on him, he could barely discern me. He stood in the hall, holding the door, looking very tall and dark, and said in that peculiar, tired and plaintive voice of his, 'Who is it?' and I answered 'St. John Ervine.' There is always something conspiratorial about the manner in which he admits you to his rooms. You feel that you want to give the countersign.

'Oh, yes!' he said, without any interest, and bade me enter.

In one[6] of his books, he writes that life seems to him to be a preparation for something that never happens; and the quality of his voice suggests that thwarted desire which is expressed in so much of his work. He is, in poetry, what Mr. Galsworthy is, in fiction: he surrenders to life. I do not know of any one who can speak verse so beautifully and yet so depressingly as he can. The very great beauty that is in all his work does not stir you: it saddens you. There is no sunrise in his writing: there is only sunset. In his lyrics, there is the cadence of fatigue and of the lethargy that comes partly from disappointment, partly from loneliness, partly from doubt, and partly from inertia. *Innisfree*, the beauty of which has not been diminished by familiarity, does not sound glad: it sounds tired. The poet's wish to return to the lake island is not due to any pleasurable emotion, but to weariness and exhaustion: he dreams of the island, not as a place in which to work and to achieve, but in which to retire from work and achievement that has not brought with it the gratification for which he hoped; and the final impression left on the mind of the reader is that the poet is too tired and disappointed to do more than wish that he might go to Innisfree. One reads the beautiful poem in the sure and certain belief that Mr. Yeats will not 'arise and go now, and go to Innisfree,' but that he will remain where he is. There is no impulse or movement in the poem: there is only a passive wish and a plaintive resignation.

And all that inertia and negation and inactive desire is sounded in his voice. It is very palpable in his manner.

He warned me not to make a noise as I ascended the uncarpeted stairs: the people on the second floor might be disturbed. They were working-people, I understood, and either there was a fretful baby asleep or the people retired early because they had to rise early, and he did not wish to break their rest. Mr. Yeats can be very harsh and inconsiderate with his associates, but his bearing to poor men and women, in my experience, is very courteous and very considerate. He could not have been more gracious to a duchess—he probably was sometimes less gracious to a duchess—than he was to the middle-aged woman who cooked his meals and kept his rooms clean. I have seen distinguished men being gracious to poor, unlettered men, but most of them had an air of . . . not exactly condescension in doing so, but of altering their attitude slightly, of relaxing and unbending, of modifying their style, as it were, and making it simpler. I did not observe any effort at condescension in his manner towards that plain and simple woman. He spoke to her in the same way that he would speak to 'A.E.' or to Lady Gregory. I suppose that Queen Victoria was the only woman in the world to whom Mr. Yeats ever spoke in a condescending fashion.

II

He is a tall man, with dark hanging hair that is now turning grey, and he has a queer way of focussing when he looks at you. I do not know what is the defect of sight from which he suffers, but it makes his way of regarding you somewhat disturbing. He has a poetic appearance, entirely physical, and owing nothing to any eccentricity of dress; for, apart from his necktie, there is nothing odd about his clothes. It is not easy to talk to him in a familiar fashion, and I imagine that he has difficulty in talking easily on common topics. I soon discovered that he is not comfortable with individuals: he needs an audience to which he can discourse in a pontifical manner. If he is compelled to remain in the company of one person for any length of time, he begins to pretend that the individual is a crowd listening to him. His talk is seldom about common-place things: it is either in a high and brilliant style or else it is full of reminiscences of dead friends. I do not believe that any one in this world has ever spoken familiarly to him or that any one has ever slapped him on the back and said 'Hello, old chap!' His relatives and near friends call him 'Willie,' but it has always seemed to me that they do so with an effort, that they feel that they ought to call him 'Mr. Yeats!' I doubt very much whether he takes any intimate interest in any human being. It may be, of course, that he took less interest in me than he took in any one else, for I am not a very interesting person; but I always felt that when I left his presence it was immaterial to him whether he ever saw me again or not. I felt that, on my hundredth meeting with him, I should be no nearer intimacy with him than I was on my first meeting. My vanity has since been soothed by the knowledge that he has given a similar impression regarding themselves to other people who know him better than I do. I have seen him come suddenly into the presence of a man whom he had known for many years, and greet him awkwardly as if he did not know what to say. He never offers his hand to a friend: he will often stand looking at one without speaking, and then bow and pass on, with perhaps a fumbled 'Good evening!' but never with a 'How are you?' or 'I'm glad to see you!'

It is, I suppose, the result of some natural clumsiness of manner. He has trained himself to an elegance of demeanour, an elaborate courteousness, which is very pleasing to a stranger, but he has spent so much time in achieving this elegance that he has forgotten or never learned how to greet a friend.

He was expecting other people to come to his rooms that Sunday evening. . . . I remember he mentioned that Madame Maud Gonne McBride[7] was expected to arrive in London from Paris on her way to Ireland, and might call on her way to Euston Station . . . but no one else came. He talked to me about my play and told me that he liked it very much, but Lady Gregory did not greatly care for it. 'She is a realist herself,' he said, 'and all realists hate each other. Synge would have disliked your play, and Robinson does not like it, but I do!' (Lennox Robinson, himself a dramatist, was then manager of the Abbey Theatre.) He asked me if I had written any other plays, and I told him that I was half-way through a four-act play, called *Mixed Marriage*,[8] and I described the theme of it to him. He urged me to complete this play and bring the MS. to his rooms and read it to him. 'The difficulty about *The Magnanimous Lover*,' he said, 'is that it may provoke some disturbance among the audience, and as our patent expires shortly we do not wish to give the authorities any ground for refusing to renew it. They were very angry over our production of Bernard Shaw's *Blanco Posnet* after the Censor refused to license it in England. We'll leave the production of *The Magnanimous Lover* until the patent has been renewed. If your new play were ready, we could do it first and create a public for you! . . .'

Mr. Yeats is one of the best advertising agents in the world, and I did not doubt his ability to 'create a public' for me, although I thought that Lady Gregory would probably be more skilful even that [*sic*] he could be. When one remembers that she has established a considerable reputation as a dramatist on two continents entirely on the strength of half-a-dozen one-act plays, it is impossible to doubt that she is at least as skilful as he in drawing attention to herself. A great amount of their advertising energy has, of course, been expended on the Abbey Theatre and the Irish Literary Renaissance, and a great many Irish writers, myself included, have derived advantage, personal and pecuniary, from their activities. It would have been better for us, perhaps, if Mr. Yeats had employed his critical ability more freely than his eulogy on our work. There is an immense amount of creative power in Ireland, but it is raw, untutored, tumid stuff, and because the critical faculty in Ireland is almost negligible, this creative power is wasted in violent, explosive plays and books or violent, explosive beliefs.

I have always believed in the interdependence of all men and minds. It seems to me that an ill-conceived, foolish political scheme must in some manner react on every other department of man's life, and that the labourer who is doing his job badly in a remote village is in some measure adversely affecting the welfare of his countrymen miles away. Violent, crude plays are inevitable in a land of violent, crude beliefs; and it is, I think, not without significance that some of the most violent, crude plays in the Abbey repertory were written by dramatists who professed the violent, crude beliefs of Sinn Fein.[9] When one thinks of the generosity and courage and nobility of many of the Sinn Feiners, it is hard not to lose faith in human perfectibility when one considers how foolish are the political schemes they devise. If men so good and exalted as these men are can produce schemes so stupid and sometimes so cruel, how can we hope for any progress in the world when we remember how many bad men there are? And have we not seen how people of lofty ideals can tumble into cruelty and become brutal ruffians in the name of patriotism?

But there is an explanation of all this crudity and violence in Ireland. For all sorts of reasons, political, social, historical and religious, the critical faculty has rarely been employed and certainly has not been developed. Either you are for a thing or you are against it. Doubt is treated as if it were antagonism. Reluctance to commit oneself to any scheme, however fantastic or ill-considered it may be, is treated as treason to the national spirit. A man who asserts his belief in the establishment of an Irish Republic, by force, if necessary, is an Irishman, even though he be a 'dago,'[10] and any one who is doubtful of the feasibility of this proposal is denounced as a West Briton, an anglicized Irishman, even, on occasions, as 'not Irish at all,' although his forebears have lived in Ireland for generations. The state of affairs in Ireland is not unlike the state of affairs in Russia, where literary criticism, as a Russian writer has stated, has always tended to be the handmaid of political faction. 'Any writer of sufficient talent,' wrote a reviewer in *The Times Literary Supplement,* 'who adopted a liberal attitude was certain of the appreciation of the *intelligentsia's* acknowledged critical leaders, and hence of a wide and enthusiastic audience. But writers whose instinct for the truth led them to doubt the sufficiency of doctrinaire discontent with the established order were debarred from the aids to literary advancement, and had to struggle against the grain of popular, and even academic, valuation.'

It is even worse than that in Ireland, for there, generally speaking, there is hardly any criticism at all, although there is plenty of abuse. In great measure this lack of criticism is due to the fact that all the mind of Ireland has been obsessed by the demand for, or the opposition to, self-government. There has not been any reality in Irish electoral contests for a great many years. Until the growth of Sinn Fein, there seldom were any contests at all. Candidates for Parliament were nearly always returned unopposed. Contests, if there were any, were between one Nationalist and another, concerned with matters of detail and not with matters of principle, or, at the most, between a Nationalist and a Unionist, concerned with the advocacy of, or opposition to, Home Rule. Sinn Fein has, indeed, brought a contest to every constituency, but even here the contest is concerned with the old obsession, self-government in one form or self-government in another: Home Rule within the British Commonwealth or a Republic outside it. If one considers that this obsession was nearly always expressed in bitter language, it is not difficult to understand how deplorable its effects have been on the general life of the Irish people. It has temporarily incapacitated them from judging any proposition in a sane and dispassionate fashion; and so the critical faculty in Ireland has languished until at times one fears that it has decayed.

Mr. Yeats is a great creative artist: he is also a great critic. Had he chosen to do so, he could have had an enormous influence on the minds of his countrymen. His pride in his craft, his desire for perfect work, his contempt for subterfuges and makeshifts and ill-considered schemes, his knowledge and his skill, all these would have affected the faith and achievements of his countrymen, imperceptibly, perhaps, but very surely. It is unfortunate that he was not appointed to the Chair of Literature[11] in Trinity College, Dublin. I know that he wished to receive this appointment and was disappointed that he did not receive it. The mind that might have disciplined and developed the imagination of young Irishmen was rejected by Trinity College, and it has turned to tiresome preoccupation with disembodied beings, to table-turning and ouija-boards and the childish investigation of what is called spiritual phenomena, but is, in fact, mere conjurer's stuff.

I saw Mr. Yeats many times after that first visit. He told me that he was always at home to his friends on Monday evening, and he invited me to dine with him on the Monday immediately following the Sunday on which I first met him. No one came on that evening. He talked about acting and the theatre, and I said something that pleased him, and he complimented me in his grave, courteous manner. 'That was well said,' he exclaimed, and I flushed with pleasure. The praise of one distinguished man is more than the applause of a multitude of common men. His talk about the theatre, though interesting, was often remote from reality. He was then interested in the more esoteric forms of drama, and was eager to put masks on the actors' faces. He wished to eliminate the personality of the player from the play, and had borrowed some foolish notions from Mr. Gordon Craig about lighting and scenery and dehumanized actors. He had a model of the Abbey Theatre in his rooms and was fond of experimenting with it. There was some inconsistency in his talk about acting: at one moment he was anxious for anonymous, masked players, 'freed' from personality, and at the next moment, he was demanding that players should act with their entire bodies, not merely with their voices and faces. Hazlitt advocates anonymity on the stage, and when one considers how excessive is the regard paid to-day to the actor in comparison with that paid to the play, one is tempted to support Hazlitt's demand; but I have never understood why one should decline to exploit a personality that is rare.

There is a school of thinkers which holds that the best theatre is that one in which a player may be the hero of the piece to-night and the 'voice off' to-morrow night. This is a ridiculous theory. Even if it were practicable, which it is not, it would be a disgraceful waste of material. The manager who consented to a proposal that Madame Sarah Bernhardt should play the part of the servant with one line to say would be an ass and a wastrel. It is, perhaps, unfair to treat a man's 'table-talk' as if it were a serious proposal, and I once got into trouble with Mr. Gordon Craig for doing this; but so much of Mr. Yeats's talk and writing is related to this matter of disembodiment and passionless action, that it is difficult not to treat it seriously. For my part, I have always been unable to understand how it is possible for a human being to behave as if he were not a human being.

Most of the talking was done by Mr. Yeats, and he talked extraordinarily well. He is one of the best talkers I have ever listened to, in spite of the fact that his conversation tends to become a monologue. But if you cannot talk well yourself, you are wise to listen to a man who can. He spoke at length about the men who had been his friends when he was a young man: of Oscar Wilde and Aubrey Beardsley and Arthur Symons and Lionel Johnson and Ernest Dowson; of Henley and Whistler and Mr. Bernard Shaw and of a host of others. He had a puzzled, bewildered admiration for 'that strange man of genius, Bernard Shaw,' but I never felt that he understood Mr. Shaw or was happy with Mr. Shaw's mind. He could not make head or tail of *John Bull's Other Island* when he read it in MS.[12] Mr. Shaw, in a debate with Mr. Belloc,[13] which I had heard a night or two before the meeting with Mr. Yeats, had said, 'I am a servant,' and this statement pleased Mr. Yeats very much. He was moved by the humility of it. Mr. Shaw, however, hardly entered into Mr. Yeats's early life, and most of the talk that evening was about Beardsley and Wilde and Lionel Johnson and Ernest Dowson and the members of the Rhymers' Club.[14] 'Most of them,' he said 'died of drink or went out of their minds!'[15]

It was late when I prepared to leave him. He had been saying that a man should always associate with his equals and superiors and never with his inferiors, when I recollected that the hour was late and that I might miss the last tram from the Thames Embankment and so have to walk several miles. I was tired, too, and a little depressed, for he seemed to be a lonely man and an uneasy man. He had survived all his friends, but had not succeeded in making any intimacy with their successors. I sometimes feel about him that he is a lost man wandering around looking for his period. When I had announced that I was going home, he astonished me by saying that he would walk part of the way with me. He had not had any exercise all day, and felt that he needed some air and movement. (He hates open windows, and always keeps his tightly closed.) We walked to the Embankment together, saying little, for silence had fallen on him, and walked along it for a short while. I said some banal thing about Waterloo Bridge, but he did not make any answer; and I did not speak again, but contented myself with observing the difference between his walk when he is moving slowly and his walk when he is moving quickly. He is very dignified in his movements when he walks slowly: he holds his head erect and carries his hands tightly clenched behind his back; but when he begins to move quickly, the dignity disappears and his walk becomes a tumbling shuffle. That, I suppose, is because of his poor sight.

My tram came along, and I said 'Good-night' to him, and he answered 'Good-night' in a vague fashion. I think he had completely forgotten me.

V

He had told me that he was going on the following day to Manchester to lecture to some society there, and I was sufficiently interested in his opinions to get a copy of the *Manchester Guardian* containing a report of what he had said. I was amused to find that his lecture was a repetition of all that he had said to me on the Monday before the day on which he lectured. He had 'tried it on the dog,' and I was the dog. All his speeches are carefully rehearsed before they are publicly delivered. He told me once that Oscar Wilde rehearsed his conversation in the morning and then, being word-perfect, went forth in the evening to speak it. I imagine that he does that, too, on occasions. It is a laudable thing to do in many respects, although it tends to make talk somewhat formal and liable to be scattered by an interruption. When Mr. Yeats rehearses a speech before making it in public, he is paying a great tribute to his audience by declining to offer them scamped or hastily-contrived opinions. Those who listen to him may be deceived into believing that he is speaking spontaneously, but they may be certain that what he says has been carefully considered, that he is speaking of things over which he has pondered, and is not 'saying the first thing that comes into his head.'

Most men of letters do something of this sort. I have listened to Mr. Moore saying things which I subsequently read in the preface to the revised version of one of his novels; and I remember meeting 'A.E.' in Nassau Street, in Dublin, one evening and being told a great deal about co-operation, which I read in his paper, *The Irish Homestead*, on the following morning.

I saw Mr. Yeats many times after that. I completed the MS. of *Mixed Marriage* and, much embarrassed, read it to him in his rooms. I read it very badly, too, and I am sure I bored him a great deal; but he was kind and patient, and he made some useful suggestions to me which I did not accept. I had too much conceit, as all young writers have, to be guided by a better man than myself. I know now that I should have done well to take his advice. He warned me against topical things and against politics and urged me to flee journalism as I would flee the devil; and he advised me to read Balzac.[16] He was always advising me to read Balzac, but I never did. . . .

VI

My memories of those days when I first knew him begin to be disconnected, and I find myself putting down things which happened after other things which I have still to relate; but I have never found a consecutive narrative very interesting, which, perhaps, is why I cannot read *Pepys' Diary* or *Evelyn's Diary*. I like to take things out of their turn, to go forward to one thing and then back to an earlier thing. I can only connect one incident or memory with another by taking them out of their order and doing violence to the natural sequence of things. Life is not so interesting when all the factors between 1 and 100 are in sequence as it is when 26 and 60 are taken out of their place and put into coherence, temporary or permanent, with each other.

He said to me one evening that a man does not make firm friendships after the age of twenty-five. There is a good deal of truth in that statement, but I doubt whether it is generally true. It is true of him, for his mind turns back continually to the men who were his contemporaries twenty-five years ago, but it was not true of Dr. Johnson, who shed his friends as he grew in stature of mind. And perhaps what Dr. Johnson said to Sir Joshua Reynolds is more generally true than what Mr. Yeats said to me. 'If a man does not make new acquaintances as he advances through life, he will soon find himself alone. A man, Sir, should keep his friendship in constant repair.' I do not think that anything is so remarkable about Mr. Yeats as his aloofness from the life of these times. He has very little knowledge of contemporary writing. I doubt whether he has read much or even anything by Mr. H. G. Wells or Mr. Arnold Bennett or Mr. John Galsworthy or Mr. Joseph Conrad. He said to me one night that after thirty a man ought to read only a few books and read them continually. Someone had said this to him—I have forgotten who said it—and he passed on the advice to me; but he added, after a while, that 'perhaps the age of thirty was too young,' and suggested that 'the age should be raised to forty.' It seemed very wrong advice to me.

An active mind will surely keep itself acquainted with new books and familiar with old books. I have heard many men, particularly schoolmasters and classical scholars, say with pride that they never read modern books. Such people boast that when a new book is published, they read an old one. They are, in my experience, dull people, sluggardly in mind, and pompous and set in manner. In many cases, particularly if they are schoolmasters, they neither read new books nor old ones. Dr. Johnson and his friends, however, appear to have been familiar with all the current literature of their time: history, fiction, poetry, drama, philosophy and theology; as well as with the ancient writings. They would not have *boasted* of their ignorance of the work of their contemporaries. In Mr. Yeats's case, however, this unfamiliarity with the work of men writing to-day is understandable when one remembers that he cannot read easily because of his sight. When I first knew him, a friend came several times a week to read to him out of a copy of the Kelmscott[17] Press edition of William Morris's *Earthly Paradise*.[18]

He had, like most young men of his time, been much influenced by William Morris,[19] the only man for whom I ever heard him profess anything like affection, but I remember hearing him say once that he no longer got pleasure from reading or listening to Morris's poetry.

VII

One night, I was at his rooms when Mr. G. M. Trevelyan, the historian and biographer of Garibaldi and John Bright, was present with his wife, a daughter of Mrs. Humphry Ward.[20] Mr. Yeats, who had first warned me to be very careful of what I said about Mrs. Humphry Ward, talked much and well, and I remember his story of a dream he had had. He often told stories of his dreams, but some of them smelt of the midnight oil. A friend of his, he said, was contemplating submission to the Catholic Church. He had tried to dissuade her from this, but she went away to another country in a state of irresolution. One night, he dreamt that he saw her entering a room full of beautiful people. She walked around the room, looking at these beautiful people who smiled and smiled and smiled, but said nothing. 'And suddenly, in my dream,' he said, 'I realized that they were all dead!' 'I woke up,' he proceeded, 'and I said to myself, "She has joined the Catholic Church," and she had.' Mr. Trevelyan thought that the description of the Catholic Church as a room full of beautiful people, all smiling and all dead, was the most apt he had ever heard. He chuckled with contented anti-clericalism. Another night, when I was in his rooms, Miss Ellen Terry's son, Mr. Gordon Craig, came to see him; and a model of the Abbey Theatre was brought down from his bedroom to the candle-lit sitting-room, where Mr. Craig experimented with lighting effects. Mr. Craig is a man of genius, but he is a very difficult and childish person, whose view of the theatre is nearly as damnable as that of the most vain of the lost tribe of actor-managers or their successors, the shop-keeper syndicates. Scenery and lighting effects were of greater consequence to Mr. Craig than the play itself! His designs for scenery were very beautiful, indeed, but they were suitable only to romantic and poetical plays, and not always to them or to anything.

I remember that when he had manipulated Mr. Yeats's model theatre to his liking, he stood back from the scene and said, 'What a good thing it would be if we were to take all the seats out of the theatre so that the audience could move about and see my shadows!' Mr. Yeats dryly replied that this was hardly a practical proposal. I was irritated by Mr. Craig's remark, which was in keeping with his general theory of the theatre. It seemed to me that he would, were he less difficult to work with, be as great a nuisance and danger to drama as any actor-manager in London. Sir Henry Irving and Sir Herbert Tree, turning the attention of the audience away from the play to the player and the scenery, were not any worse than Mr. Craig, anxious to turn the attention of the audience to his shadows. I was glad when this remarkable man was carried off by Mr. Albert Rutherston[21] and Mr. Ernest Rhys[22] to exhibit himself somewhere else.

Mr. Yeats was bitten with Mr. Craig's theories about lighting and scenery, and a large sum of money for so poor a theatre as the Abbey, was spent on some of his 'screens' for use in plays like *Deirdre*. They were never used for anything else. When I went to Dublin to manage[23] the Abbey, I was very anxious that we should employ a competent scene-builder to make some good 'sets' for us, but Mr. Yeats said that scenery was of no consequence: the dirty hovel which we always employed to represent an Irish cottage or farm house would do well enough. I thought there was some oddness in this opinion when I remembered that the theatre had been almost bankrupted in order to purchase 'screens' for occasional performances of his own one-act plays. He would spend hours in rehearsing the lighting of a scene for one of them: this 'lime' was too strong and that 'lime' was too weak or there was too much colour or there was not enough or the mingling of colours was not sufficiently delicate. One day, when he had worn out the patience of every one in the theatre, with his fussing over the lighting, he suddenly called out to the stage-manager, 'That's it! That's it! You've got it right now!' 'Ah, sure the damned thing's on fire,' the stage-manager answered.

VIII

I have written already that he is not happy with an individual: he must have an audience; and I remember now something that he said to me which supports my belief. We had been talking about Synge and his habit of listening at key-holes and cracks in the floor in order to hear scraps of conversation that he might put into his plays.[24] I said I had been told that Synge, though excessively shy and silent in company, was a very companionable person with an individual. He was a good comrade on a country road, talking easily and naturally, and had the gift of friendliness with plain and simple people. Labourers and countrymen would talk to him as easily as they talked to one another, and would confide in him. I wondered whether there were as many entertaining tales to be heard from working-people in England as were to be heard from working-people in Ireland. Mr. Yeats thought that perhaps there were. He told me that the woman who cooked his meals and cleaned his rooms had begun to tell some story of a love affair to him, but that he had been too diffident to encourage her to go on with it. He thought that if he had talked to her more than he had, she would have told him many stories of her youth in the country; but all his talk to her had been of food and household things. He is not a man in whom poor men and women confide. His civility to them is magnificent, but it overawes them and makes them as uneasy in one way as it pleases them in another. He is an excellent entertainer in a crowded room, but he is a poor companion on a road. He can talk well to a company of educated men and women, but he is tongue-tied in the presence of those who have little learning. When I survey my acquaintance with Yeats, I find strangely diverse thoughts rising in my mind. I am drawn to him and repelled by him. He stimulates me and depresses me. I am moved by the beauty of his work and distracted by its vagueness. I find, in his writing and in his speech, great spiritual loveliness but curiously little humanity, and I have often wondered why it is that while Irishmen, even such as I am, are deeply moved by his little play, *Kathleen ni Houlihan*, men of other countries—not only Englishmen—are left unmoved by it, unable, without a note in the programme, to understand it. I have seen this play performed very many times. I never missed seeing it, when it was done at the Abbey during the time that I was manager there. It moved me as much when I last saw it as it did when I first saw it; and I do not doubt that if I live to be an old man, it will move me as much in my old age as it has moved me in my youth. But it does not move men of other races. That is a singular thing. It denotes, I suppose, that while there is much that is national in Mr. Yeats's work, there is less that is universal.

One rises from his work, as one comes from his company, with a feeling of chilled respect that may settle into disappointment. It is as if one had been taken into a richly-decorated drawing-room when one had hoped to be taken into a green field. I have read Blake's poems and then I have read his and sought to see the resemblance that I am told is between them, but have not always found it. Blake wrote about things that he felt, but Mr. Yeats writes about things that he thinks; and thought changes and perishes, but feeling is permanent and unchangeable; thought separates and divides men, but feeling brings them together; and it may be that Mr. Yeats's aloofness from men is due to the fact that he thinks too much and feels too little.

IX

I think of him as a very lonely, isolated, aloof man. He is, so far as I am aware, the only English-speaking poet who did not write a poem about the War, a fact which is at once significant of the restraint he imposes upon himself and of his isolation from the common life of his time. I have never met any one who seems so unaware of contemporary affairs as Mr. Yeats, and this unawareness is due, not to affectation, but to sheer lack of interest. He probably would not have known of the War at all had not the Germans dropped a bomb near his lodgings off the Euston Road. When Macaulay's New Zealander comes to examine the ruins of London, he will probably see Mr. Yeats, disembodied and unaware that he is disembodied or that London is in ruins, sitting on a slab with a planchette. He is younger than Mr. Shaw by ten years, but might be ten years older. His verse and his speech and his manner are all elderly, and his conversation is composed chiefly of reminiscences of men who have been dead for many years, so that one imagines he has not had a friend since 1890. There is absolutely no suggestion of youth in his writings. In the poem entitled, *To a Child Dancing in the Wind,* he says:

> I could have warned you, but you are young,
> So we speak a different tongue.

and again:

> But I am old and you are young,
> And I speak a barbarous tongue.

I do not know what age Mr. Yeats was when he wrote those lines, but they are included in a collection of poems, dated '1912–1914,' and at most he could not have been fifty, for he was born in Dublin in 1865.

The sense of age seems to have oppressed his mind for many years, perhaps for the whole of his creative life. He feels that he has outlived his generation and is lost in a period of time peculiarly alien to him.

> When I was young,
> I had not given a penny for a song
> Did not the poet sing it with such airs
> That one believed he had a sword upstairs:
> Yet would be now, could I but have my wish,
> Colder and dumber and deafer than a fish.

This coldness closing on his heart and congealing all his generous emotions, causes him, at the end of a graceful book, *Reveries Over Childhood and Youth* (in itself, significant of the age-obsession which possesses his mind) to declare that 'all life, weighed in the scales of my own life, seems to me a preparation for something that never happens,' and leaves his readers wondering why a man who began his life by singing songs with such airs 'that one believed he had a sword upstairs,' should stumble into dismal prose towards the end of it, pronouncing life to be a cheerless deceit.

His effect on young men is peculiar. His brilliant conversation is very attractive to them, but his insensibility to the presence of human beings repels them. 'A.E.' once told me that Arthur Griffith, the founder of the Sinn Fein movement, drew young people to him by the strength of his hatred, but finally repelled them by his complete lack of charity and love. A nature compounded principally or exclusively of hatred must be destructive. No man can construct anything unless love and charity predominate in his heart. Griffith, throughout his career, was never notable for his power to make things. He could not even make his own movement grow, for Sinn Fein became a popular and appealing force only after Padraic Pearse[25] and Thomas Macdonagh[26] and James Connolly[27] had put a fire into the machinery of it on Easter Monday, 1916.[28] There is something terribly ironical in the fact that James Connolly, to whom Griffith offered every possible opposition in his lifetime, should by his death have helped to put Griffith in a position of authority to which his own intellectual and spiritual qualities could never have raised him. Mr. Yeats has something of the inhumanity of Arthur Griffith. His talk is brilliant, indeed, but it is not comradely talk. It never lapses from high quality to the easy familiarities which humanize all relationships. He is more fastidious about his speech than he is about his friends. It would shock him more to use a bad word than to make a bad friend, because he is more aware of bad words than of bad men; and he would be quicker to forgive a crime than to forgive a vulgar phrase. I have never heard him use a common expression. He once repeated an angry speech of William Morris to me with an air almost apologetic for using profane language, not because it was profane, but because it was inelegant. He never says 'Damn!'or 'Blast!' when he is angry. . . . He is one of the loneliest men in the world, for he cannot express himself except in a crowd. Dr. Stockman said that the strongest man in the world is the man who stands absolutely alone—a feat which is surely impossible—and this specious statement has supported many ineffective egoists in their belief that neurosis is strength and misbehaviour a sign of individuality. But the penalty of isolation is that the isolated cannot dispense with an amenable crowd. The hermit must have a succession of respectful pilgrims to his cave, each one murmuring, 'There is but one God, and Thou art His Prophet!' until at last the hermit begins to believe that *he* is God and God is *his* prophet. Hermits have followers, or, perhaps one ought to say, curious visitors, but they have no friends. Why should they have friends? They have not got the social sense nor can they take part in the common labours of mankind. They live in caves and desert places because they are not fit to live in houses and places that are inhabited. But even the hermits, wrapped in self-sufficiency, realize that no man is effective without his fellows, and so, though they cannot make friends, they make disciples. This is a truth which all the great lonely men from Adam to Robinson Crusoe have discovered, that a man by himself is ineffective and without interest. Life for Adam remained uneventful until the arrival of Eve: the island of Juan Fernandez was livelier after Man Friday came to keep Crusoe company. For fellowship is life, as Morris said, and lack of fellowship is death.

There is no poet, not even Keats or Shelley, who has so much of pure poetry in his work as Mr. Yeats has in his, and perhaps that is enough; but there is no other poet, not even Mr. Kipling, who has so little understanding of human kind. It is an odd commentary on his relationship to his countrymen that while he was writing the bitter poem, entitled *September, 1913*, with the desolating refrain:

> Romantic Ireland's dead and gone—
> It's with O'Leary in the grave.

Thomas Macdonagh and Padraic Pearse and James Connolly were preparing themselves for a romantic death.

John Davidson, in a book called *Sentences and Paragraphs*, writes of Keats that, 'beginning and ending his intemperate period with the too ample verge and room, the trailing fringe and samplelike embroidery of *Endymion*, he was soon writing the most perfect odes in the language.' Mr. Yeats, in spite of some reluctant intrusions into enthusiastic movements, escaped 'the intemperate period'; but he did so at the cost of his youth and ardour. Like the Magi in his poem of that name, he, 'being by Calvary's turbulence unsatisfied,' seeks 'to find once more' 'the uncontrollable mystery on the bestial floor'; but it eludes him, and will always elude him, because he thinks of its habitation as 'a bestial floor.' It can only be found by a poet who, whatever happens, still believes that the earth is a place where God may yet walk in safety. Mr. Yeats is the greatest poet that Ireland has produced, but he has meant very little to the people of Ireland, for he has forgotten the ancient purpose of the bards, to urge men to a higher destiny by reminding them of their high origin, and has lived, aloof and disdainful, as far from human kind as he can conveniently get.

NOTES

St John Greer Ervine (1883–1971) was born in Belfast but moved to Dublin as a young man and was associated with the Abbey Theatre, becoming its manager for a short time in 1915. His best-known plays of this period are *Mixed Marriage* (1911), *Jane Clegg* (1913) and *John Ferguson* (1915). In World War I he served with the Dublin Fusiliers and lost a leg. After the war he settled in London and wrote *Mary, Mary, Quite Contrary* (1923), *The First Mrs. Fraser* (1929), *Robert's Wife* (1937) and *Private Enterprise* (1947). Ervine also wrote novels, biographies and several books on the theatre including *How To Write a Play* (1928) and *The Theatre in My Time* (1933). He served as dramatic critic on a number of papers, notably the *Morning Post* and the *Observer*, while from 1928 to 1929 he was guest critic of the *New York World*. From 1933 to 1936 he was Professor of Dramatic Literature for the Royal Society of Literature, of which he was made a Fellow. He has received honorary degrees from St Andrews and Belfast, and in 1937 became President of the League of British Dramatists.

According to A. E. Malone (*Irish Drama*, p. 198), 'It is only incidentally, and perhaps accidentally, that St. John Ervine is to be regarded as an Irish Dramatist.' He always regarded the Abbey merely as one of a chain of repertory theatres throughout the British Isles rather than the expression of a separate national consciousness which it was founded to be. In the course of a lecture to the members of the Dublin Literary Society shortly after he assumed the management of the Abbey, he announced his intention of making some radical departure from the accepted tradition of the Theatre. During the short term of his management (1915–16) he avowed his intention to produce such works as *Samson Agonistes* and *The Knight of the Burning Pestle*, at the same time announcing that no acceptable plays were being written in Ireland. The fact that the Abbey Theatre was an expression of Irish national culture in terms of dramatic art, was either not understood or was ignored by Ervine. In the end the company revolted, the majority of the players left the Abbey and never returned, and Ervine left Ireland to write *The Island of Saints, and the Way to Get out of It*. See Ervine's references to the Abbey Theatre in his book *The Organised Theatre; A Plea in Civics* (London: George Allen and Unwin, 1924).

1. First produced on 17 October 1912.
2. Not included in *The Letters of W. B. Yeats*, ed. Allan Wade (London: Macmillan, 1954).
3. First produced on 30 November 1915.
4. Not included in *The Letters of W. B. Yeats*, ed. Allan Wade (London: Macmillan, 1954).

5. 'He seems to have no practical sense,' Yeats wrote to Lady Gregory. 'He is a logician, and a logician is a fool when life, which is a thing of emotion, is in question; it is as if a watch were to try to understand a bullock.'

6. *Reveries over Childhood and Youth* (Churchtown, Dublin: Cuala Press, 1915).

7. Maud Gonne, who had refused Yeats's repeated proposals, married John MacBride, who had led the Irish Brigade with the Boers and was Secretary of Laffan's Bureau in Paris, where the wedding took place.

8. First produced on 30 March 1911.

9. Founded by the Irish political leader Arthur Griffith (1872–1922), who withdrew from the Irish Republican Brotherhood to move for establishment of an Irish parliament united to the English parliament only by the link of the Crown. In 1902 he organised a group to forward this movement and thus founded what became known as Sinn Fein. In 1906 he changed the name of his journal the *United Irishman* (1899) to *Sinn Fein*. To keep the literary movement on the Nationalist path, Maud Gonne aimed at forming a link between Yeats and Griffith, who had some taste in letters. She established or rejuvenated 'Young Ireland' societies, one of these being Inghinnide na h'Eireann [Daughters of Ireland]. Yeats assisted Maud Gonne in drawing up rules for this organisation, though he had little belief in the new political programme. He had had enough of the turmoil of politics. Besides, other interests were absorbing more of his time.

10. Slang. An Italian, Spaniard or Portuguese. An offensive term, used derogatorily.

11. At the time when there was a chance of Yeats's getting the professorship of English at Trinity College, he had come to a greater admiration of the classical English poets. In a letter (3 January 1913) to Lady Gregory he tells her that he was 'writing with new confidence having got Milton off my back'. Another letter (7 May 1913) tells of Gogarty advising him to go to Dublin, but the very thought 'fills me with gloom and fury'. See Austin Clarke, 'W. B. Yeats', *Dublin Magazine*, xiv, no. 2 (Apr–June 1939) 6–10 and John Eglinton, 'Life and Letters', *Irish Statesman* (Dublin) ii (Feb 1920) 181.

12. Bernard Shaw offered this play to the Abbey in 1905, but the directors refused it on the ground that there was no one in the company who could play the Englishman, Broadbent. (Actually, the part was magnificently played many years later by the Irish actor Barry Fitzgerald.) The Abbey, however, accepted Shaw's *The Shewing-up of Blanco Posnet* a few years later when the Lord Chamberlain refused to license it.

13. Hilaire Belloc (1870–1953), English author of essays, verse, novels, history, biography and criticism.

14. In London Yeats met the poets whom he organised into creating the Rhymers' Club. The Rhymers furnished much of the talent for the *fin-de-siècle* reviews, the *Yellow Book* and the *Savoy*. Among the members were Ernest Dowson, Victor Plarr, Richard Le Gallienne, Aubrey Beardsley, John Davidson, Lionel Johnson, Arthur Symons and Ernest Rhys. One thing they all had in common, an admiration for the traditions of Rosetti in verse and of Pater in prose. For a time Yeats was heavily, though never wholeheartedly, affected by them. He was especially friendly during the years 1890 to 1895 with Lionel Johnson, and after that until the end of the century with Arthur Symons, with whom he shared lodgings in the last months of 1895 and in January 1896. See R. K. R. Thornton, 'The Poets of Rhymers Club', MA thesis (University of Manchester, 1963).

15. Yeats appropriately labelled the men of letters of the 1890s the 'tragic generation', for many of them came to untimely ends. Oscar Wilde's death at the age of forty-six removed him from the theatre when his contribution might have been so much more ample and varied. Lionel Johnson became an incurable drug addict. One day he fell over backwards from a stool in a London tavern and was carried off to hospital insensible; he never recovered consciousness and died aged thirty-five. A hopeless love with a waitress at a little restaurant almost unbalanced Ernest Dowson; feverish spells of drinking and drugging alternated with spells of hard literary work, but the evil cravings conquered, and he died at the age of thirty-three. Aubrey Beardsley died, aged twenty-six, of tuberculosis. Oppressed by his wife's goodness and simple faith, Hubert Crackanthorpe took a perverse pleasure in a liaison with

the daring and gifted wife of a friend; he finally committed suicide in the Seine at the age of thirty-one. Death came to Charles Conder in a private asylum at the age of forty-one. When he died Arthur Symons was a patient in the same institution. Henry Harland was dogged by ill-health, and he finally took up residence in Italy where his career was cut short at the age of forty-four. Disease and his own incapacity to earn a living inclined Francis Thompson to self-indulgence and self-destruction; he died at the age of forty-eight in a cottage on an estate which Wilfrid Blunt allowed him to occupy rent-free. One day John Davidson was reported missing from his house; six months later a fisherman found his body washed up by the sea.

16. In his teens Yeats learned from his father to admire the French novelist Honoré de Balzac (1799–1850). In the last stages of Lady Gregory's illness Yeats was constantly at Coole. There he read during the winter of 1931–2 all Balzac again 'with all my old delight.' Yeats makes several allusions to Balzac in his *Autobiographies*.

17. At twenty-one Yeats found his way to Kelmscott House in Hammersmith, the home of the English poet and artist William Morris (1834–96). He went there on Sunday evenings to hear the socialist lectures and was soon asked to join the little group who were invited to stay to supper.

18. As a boy Yeats had greatly liked *The Earthly Paradise* (1868–70).

19. On finding that the socialists made no effort to understand his thought, Yeats ceased after a while to attend the debates and lectures at Kelmscott House and seldom saw Morris, who, however, remained an enduring literary influence and was perhaps the only nineteenth-century poet to whose mood he could always adapt himself. He once described the prose romances *The Story of the Sundering Flood* (1898) and *News from Nowhere* (1891) as 'the only books I ever read slowly so that I might not come quickly to the end'. See Yeats's various references to William Morris in his *Autobiographies*.

20. Mary Augusta Ward (1851–1920), English novelist; niece of Matthew Arnold; opponent of woman suffrage. Her novels include *Robert Elsmere* (1888), *David Grieve* (1892), *Marcella* (1894), *Lady Rose's Daughter* (1903), *The Marriage of William Ashe* (1905), *Daphine* (1909), *The Case of Richard Meynell* (1911), *The Coryston Family* (1913), *Missing* (1917) and *Harvest* (1920).

21. Albert Daniel Rutherston (1881–1953), English painter, illustrator, and stage designer.

22. Ernest Rhys (1859–1946), English editor and writer. For further information on him see p. 39.

23. During World War I the Abbey Theatre was under the control of four different managers, each of whom occupied the position for about a year. In the season 1914–15 A. Patrick Wilson had control; on his departure the management was assumed by St John Ervine.

24. 'When I was writing *The Shadow of the Glen*, some years ago,' says Synge in his preface to *The Playboy of the Western World*, 'I got more aid than any learning could have given me from a chink in the floor of the old Wicklow house where I was staying, that let me hear what was being said by the servant girls in the kitchen.'

25. Padraic Pearse (1879–1916), Irish educationist, author and Sinn Fein leader; Commander-in-Chief of Irish forces in the Easter Rebellion in 1916; executed after surrendering troops.

26. Thomas MacDonagh (1878–1916), Irish poet involved in the Easter Rebellion and executed. He wrote *Literature in Ireland* (1916).

27. James Connolly (1870–1916), a trade union organiser and Irish socialist. He wrote *Labour in Irish History*, founded the *Irish Worker* and the *Worker's Republic*, organised the Irish Citizen Army, and was Commandant in the Post Office in the 1916 Rising. He was executed for his part in this.

28. The Sinn Fein called on its members to rebel on Easter Sunday 1916. Fighting raged in Dublin for seven days, as a small group of poorly armed Irish patriots defied British police and army units. The rebels were finally defeated.

Meetings with W. B. Yeats*

BURTON RASCOE

I met William Butler Yeats, the winner of the Nobel Prize for Literature for 1923, on several occasions during his second and third visits to this country.[1] Miss Harriet Monroe, the editor of 'Poetry: A Magazine of Verse,' arranged that I should meet him alone in her apartment in Cass Street, Chicago; and I was a little self-conscious when I was introduced to him because I had just been reading George Moore's delightfully malicious stuff about Yeats in 'Hail and Farewell,' and Moore's jibes were running through my mind. This tall, stooped, very poetical (and professorial) looking man with his black hair streaked white and his beribboned glasses, however, was very gracious to me and (such was his absent-minded habit) since I had now and then to remind him by interrogations that I was there, I had no difficulty in conquering my self-consciousness. Sometimes he did not hear my question or heard only part of it, but when I asked him about the Moore book in which he was lampooned he said something about Moore's 'jealousy' and went ahead with his monologue about the Abbey Players in Dublin which I had not asked him about at all.

They relate an anecdote of Yeats that I can easily believe which is that at a reception given for him at the University of Chicago, he soared up into the clouds again and automatically repeated to everyone who came up to him, no matter with what words or questions, 'So glad you like them, so glad you like them.' And at a dinner given for him, he so far forgot where he was as to begin chanting some verse while a brother poet was paying an eloquent and thoughtful tribute to him, and continued so audibly and monotonously that the other poet forgot the conclusion to his talk and had to sit down in great confusion.

Still on this first occasion of my meeting him Yeats responded with what was to him a considerable discourse in reply to my question about the value of national institutes of arts and letters. 'I am a member of the academic committee of such a body in England, a committee consisting of thirty men, all of them the most consequential men of letters. The business of such an institution is to set standards and to exist for the younger generation to attack. The quarrels between the academic standard bearers and the

---

* Extracted from 'Contemporary Reminiscences', *Arts and Decoration* (New York) XXI (May 1924) 31, 62, 68.

revolutionary young men bears the fruit of progress. If such an institution served only as something for the younger men to attack it would have a worthy motive for existing.'

Yeats's interest in spiritism and the occult at that time was very intense and on the afternoon of his arrival in Chicago he paid a visit to a clairvoyant, about whom he had heard. The story of the seance was shielded from the newspapers by Miss Monroe, for Yeats was beginning to be the butt of many facetious paragraphs because of his stated belief in fairies. Like most poets, Yeats reads his own incomparably beautiful verses badly; indeed, he mangles them by reciting them in a dreary monotone, with care only for the beat of a measure.

When he was in America on his last visit, I went to lunch one day in Chicago with him and Mrs. Yeats (for he had married then) and Mary M. (Mrs. Padraic) Colum and St. John Ervine. Marriage, it seems, had cured a great deal of his absent-mindedness and he talked during that luncheon with a great deal of animated attention to the general trend of conversation.

Bernard Shaw, he said, had been terribly frightened by the bombing raids of the German aircraft over London and he confessed himself guilty of a great degree of physical cowardice. He said he had agreed with the French historian, Salomon Reinach, on a walk in the Luxembourg Gardens, that late middle age and old age is the happiest time of life, holding that youth and especially adolescence is the unhappiest period of life. He wondered how Americans continued to eat hot bread and hot rolls without ruining their stomachs, saying that Europeans would not think of eating bread so fresh from the ovens.

Mrs. Yeats, an energetic, auburn-haired, efficient-looking little woman, appeared to serve as an adequate balance of practicality in a marriage where there was so much ethereality.

NOTE

1. Yeats visited America in 1903, 1912, 1914, 1920 and 1932.

Irish Literature Discussed by William Butler Yeats in an Interview*

MARGUERITE WILKINSON

'I call to the mysterious one who yet
Shall walk the wet sand by the water's edge,
And look most like me, being indeed my double,
And prove of all imaginable things
The most unlike, being my anti-self.'
WILLIAM BUTLER YEATS.

In every generation a few men and women seek the roots of genius and try to learn how they are interwoven with the roots of the tree of life. They would know what relation exists between the human spirit and its achievements and would find the sources of such beauty as man is able to make. What is it, they ask, that gives unique form and flavor to any creation? William Butler Yeats has given his answer to this question most concisely in the five lines of verse which I have quoted. He has explained his theory at greater length in a small grey book published about two years ago and called 'Per Amica Silentia Lunae' (Macmillan).

The argument of the book—if such serene and simple speech can be called argument—is founded on the belief that the artist is the man who succeeds in giving expression to a self that is the antithesis of his every-day self. 'When I think of any great poetical writer of the past,' says Mr. Yeats, 'I comprehend, if I know the lineaments of his life, that the work is the man's flight from his entire horoscope, his blind struggle in the network of the stars.' Landor, he says, 'topped us all in calm nobility when the pen was in his hand, as in the daily violence of his passion when he had laid it down.'[1] Keats, he believes, was born with a thirst for luxury which he was never able 'to slake with beautiful and strange objects,' and therefore created an imaginary luxuriance.[2]

The theory is one that might easily be misinterpreted and made a menace to talented youth. It would become comic in a crude mind and ridiculous in the mouth of the unwary. Must a man be a felon to praise

* *Touchstone* (New York) VIII, no. 2 (Nov 1920) 81–5.

honesty in his verse, or a poltroon to exalt valor? Or, conversely, will the strong and virtuous man necessarily write weak and base poetry? Must we alter the words of Christ and look for figs only among the coarse spines of the thistle? These are questions which, lacking discernment, or leisure for the understanding of complex psychological processes, we might be tempted to ask.

But 'Per Amica Silentia Lunae,' obviously, was written for those who can and will take time for discrimination and the discovery of exact meanings. The doctrine of the antithetical self may be better founded than such casual questioning would suggest. It is not very remote, after all, from certain other doctrines current among plain people everywhere. What country parson has not told his flock that when a fault is conquered the opposite virtue rules in its stead? Or what nation is without some saw or catchword telling everybody that men and women desire and admire only, or chiefly, what they do not already possess?

Moreover, Mr. Yeats greatly modifies his theory when he says, 'The other self, the anti-self or the antithetical self, as one may choose to name it, comes but to those who are no longer deceived, whose passion is reality.' The winning of power to express this anti-self, then, is not cheap, but costly. The thews of the spirit grow strong by pulling against the current, not by drifting with it. As Mr. Yeats says again, 'We make out of the quarrel with others, rhetoric, but of the quarrel with ourselves, poetry.'

A man's poetry may be (if Mr. Yeats be right) a record of the endeavor to satisfy that in his nature which must live unsatisfied, a witness to the fact that he shares, through insight, much that he can never possess in actuality. Perhaps the songs of men and of nations come out of their great needs. To quote once more from 'Per Amica Silentia Lunae,' 'Each Daemon is drawn to whatever man or, if its nature is more general, to whatever nation it most differs from, and it shapes into its own image the antithetical dream of man or nation.'

Because I had heard something of Mr. Yeats' theory of genius I thought that readers of THE TOUCHSTONE might be glad to know how he would relate it to the progress of modern Irish literature, about which he undoubtedly knows more than anyone else can know, since he has been the most important single influence to make it what it is. Therefore, when opportunity came, I said:

'I have heard you say that the great dream poetry of England has come as a result of England's very practical every-day life, because the English people had great need of it. Will you tell me how you think modern Irish literature is the antithesis of Irish life? It is a proud literature, we know. Is that because the Irish must live humbly, for the most part?'

'Pride is not the antithesis of humility,' said Mr. Yeats, 'but the antithesis of vanity. The vain man cares for the good opinion of the crowd. The proud man is content with his own good opinion, because he respects himself. The vain man loves rhetoric because it pleases the crowd. The proud man speaks simply. And Ireland has a proud and aristocratic literature today because she has needed it.'

'In forty-eight,' Mr. Yeats continued, 'the poetry of Ireland was the most rhetorical poetry in the world, full of harps and shamrocks and green flags. They were all trying to express Ireland. Up to the early nineties everybody spoke for everybody to everybody. T. D. Sullivan[3] wrote the sort of thing that typified that period. One of his poems, I remember, was made to the tune of a popular song, and on the day when it was printed in a Dublin newspaper he heard people singing it on the streets.'

'There has been a great change since then,' I suggested.

'Today,' said Mr. Yeats, 'no poetry is less rhetorical than Irish poetry. Poets and dramatists express themselves, asserting the right to a personal point of view, and they are more Irish than the people who used to try to express Ireland. When people, or nations, will tolerate an idea peculiar to one man, even if that idea can never be their own, then they are intellectually aristocratic. Ireland is now associated with the aristocratic intellect. The controversy over Synge's "Playboy" was really a controversy between two Irelands, the normal Ireland of the crowd and the antithetical Ireland of the proud, personal, solitary intellect.'

'The Abbey Theater must have done a great deal to bring this about,' said I.

Mr. Yeats admitted that the change in temper had been much helped by dramatists, but went on to say that the young men of today are writing poems and novels also.

'Standish O'Grady,[4] who is now a very old man, had more influence than anyone else in bringing about the change,' said Mr. Yeats. 'His books dealt with the heroic age of Ireland and he took the old legends and set them down in the style of Homer. Then there was John O'Leary,[5] a very proud man. He was imprisoned for five years for joining the Fenians and put up with conditions that might have been changed, since he was a political prisoner, if he would have complained. But he would not complain. Later, when someone asked him why he had not done so, he said, 'A man does not complain when he is in the hands of his enemies.'

Mr. Yeats went on to say that the same change had taken place in Irish public life.

'Daniel O'Connell[6] represented normal Ireland, Ireland of the crowd, but Parnell[7]—there was never a man less of the crowd than Parnell. It is recorded of him that the members of Parliament did not salute him first, but awaited his recognition, according him the position of a superior, as of natural right. The old leaders used to exaggerate. But Padraic Pearse and the others who worked with him could speak very simply.'

I asked Mr. Yeats to tell me something of the Irish writers of today in whose work he has faith.

'James Stephens[8] is by far the biggest literary man in Dublin,' he said. 'Everybody should know his "Crock of Gold" and "Mary, Mary"[9] and his latest book of verses, "Reincarnations," in which his best poems can be found. His prose style is very beautiful. He is at work now on what will probably be his finest book, a collection of fragments of old Irish legends in prose, like an Irish Arabian Nights.'

I asked about younger writers.

'Of the younger men I might mention Brindsley [sic] McNamara,[10] who has written a novel called "The Valley of the Squinting Windows." Then there is James Joyce, who wrote a realistic novel called "Portrait of an Artist as a Young Man," full of the most strange, poignant, powerful, but sordid descriptions. He has made a small book of lyrics utterly unlike his novel. They are like bird-songs, slight, but with faint, exquisite rhythm. The book is called "Chamber Music" and is little known.'

When Mr. Yeats spoke of James Joyce I remembered that I had tried to read 'Portrait of an Artist as a Young Man' and failed. The realism of it was too utterly sordid. But I have found 'Chamber Music' since talking with Mr. Yeats, and it is a pleasure to quote one of these thirty-six lyrics which has a delicate loveliness of the kind often associated with the Elizabethans. It is the eighth.

> Who goes amid the greenwood
>   With springtide all adorning her?
> Who goes amid the merry greenwood
>   To make it merrier?
>
> Who passes in the sunlight
>   By ways that know the light footfall?
> Who passes in the sweet sunlight
>   With mien so virginal?
>
> The ways of all the woodland
>   Gleam with a soft and golden fire—
> For whom does all the sunny woodland
>   Carry so brave attire?
>
> O, it is for my true love
>   The woods their rich apparel wear—
> O, it is for my own true love,
>   That is so young and fair.

It is not difficult to find in such a lyric the personal quality which Mr. Yeats praises as belonging to the antithetical self of modern Ireland.

'Lady Gregory, John Synge, Lord Dunsany, James Stephens—all solitaries,' he said, 'and not one of them ever modified a line or a word for the sake of the crowd.'

It came into my mind that none of those whom he mentioned was more remote from the crowd than he, and that none put into his poetry a more austere and single-hearted pride. I remembered a lyric like the voice of an oracle that Mr. Yeats wrote a long time ago. It appeared (the original version) in a beautiful English magazine edited by Arthur Symons and no longer in existence, called *The Savoy*. It seems to me to round out and make complete the philosophy of genius given in 'Per Amica Silentia Lunae,' for the winds blowing evil and good and the flame and the flood are of the crowd, and those who are cowardly before them will be hidden from the world of tomorrow.

> Be you still, be you still, trembling heart;
> Remember the wisdom out of the old days:
> Him who trembles before the flame and the flood
> And the winds that blow through the starry ways,
> Let the starry winds and the flame and the flood
> Cover over and hide, for he has no part
> With the proud, majestical multitude.[11]

NOTES

Marguerite Ogden Wilkinson (1883–1928) was a writer and compiler of the poetry anthology *New Voices*. Among her works are *The Great Dream* (1923) and *Yule Fire* (1925).

Yeats's book *Per Amica Silentia Lunae*, which is the subject of this interview, was published in 1918. It is a series of philosophical essays completed during the winter of 1916–17. With them he included 'Ego Dominus Tuus', the first manuscript of which is dated October 1915, the second December 1915. In this little book, which was first called 'An Alphabet', Yeats outlined in terms of spiritism the doctrine of the antithetical self—or of philosophy as drama. 'Each daemon is drawn to whatever man or, if its nature is more general, to whatever nation it most differs from and it shapes into its own image the antithetical dream of man or nation.' In his early letters to Mrs Shakespear there are passages which show that he was already feeling his way towards his doctrine of the self and anti-self set out in this book and expressed in his poetry.

1. Yeats's ambition for his old age was that of the English poet and prose writer Walter Savage Landor (1775–1864), rather than of Wordsworth, a possible mask he had considered in middle age. In his *Essays* (p. 506) he says: 'Could he, if he would, knowing how frail his vigour from youth up, copy Landor who lived loving and hating, ridiculous and conquered, into extreme old age, all lost but the favour of his muses?

> The mother of the muses are taught
> Is memory; she has left me; they remain
> And shake my shoulder urging me to sing.'

2. 'I think Keats', Yeats wrote to his father, John Butler Yeats, 'perhaps greater than Shelley and beyond words greater than Swinburne because he makes pictures one cannot forget and sees them as full of rhythm as a Chinese painting.' In his poem 'Ego Dominus Tuus' he explains that Keats, because he was 'the course-bred son of a livery-stable keeper', developed his 'luxuriant song'.

3. 'Another member of the party,' says Stephen Gwynn in *Irish Literature and Drama* (p. 113), 'T. D. Sullivan, one of a brilliant clan, was the song writer of the movement; and his verses in praise of the Manchester Martyrs—(three Fenians hanged for a death inflicted

during an attempted rescue)—became the nationalist anthem. "God Save Ireland" had at least as much literary merit as "The Soldiers' Song" of our day—or, for that matter, as "God Save the King".'

4. Standish James O'Grady (1846–1928), Irish man of letters; author of *History of Ireland: Heroic Period* (1878); wrote Irish historical romances. His passionate interest in the heroic aspects of Irish history made him a strong influence on the generation growing up between 1890 and 1916, and he has been called 'the Father of the Irish Revival'. In his contributions to the *Pilot*, Yeats continually set nationalism against internationalism; he drew attention to the romances of Standish O'Grady and to Douglas Hyde's Gaelic translations. He is also quoted in E. A. Boyd's *Irish Literary Renaissance* as having said that Russell and the theosophists on the one hand, and Standish O'Grady on the other, had done more for Irish literature than Trinity College in the course of three centuries.

5. For a note on John O'Leary see p. 12.

6. Daniel O'Connell (1775–1847), Irish nationalist leader; known as 'the Liberator'. United Irish Roman Catholics under leadership of their priests into a league for urging Irish claims; originated the Catholic Association (1823) and perfected its constitutional method of agitation for repeal of civil disabilities by mass meetings; fought Coercion Act (1833); led agitation for abolition of tithes and of established church in Ireland; revived earlier demand for repeal of union of Great Britain and Ireland; re-created the Catholic Association and held monstrous mass meetings (1842–3); arrested for seditious conspiracy (1843) but released (1884) on writ of error by House of Lords; found his power broken by dissension, opposition by revolutionaries of Young Ireland (1845), distress from potato famine and ill-health. In a speech on the subject of divorce in the Senate in June 1925, Yeats introduced the private lives of the three public figures, Nelson, O'Connell and Parnell, whose statues decorate Dublin's main street, of whom he wrote in 'The Three Monuments' with some bitterness after his speech. The poem ridicules the Senate's reluctance to pass a Divorce Bill.

7. Charles Stuart Parnell (1846–91), Irish Nationalist leader. See note on him p. 57.

8. James Stephens (1882–1950), Irish poet and novelist. His poetry includes *Insurrections* (1909), *The Hill of Vision* (1912) and *Reincarnation* (1918). Among his other works are *The Charwoman's Daughter* (1912), *The Crock of Gold* (1912), *Here Are Ladies* (1913), *The Demi-Gods* (1914), *The Rocky Road to Dublin* (1915), *Songs from the Clay* (1915), *Deirdre* (1923), *In the Land of Youth* (1924), *Etched in Moonlight* (1928) and *Kings and the Moon* (1938). Almost all these books, except *The Crock of Gold*, are out of print. But his eye-witness account of the Easter Rising, *The Insurrection in Dublin*, was reprinted in 1965. When Stephens received the Polignac award for imaginative literature in 1913, Yeats, who was staying in Sussex because of a digestive disorder, went to London to make a speech on his compatriot's work at the Academic Committee.

9. The American title of *The Charwoman's Daughter* (1912).

10. Brinsley MacNamara (1890–1963), pen name of John Weldon; joined Abbey Theatre company in 1909 and toured with it in USA; left company in 1912 to give all his time to writing; became a centre of national controversy with his first novel, *The Valley of the Squinting Windows* (1918). The following year the Abbey produced his first play, *The Rebellion in Ballycullion* and he published a second novel, *The Clanking of Chains*; became director of the Abbey Theatre and wrote several more plays for the company, of which the best known include *Look at the Heffernans* (1926), *Margaret Gillian* (1935), *The Glorious Uncertainty* (1923) and *The London for the People* (1920). He also published three collections of short stories. McNamara resigned as director of the Abbey after a disagreement over Sean O'Casey's *The Silver Tassie*, which he did not think good enough for production. He was also for a time drama critic of the *Irish Times*, and compiled a useful indexed guide, *Abbey Plays, 1899–1948* (1949).

11. 'To His Heart, Bidding It Have No Fear', in *The Wind Among the Reeds* (1899).

With William Butler Yeats*

MONTROSE J. MOSES

Many years ago, when I first met William Butler Yeats, he was tall and lithe; with a boyish quality to him which carried enthusiasm. There was a look of constant inquiry arching his eyebrows over the straight bar of his eyeglasses. He had the sensitive face of a poet alive, not to the moment, but to the mystic stretch of the moments in the past. Yet, at that time, he was intent on establishing a theatre—which carried with it a multitude of worldly arrangements. He came to America[1] to talk of the Irish Revival—and he did talk, glowingly, confidently. He was the flaming flower of that rebirth: to him we owe the stirring of the rich soil of Irish folk tradition; it was he who went to Paris and uprooted Synge, and transplanted him in the Aran Islands; through his encouragement it was that Lady Gregory turned playwright, and became mother of the movement which he had fathered in his mind so many years.

I saw Yeats the second time when the Irish Players came to America,[2] after they had won their spurs at home and abroad—meaning London—and there was the same resilience, the same rush of energy,—not the energy of action so much as a spiritual energy directed toward an ever-present ideal. I had never seen a visitor to America more oblivious to the country he was visiting. A child chasing butterflies could not have been as completely impervious to surrounding condition. It was during this time that I had a taste of the golden tongue of Yeats—which, in the early days of the Celtic Revival, was the cause of so many friends losing their sleep, for he insisted on talking to them far into the morning on the principles of poetry and on theosophy, which has interested him from his earliest days. His *Cathleen ni Houlihan* had been given an excellent performance in Boston,[3] and three or four of us met afterward in the lobby of the hotel. Yeats began talking of the Irish peasantry, what their adoption of the Gaelic tongue had done for them in decreasing drunkenness; he passed to memories of Synge and their meeting in the Paris days; he touched on the richness of legendary Ireland and what he owed to it. Such talk was an overflow of thanksgiving for a successful evening. Yeats was in his element. The Irish Theatre was flourishing in his mind and his heart was full.

That same evening, at the Boston Playhouse, I had seen Lady Gregory in black lace, with a royal assemblage of red roses in her arms, standing in

* *Theatre Arts Monthly* (New York) VIII (June 1924) 383–8.

the lobby of the theatre, watching her audience coming in, smiling graciously whenever someone paused at the bookstall by the door to buy a volume of Irish plays—it made no difference whether hers, or Yeats', or Synge's, or Lennox Robinson's. She was the hostess, and every one was a friend. There was an onslaught of a tall figure with somewhat stooped shoulders, a flowing tie, a thick black ribbon to the eyeglasses, a nervous greeting, and Yeats himself sped down the aisle to his seat. I could see then that the best way of announcing the presence of these literary folk would have been as follows: 'Lady Gregory and William Butler Yeats with their child—The Irish Literary Revival—are staying for a few days at the Plymouth Theatre in Boston. They welcome their friends and challenge their enemies.'

The next time Mr. Yeats came to America,[4] the theatre of his enthusiasm had grown to be over twenty years old and was left at home, to cope with the spirit of modernism which was creeping into Ireland. The shock of black hair had turned gray; the lithe figure had become heavy; the enthusiasm of youth had settled into a glow of wisdom. William Butler Yeats was fifty-four.

I have just come across the notes of our conversation at that time. They are interesting in view of what has recently happened to Yeats. He is now a senator attending to the ordering of the Irish Republic. He is now a recipient of the Nobel Prize,[5] the award having been made in recognition of his devotion to Art. We do not hear as much of the Irish Theatre as we used to. Is it that Mr. Yeats is being caught at last in the maelstrom of world affairs? If so, what he said to me will be enlightening.

An interesting contrast—the three stages in which I have seen him in the past. I am now able to read his delightfully refreshing *Reveries of Childhood and Youth* and the letters[6] written in his early poetic years to Katherine Tynan,[7] the poet, and see what there is of the boy which has persisted; what there is of his ambition that has ripened into accomplishment. I found him on this last trip to America still the absent-minded fellow who, in younger days, would forget to eat, would go walking when it rained and forget to open the umbrella he carried in his hand. Years had not quenched his dreams; I found him living in a past which was strictly his own. It was strange to hear him speak of The Art and Poetry of *his* generation. Yeats was viewing himself and his contemporaries in perspective—he and Lionel Johnson and George Moore, and 'Æ'; Shaw; Arthur Symons·, Maeterlinck—to mention names which once represented the youth of literary theories now either established or rejected. We faced Yeats now with his gray hair; Maeterlinck with his youthful countenance grown wise; Shaw with his fiery beard grown gray, the figure of a satyr domesticated. And we realize that literary movements, as well as literary people, have a habit of growing old. The Irish Revival is no longer a child.

It struck me in my talk with Yeats that he still held to his love of fantasy; his nationalism was bound up in tradition, not in political programs.

'What's the matter with the world,' he said to me, 'is that intellect has destroyed dignity, nobility. People become restless and emphatic when they are in conscious pursuit of things.' And he still longed,—as he did when he first welcomed Tagore,[8] in an introduction written[9] to *Gitanjali*,—for the age of innocence, the age of saints. I heard him declare that what differentiated the present time from *his* age was that poets today are objective, while he and his contemporaries were subjective. In that sense—not in the philosophic—there is a personal note to Yeats' poetry and prose which recalls Wordsworth; he treasures in memory the small manifestations of the spirit; he describes places through feeling rather than through his eyes. He is ever the mystic.

'Thank God!' he exclaimed, 'we have passed the age of photographic realism. There was a period at the Abbey Theatre, when we ran peasant life plays into the ground, making a formula of them. But there is now a new rush of life in the world; audiences are more imaginative than ever; they are demanding fantasy. I may safely say that during the war the Dublin Abbey Theatre was the only place in all Ireland where free speech actually reigned. But now that the war is over, a great deal of valuable energy is unfortunately being directed into political channels. When the Irish Republic[10] comes, I suppose the modern mind will be all over the place! I wish that it would come that we might attend to more vital things!' Strange words from a future senator of the Irish Republic.

The Irish Theatre did not seem to be as much on the mind of Yeats during his last visit as it was in years passed. I recall directing our talk to the Abbey Theatre and the importance it had in quickening belief in a folk theatre.

'I think the Abbey is a folk theatre, a playhouse of the people, in a way not understood by America. The American and European stages have been occupied too constantly with the well-to-do and educated classes. But Ireland has pulled away from the drawing-room. When I come to think of it, possibly a theatre of the people is dependent for its richness on whether a country has a peasantry or not. Is it not true that every country must aim for a drama that deals with a life appealing to the greatest number of its people?'

'Has that been the chief aim of the Irish Literary Revival?' I asked.

'Ireland has an imaginative peasantry,' he rejoined, 'and there is a predominant tendency on our part to lay stress on association. Poetry comes, I believe, from associative values. Among a peasantry, life changes so little from generation to generation that every article one possesses takes on a heavy charge of personal meaning. Note, for instance, what a host of human experiences is called forth by the mere mention of a wooden spade. The very word "spade" has a value strictly spiritual which the word "sewing-machine" has not. To your own self repeat the words "spinning-wheel" and "thread factory." Which one has its associative value? The one is saturated with poetic meaning; the other conjures up industrial slavery.'

'You have a charge to make against Industrialism?' I asked.

'Yes,' Mr. Yeats replied, 'a charge outside the channels of economics and social history. I believe that an industrial population uses a form of machinery which does not profoundly affect the subconscious. This machinery creates restlessness. It is continually changing; what is used in one decade is out of date in another. The modern world is prosaic merely because it is continually changing. That is why we are so objective. All modern life tends to make us so. But agriculture depends on growing things; sentiment can grow in the soil but never in machinery.'

'Then you deplore this objective phase through which we are passing?'

'I don't say that, quite,' Mr. Yeats replied. 'But I do say that I am content with the style of my generation—with the subjective mood of Lionel Johnson and the rest. One must not deny merely because one is not of the thing which is new. For instance, my habit of ear, as a poet, makes *vers libre* unsatisfactory. But I do not see why *vers libre* should not do better what beautiful prose has already done. There are some who practice this *vers libre* delightfully, but there are others who use it merely in a bizarre fashion,—aiming only at originality and cleverness. I hate the search for originality; it is always journalistic and a form of advertisement. After all, what counts is quality; it is the only thing that interests me.'

I have never met a man whose life was more completely bound up in spiritual reactions, at the moment transcending political and social problems. When Yeats was here on his last visit,[11] Sir Horace Plunkett, St. John Ervine, and the 'President of the Irish Republic' were in this country and all of them were talking on nationalism, yet never once did their subject draw from Mr. Yeats any pronounced enthusiastic retort. He said to me:

'I know we are approaching some kind of philosophy which will deal with the social state. But I avoid politics merely because I feel that our opinions will not long hold. To my way of thinking, speculative interests are our true interests for the time being. The more I ponder it, the more I am confident that the only salvation for the world is to regain its feeling for revelation. That is the criterion to live by. But it is not the criterion of a thinking age. What a democracy needs is a great system of education, not great school-masters; a system of Art, not great artists alone. We must bring ourselves to distrust general principles, and strive to get some sort of spiritual basis. Until we do there is no hope.'

We do not know what he may be, now that he is a senator.[12] But assuredly before these public honors were thrust upon him, Yeats had dreamed himself into Life. To him speech was music and music was poetry. Read his essay *On Speaking to the Psaltery*, and you say, 'Yeats should have lived in the age of minstrelsy.' Read certain purple passages on his favorite poet, Blake[13] and there is, as one of Yeats' critics has asserted, a mediaeval touch to his prose. He is as far removed from the present as these.

I recall a passage from a prose piece written by Yeats and culled from a story entitled *John Sherman*.[14] It reads as follows:

'If my voice at whiles grows distant and dreamy when I talk of the world's affairs, remember that I have seen all from my hole in the hedge. I hear continually the songs of my own people who dance upon the hillside, and am content.'

I left Mr. Yeats when I saw him on that last visit of his to America thoroughly confident that he would never remember that I had called upon him. His eloquence was the eloquence of beautiful talk; there was no trace of social intercourse about it.

NOTES

Montrose Jonas Moses (1878–1934) was the author of *The American Dramatist* (1911), *The Fabulous Forrest; The Record of an American Actor* (1929) and *Henrik Ibsen: the Man and His Plays* (1908). He also edited several books including *British Plays from the Restoration to 1820* (1929), *Representative American Dramas* (1925), *Representative British Dramas, Victorian and Modern* (1918) and *Representative Plays by American Dramatists* (1918).

1. Yeats's first American lecture tour began in November 1903 and was arranged for him by his friend John Quinn. He spoke before dozens of societies, mostly Irish, and before more than thirty schools and universities; he also penetrated into Canada. His honorarium for college lectures was the modest one of $75, but he returned with money in his purse, and his first thought was to repay Lady Gregory, who had rendered him some financial assistance at the time that she had persuaded him to give up journalism. It was only after his third American tour in 1914 that she would accept repayment of a debt which then amounted to £500.

2. From 23 September 1911 to 4 March 1912.

3. On 20 November 1911.

4. In 1914.

5. Yeats was awarded the Nobel Prize for Literature in 1923. See W. B. Yeats, *The Bounty of Sweden: A Meditation, and a Lecture Delivered before the Royal Swedish Academy* (Dublin: Cuala Press, 1925). Reprinted in *Autobiographies* (London: Macmillan, 1955).

6. W. B. Yeats, *Letters to Katherine Tynan*, ed. R. F. McHugh (Dublin, 1955).

7. Katherine Tynan (1861–1931), Irish poet and novelist; one of the leaders of the Irish literary renaissance. Among her many works are *Shamrocks* (1887), *Ballads and Lyrics* (1890), *A Nun . . .* (1892), *Cuckoo Songs* (1894), *The Handsome Brandons* (1898), *The Honorable Mollie* (1903), *The Luck of the Fairfaxes* (1904), *Irish Poems* (1913), *The Story of Margery Dawe* (1915), *Herb O'Grace* (1918), *The Second Wife* (1920), *Wives* (1924), *The Wild Adventure* (1928) and *A Fine Gentleman* (1929). She also wrote a five-volume autobiography, *Twenty-Five Years, Reminiscences* (1913). A well-known portrait of her by Jack B. Yeats painted in 1896 is in the National Gallery, Dublin. One day Yeats overheard somebody say that she was the sort of woman who might make herself very unhappy about a man, and he began to wonder if it was his duty to propose to her. Yet she never gave him reason to believe that she thought of him otherwise than as a friend. In her books of memories Yeats is portrayed as the gentlest of creatures, the most sympathetic and helpful of critics. 'I want you', Yeats wrote to Lady Gregory on 11 November 1913, 'to get from the Library . . . *Twenty-Five Years*' Reminiscences. It contains—without permission—pages of my letters written when I was twenty-one or two, to me very curious letters. I recognise the thought, but the personality seems to me someone else. The book contains a great deal that moves me, for it is a very vivid picture of the Dublin of my youth . . .'

8. Rabindranath Tagore (1861–1941), Hindu poet; established school in Bengal which developed into an international university called Visva-Bharati; translated some of his

Bengali works into English (1912); awarded Nobel Prize for Literature (1913); wrote about sixty poetical works besides volumes of stories, plays and novels. Amongst his last-known works are *Gitanjali* (1912), *The Gardener, The Crescent Moon, Chitra* (1913), *Sadhana* (1914), *Songs of Kabir* (1915), *Fruit Gathering, Stray Birds, Hungry Stones* (1916), *Nationalism* (1917), *Lover's Gift, Parrot's Training* (1918), *The Wreck, Thought Relics, The Fugitive* (1921), *Creative Unity* (1922) and *Fireflies* (1928). Yeats helped Tagore, when he visited London for the first time, to revise and improve his translations from his own Bengali; and Tagore was to write to him years later of the 'greater mastery of the English language' which he owed to 'intimate instruction in a quiet little room off Euston Road.' Encouraged by the reception of *Gitanjali*, Tagore made further English translations of his own work, and presently Yeats produced his *The Post Office* (1913) at the Abbey Theatre. Later, in his old age, Yeats said that Tagore wrote 'too much about God'.

9. Yeats wrote his enthusiastic introduction to Tagore's *Gitanjali* while with the Gonnes in Normandy in August 1912.

10. The Irish Free State was established in 1922, and the Republic of Ireland in 1949.

11. Yeats made an American tour with his wife in 1920, its object being to earn money to provide for a roof for Ballylee Tower. During the visit he saw his father in New York for the last time. Actually, this was not his last visit; in 1932 he made a lecture tour, the proceeds of which went to the Irish Academy.

12. Yeats was appointed as a Senator of the Irish Free State in 1922. This had been brought about by the activity of his friend Dr Oliver Gogarty; ironically the appointment rested more upon his having once been a member of the Irish Republican Brotherhood than upon his work for Irish literature.

13. When Yeats was fifteen or sixteen his father had talked to him of Blake and Rossetti, given him their works to read, and told him of his own essentially pre-Raphaelite literary principles. An edition of Blake undertaken by Yeats in collaboration with Edwin J. Ellis appeared in 1893 and was followed by a selection of Blake's poems edited by Yeats with an enthusiastic introduction.

14. Yeats's only published novel, in *Ganconagh, John Sherman and Dhoya* (London: T. Fisher Unwin, 1891). Yeats put his longing for Sligo into the novel. His cousin and playfellow, Henry Middleton, was the original of John Sherman in the novel. 'It is West rather than National,' Yeats wrote to Katherine Tynan. 'Sherman belongs, like Allingham, to the small gentry, who in the West at any rate, love their native place without perhaps loving Ireland.'

Meeting Yeats*

F. H.

I am sorry now not to have treasured every word that came from my poet. At the moment I disliked to play Boswell, I thought it beneath my dignity. But artists like Arnold Bennett who ply the note-book are not ashamed to be the Boswells of mediocrity. Why should I have hesitated to take notes of William Butler Yeats?

In the Pennsylvania station I had met him, as his host agreed, and I intruded on him as far as Philadelphia. I say intruded, his forehead wrinkled in tolerant endurance too often for me to feel that I was welcome.

* 'Books and Things', *New Republic* (New York) XIII (24 Nov 1917) 100.

And yet, once we were settled, he was not unwilling to speak. His dark eyes, oblique and set far into his head, gave him a cryptic and remote suggestion. His pursed lips closed as on a secret. He opened them for utterance almost as in a dream. As if he were spokesman of some sacred book spread in front of him but raptly remembered, he pronounced his opinions seriously, occasionally raising his hands to fend his words. He was, I think, inwardly satisfied that I was attentive. I was indeed attentive. I had never listened to more distinguished conversation. Or, rather, monologue—for when I talked he suspended his animation, like a singer waiting for the accompanist to run down.

It was on the eve of The New Republic. I asked him if he'd write for it and he answered characteristically. He said that journalism was action and that nothing except the last stage of exasperation could make him want to write for a journal as he had written about Blanco Posnet[1] or The Playboy. The word 'journalism' he uttered as the ex-Czar Nicholas might now utter 'vaudeville.' He was reminded, he said, of an offer that was made to Oscar Wilde of the editorship of a fashion paper, to include court gossip. Wouldn't it interest Wilde? Ah, yes, responded Wilde, I am deeply interested in a court scandal at present. The journalist (devourer of carrion, of course) was immediately eager. Yes, said Wilde, the scandal of the Persian court in the year 400 B.C.

It was telling. It made me ashamed for my profession. I could not forget, however, pillars of the Ladies' World edited by Oscar Wilde which I used to store in an outhouse. Wilde had condescended in the end.

Yeats's mind was bemused by his recollection of his fellow-Irishman. Once he completed his lectures he would go home and a 'fury of preoccupation' would keep him from being caught in those activities that lead to occasional writing. His lectures would not go into essays but into dialogues, 'of a man wandering through the antique city of Fez.' In the cavern blackness of those eyes I could feel that there was a mysterious gaze fixed on the passing crowd of the moment, the gaze of a stranger to fashion who might as well write of Persia, a dreamer beyond space and time.

'And humanitarian writing,' he concluded, with a weary limp motion of his hand, 'the writing of reformers, "uplifters," with a narrow view of democracy I find dull. The Webbs are dull. And truistic.'

I spoke of the Irish John Mitchel's[2] narrow anti-democracy and belief in the non-existence of progress, such as he had argued in Virginia during the Civil War. Mitchel, he protested, was a passionate nature. The progress he denied was a progress wrongly conceived by Macaulay and the early Victorians. It was founded on 'truisms' not really true. Whether Carlyle or Mitchel was the first to repudiate these ideas he didn't know: possibly Mitchel was.

Yeats's one political interest at that time, before the war, was the Irish question. He believed in home rule. He believed the British democracy was then definitely making the question its own, and 'this is fortunate.' I spoke of Jung's[3] belief in England's national complex. He was greatly interested. Ulster opposition to home rule he regretted. 'The Scarlet Woman is of course a great inspiration,' he said, 'and Carson[4] has stimulated this. His one desire is to wreck home rule, and so there cannot be arrangement by consent. I agree with Redmond[5] that Carson has gone ahead on a military conspiracy. Personally, I do not say so far a party reason. I am neither radical nor tory. I think Asquith[6] is a better man than Lloyd George[7]—less inflated. He is a moderate, not puffed up with big phrases. He meets the issue that arises when it arises. . . . I object to the uplifter who makes other people's sins his business, and forgets his chief business, his own sins. Jane Addams?[8] Ah, that is different.'

His lectures he would not discuss but he spoke a good deal of audiences. In his own audiences he found no one more eager, no one who more knows, than an occasional old man, a man of sixty. He was surprised and somewhat disappointed to find prosperity go hand in hand with culture in this country. In the city where the hotel is bad there is likely to be a poor audience. Where it is good, the audience is good. In his own country the happiest woman he could name was a woman living in a Dublin slum whose mind is full of beautiful imaginings and fantasies. Is poverty an evil? We should desire a condition of life which would satisfy the need for food and shelter, and, for the rest, be rich in imagination. The merchant builds himself a palace only for auto-suggestion. The poor woman is as rich as the merchant. I said yes, but a brute or a Bismarck[9] comes in and overrides the imagination. He agreed. 'Life is the warring of forces and these forces seem to be irreconcilable.'

It could cost an artist too much to escape poverty. I spoke of the deadness of so much of the work done by William Sharp[10] and Grant Allen.[11] He said it was Allen's own fault. He, or his wife, wanted too many thousand dollars a year. They had to bring up their children on the same scale as their friends' children! And he kindled at this folly. 'A woman who marries an artist,' he said with much animation, 'is either a goose, or mad, or a hero. If she's a goose, she drives him to earn money. If she's mad she drives him mad. If she's a hero, they suffer together, and they come out all right.'

Phrases like this were not alone. There was the keen observation that the Pennsylvania station is 'free from the vulgarity of advertisement'; the admission of second hand expression in Irish poetry except in The Dark Rosaleen and Hussey's Ode; a generalization on Chicago to the effect that 'courts love poetry, plutocracies love tangible art.' Not for a moment did this mind cease to move over the face of realities and read their legend and interpret its meaning. Meeting him was not like Hazlitt's meeting Coleridge. I could not say, 'my heart, shut up in the prison-house of this rude clay, has never found, nor will it ever find, a heart to speak to; but that my understanding also did not remain dumb and brutish, or at length found a language to express itself, I owe to Coleridge.' But the Yeats I met did not meet me. I remained on the periphery. Yet from what I learned there I can believe in the sesame of poets. I hope that some one to-day, nearer to him than a journalist, is wise enough to treasure his words.

NOTES

1. *The Shewing-up of Blanco Posnet*, by Bernard Shaw. The play was intended to be done by the Afternoon Theatre at His Majesty's Theatre, London in 1909, but a licence was refused by the censor because its references to the Almighty were considered to be blasphemous. Yeats thought Shaw's theology 'absurd', but he pressed Shaw to give the Abbey the play. The Lord Chamberlain had no jurisdiction in Ireland; so the first production was that at the Abbey Theatre on 26 August 1909. Later the production was brought to London and given privately for the Stage Society. The Irish Players took it to the United States and performed it in Boston in 1911.

2. John Mitchel (1815–75), Irish solicitor who became Thomas Davis's friend and joined him in editing the *Nation* and in 1848 founded the *United Irishman*. Condemned to fourteen years' transportation the same year for treasonous articles, he was sent to Bermuda. He escaped in 1853, went to San Francisco, and later to New York. There he published his most famous work, *Jail Journal, or Five Years in British Prisons* (1854). Yeats loved to roll the heroic names over his tongue. In a speech he gave to a Wolfe Tone banquet in London on 13 April 1898 he said: 'Ireland is coming to her own and better self. She is turning to the great men of her past—to Emmet and Wolfe Tone, to Grattan and to Burke, to Davis and to Mitchell. . . .'

3. Carl Gustav Jung (1875–1961), Swiss psychologist and psychiatrist; founded analytic psychology.

4. Edward Henry Carson (1854–1935), British jurist and politician; Queen's Counsel at Irish bar (1889) and English bar (1894); Solicitor-General for Ireland (1892); Solicitor-General (1900–6); Attorney-General (1915); First Lord of Admiralty (1917); member of war cabinet, without portfolio (1917–18); Lord of Appeal in Ordinary (1921–9).

5. John Redmond (1856–1918), Irish political leader. See note on him p. 77.

6. Herbert Henry Asquith (1852–1928), English statesman; Home Secretary (1892–5); Chancellor of the Exchequer (1905–8); Prime Minister (1908–16). Obtained passage of Parliament Act (1911), abolishing veto power of House of Lords, Home Rule Bill for Ireland and Welsh Disestablishment Act. Formed (1915) coalition cabinet with Unionists; forced out by Lloyd George (1916). Yeats met Asquith at a men's dinner party, given by Edmund Gosse: 'I found him an exceedingly well-read man, especially, curiously enough, in poetry . . . Not a man of really fine culture, I think, but exceedingly charming. . . .'—Joseph Hone, *W. B. Yeats 1865–1939* (London: Macmillan, 1943) p. 234.

7. David Lloyd George (1863–1945), British statesman. MP (from 1890); won recognition by brilliancy in debate; President of Board of Trade (1905–8); Chancellor of the Exchequer (1908–15); Minister of Munitions (1915–16); Secretary of State for War (1916). Replaced Asquith as Prime Minister (1916–22) and, as virtual dictator, directed Britain's policies to victory in war and in settlement of terms of peace; also arranged conference (1921) with Irish leaders and instituted negotiations which resulted in founding of Irish Free State. A furious Irish civil war broke out in June 1922 as the result of de Valera's refusal to accept the treaty signed by Arthur Griffith and others with Lloyd George, which guaranteed the independence of Ireland under the Crown. The war lasted until about the end of May 1923, and affected Yeats deeply, for he had always closely identified his country's troubles with his own.

8. Jane Addams (1860–1935), American social settlement worker and peace advocate.

9. Bismarck (1815–98), Prussian statesman and first Chancellor of German Empire; called 'the Iron Chancellor'.

10. William Sharp (1856–1905). Pseudonym Fiona Macleod. Scottish poet and man of letters; promoter of Celtic revival; intimate of the Rossettis. In Sharp, one of the most typical

writers of the 1890s, the pseudonym reached its furthest development; he eventually almost collapsed under the strain of double life. Sharp was a friend of Yeats, shared his occult theories and helped him in his meditation which Yeats called 'vision'.

11. Grant Allen (1848–1899), British author. His books include *Physiological Aesthetics* (1877), *The Evolutionist at Large* (1881), and thirty works of fiction, beginning with *Philistia* (1884) and including *The Devil's Die* (1888), *The Woman Who Did* (1895) and *The British Barbarians* (1896).

Yeats at Oxford*

BEVERLEY NICHOLS

In January, 1919, I went to Oxford. That seems about the shortest way of relating a fact that is of singularly little interest to anybody but myself. What *is* of interest is that Oxford, at that time, was a regular nest of famous singing birds gathered together in the aftermath of the War, choosing Oxford as a sheltered resting-place, as though their wings were a little weary and their feathers rather draggled.

W. B. Yeats had come to rest from the storms of Ireland in a quiet, green-shuttered house in Broad Street. . . .

*   *   *

Yeats always seemed to me to move in a mist. He was like 'men as trees walking.' He certainly did not do it on purpose, as Bridges may have done. He would wander along the street with his head in the air and his hands behind his back, always wearing an overcoat, even in the warmest weather, with a long loose bow, and a mouth perpetually open. To walk behind him was in itself an adventure, for when he crossed the street he never took the faintest notice of any traffic that might be bearing down upon him, but dawdled over oblivious of the stream of cars, bicycles, horses and motor-lorries that were rushing past.

A lovable man, Yeats, but, I should imagine, that some people would have found him a trying fellow to live with. When I left my college rooms I went to a divine old house with a rickety staircase, and low ceilings, which looked out onto one of the fairest views in Oxford, the Sheldonian library. To this house after a little time, drifted Yeats, complete with his wife and his baby. It was a time when the servant problem was at its height, and occasionally, if the house was more than usually under-staffed, all the undergraduates and other occupants of rooms, including Yeats himself, used to gather to eat a communal luncheon.

* Extracted from *Twenty-Five; Being a Young Man's Candid Recollections of His Elders and Betters* (London: Jonathan Cape, 1926) pp. 36–44.

On the first of these luncheons, Yeats arrived very late, and after absently toying for a few moments with a little cold asparagus, turned to me and said:

'Were you at the Union last night?'

'Yes.'

'Well, what did you think of it?'

It was difficult to say what one thought of it. The debate had centred round the ever-green subject of Ireland. There had been a great deal of bad temper, and not very many arguments. Before I could reply Yeats said:

'I thought it was terrible. The appalling ignorance of English Youth about anything remotely connected with Ireland. I was astonished. Why, they don't know the first thing about us.'

He darted a limp stick of asparagus into the open mouth, looked away for a moment and then said:

'Why can't they understand that the Irish people are Irish, and not English? Why can't they realize that over there they've got a race of peasants who believes in fairies, and such-like, and are quite right to do so? Why, I've seen myself the saucers of milk which the Irish peasants have put outside their doors for the pixies to drink.'

He talked absently for a little longer, and then said, in a dreamy voice:

'*If the English could only learn to believe in fairies, there wouldn't ever have been any Irish problem.*'

However, Yeats was not made entirely from dreams. He had a good business streak in him as well. He knew to a 'T' the best market for his poems, although like all poets he also knew from bitter experience that verse as a means of livelihood was impossible.

'America pays best for poetry,' he said to me once; 'but even America pays badly. They will give you twice as much for a poem in America as in England. But for an article they will give you three times as much. I wonder why?'

NOTE

John Beverley Nichols (1898–   ), English author and journalist, was educated at Marlborough and Oxford, where he edited the *Isis*, founded and edited the *Oxford Outlook*, was President of the Union, and published his first novel. Thereafter he combined writing with travel and gained a reputation as a brilliant and unorthodox interviewer. To this period belong *Are They the Same at Home?* (1927), *The Star Spangled Manner* (1928), *Oxford – London – Hollywood* (1931) and his early autobiography, from which these recollections are extracted, written when he was twenty-five. *All I Could Never Be* (1949) is a continuation of his autobiography. He also wrote plays, including *The Stag* (1929), *Dr. Mesmer* (1935) and *Shadow of the Vine* (1949); and some detective stories.

Conversations with W. B. Yeats*

LOUIS ESSON

I have just returned from Oxford, where I have had some long, elaborate and stimulating conversations with W. B. Yeats.

*   *   *

I must get my boasting over, though it is necessary to state it. Yeats asked me up to see him and put me up for the night. I landed late afternoon, and he talked for an hour on my plays, theories, etc., before dinner. At dinner he told good stories. After that we talked till past midnight. Next morning he took me into his study, and he was very sympathetic. I then took a walk round the town, had lunch with them, and returned.

He thought more of my little plays than I could possibly have dared to hope. He thought the dialogue excellent, the 'atmosphere' as suggestive as could be. I told him I didn't think much of myself as a 'plotter,' but he said the four little plots were perfect. The only adverse criticism made was that near the end of The Woman-Tamer[1] the woman might have pretended to relax to make the end more surprising. He said he thought the element of surprise was necessary in comedy, but not in tragedy. (He doesn't mean 'surprise' in the American magazine-editor's sense.) On the whole, he thought, I might do my best things in tragedy. There it doesn't matter if the end is foreseen, the emotion should carry the interest through. He thought success would come to me some day, though I don't believe that. I mention this not to skite, but to indicate the principle of sound literature.

Plays on really national themes, he said (not 'popular plays' in the ordinary sense)—and this is his important principle—help to *build a nation* in the spiritual sense; while the other type of play, so-called intellectual drama, abstract and cosmopolitan—Galsworthy, Bennett, etc., and the husband, wife, lover triangle (not on moral, but artistic grounds) will 'shatter a nation.' That is what our scholars fail to realise. Their arguments look good on the surface, rather difficult to meet sometimes, though they are quite unsound. We are on the side of life, and they ('they' means too

---

* Extracted from a letter in Vance Palmer, *Louis Esson and the Australian Theatre* (Melbourne: Meanjin Press, 1948) pp. 26–8.

many people in Melbourne) are on the side of death and desolation. And yet most people would be against us.

He thought we ought to get the theatre going, no matter how small. A good 50 enthusiasts are better than 500 indifferents. You must see Stewart Macky[2] about this. He has a sympathetic philosophical personality. He will feel what is right. The plays we give should all be national. Academics will say we haven't got them. Well, we've got to get them: they'll never get them or anything else. At the beginning of the Abbey Theatre Miss Horniman wanted to do, with the local plays, the European masterpieces. That is what our repertory theatres have tried to do. Yeats said he wavered, but that 'inquiring man,' Mr. Synge, objected, and Irish drama was saved. '*A theatre like that,*' said Synge, '*never creates anything.*' Isn't that true? What did MacMahon[3] create? What did Hilda's University Society that did Shaw, Galsworthy, etc., create? They should have discovered me for a start, but they didn't! What has Adelaide ever done, with all its list of plays?

The same applies to the writing of novels.

Stewart's[4] English plays, if he does them, are all in vain. The local play, he [Yeats] says, will also produce a better type of acting; there are no bad models to imitate.

If Stewart's show is still going he'd better get a definite policy to begin with. A small sheet, stating some definite aims, needs to be drawn up. I would anticipate a startling success, not a failure, if some energy were put into the movement. But there must be no bloody lectures about it. They darken counsel. Also B. or people like that mustn't say anything until they're asked.

Yeats said they had to kill the pompous literary humbugs for a start. Their idiom was objected to as not being English; they retorted by showing that the professors couldn't write at all. It is really the same battle; it always is.

I wish I could give you the faintest suggestion of his intellectual power, the strongest I've ever met, even apart from his imaginative insight, vast erudition, and wonderful humour. In the midst of some elaborate discussion he'll drop in an outrageous story, but it always has an application and is not given for its own sake.

NOTES

Not until the first decade of this century were there Australian playwrights who possessed both dramaturgic and literary skill. Louis Esson (1879–1943) was the most important talent who made his presence felt in the Australian theatre. While overseas Esson met Yeats and Synge, both of whom advised the young Australian dramatists to keep to their own background and disregard current, overseas developments in the theatre. Esson formed the Pioneer Players in Melbourne in 1921. See Leslie Rees, *Towards an Australian Drama* (1953) and Keith Macartney, 'Louis Esson and the Australian Drama', *Meanjin Quarterly*, no. 2 (1947).

1. *The Woman Tamer* was first produced in 1909. The play is set in a downtown Melbourne slum.

2. Dr Stewart Macky, Louis Esson and Vance Palmer formed the Pioneer players in Melbourne in 1921. The Pioneer Players lasted until 1923, presenting only Australian plays. The organisers were not able to sustain outside interest in their productions, but they succeeded in creating a favourable climate for indigenous drama.

3. From 1910 to 1917 Gregan MacMahon managed a repertory theatre in Melbourne, producing thirteen plays by Australian authors, including Louis Esson's *Dead Timber* (1911) and his political comedy *The Time Is Not Yet Ripe* (1912).

4. Australia's best radio dramatist is perhaps Douglas Stewart (1913–   ), who, in such plays as *The Fire on the Snow* (1943) and *The Golden Lover* (1944), wrote in a theatrical if heavy-handed verse. Stewart is best known, however, for his stage play *Ned Kelly* (1956), a highly praised verse tragedy.

Recollections of W. B. Yeats in Rapallo*

DESMOND CHUTE

The gods in due time, before the first world war, lent me a little tobacco shop in London where we used to go and telephone, and where I chanced once to set eyes on two memorable figures, Parnassian presences for an adolescent frequenter of the nearby Slade to catch sight of in a Bloomsbury lake isle; one an established bard, the other an experimenter in imagism and vorticism: William Butler Yeats and Ezra Pound.

A couple of decades, however, were to ensue since that casual encounter before I first met either of them. By then the time had changed to the nineteen-twenties, and the place to the Italian Riviera. Ezra and Dorothy Pound were living on the top floor of a cliff-like building facing the sea, in a narrow pergola of a flat, giving on to a vast roof terrace and chiefly remarkable for its wealth of works by Gaudier-Brzeska. It was their custom to take their meals at the Albergo Rapallo below, and there to meet and entertain their friends. And there it was that Pound introduced me to Yeats with, 'Come and tell William what he ought to believe'.

The first subject I heard Yeats discuss was English *versus* French poetry, he conducting a brilliant defence of the virility of Racine's style. No one ever spoke oftener, longer, or more enthrallingly than he about the art and craftsmanship of poetry. The very voluminosity of his conversation makes it hard to quote. Likewise, his whole figure was so memorable that it is not easy to pick out individual aspects without their seeming trivial in

* Extracted from 'Poets in Paradise: Recollections of W. B. Yeats and Ezra Pound in Rapallo', *Listener* (London) LV, 5 Jan 1956, 14–15.

comparison with his stature. For instance, his sense of humour: how amused he was over the difficulty of finding plain furniture in Liguria, and how he finally enjoyed getting what he wanted by ordering it 'as ugly as possible, *proprio brutto*'.

Two memories are particularly vivid. One is of drawing his portrait in a meditative attitude I had admired him in the day before. As I enter, the harmonious voice is speaking; the pose is graciously resumed, and effortlessly kept. The monologue continues. No one ever needed any interlocutor less. The only phrase I remember was: 'Now who was it drew me last? Manicini, or was it John?' No answer is expected; and as I leave, the harmonious voice is still speaking. An ideal sitter. The other occasion is a glimpse from above of a figure in a dressing gown, sitting motionless in the winter sunshine. Only a hand moves, writes, from time to time, with a gold fountain-pen in a leather-bound book. Are we present at the generation of an immortal?

Sidelight*

COMPTON MACKENZIE

Just after Yeats was awarded the Nobel Prize in 1923 Edmund Gosse[1] in that mood of conventional patriotism which he thought he owed to his Librarianship at the House of Lords[2] pointed at the poet an accusing finger, rather like a feline claw on such occasions, in the drawing-room of the old Savile Club.

'I hope, Yeats, you don't imagine that you have been given the Nobel Prize for your services to literature,' he fizzed.

Yeats backed away from the sudden attack, looking, as George Moore once described him, like a rook backing in a south-west gale.

'Oh, no, Yeats,' Gosse persisted. 'You have been given the Nobel Prize on account of your hatred of us.'

No doubt Gosse was thinking of that Civil List Pension of £150 which he had been chiefly instrumental in obtaining for Yeats in 1910, though in justice to the poet he had stipulated that its acceptance must not prejudice his liberty to express his opinions on the state of Ireland. To Yeats's rescue came Ray Lankester,[3] the rockbound materialist, with his burly form and big square head, 'Why can't you leave the poor wild Irishman alone, Gosse?' he protested.

* Extracted from *Spectator* (London) cxciii, 1 Oct 1954, 395.

Gosse must have thought better of it later, and written to Yeats, for there is a letter from him to Gosse from Dublin with the date of November 23, 1923:

'Of course I know quite well that this honour is not given to me as an individual but as a representative of a literary movement and of a nation, and I am glad to have it so. People are grateful to me for having won them this recognition and life is pleasant.'

This collection of letters[4] shows clearly how hardly and how long Yeats was harassed and oppressed by financial worries, and yet in not one letter is there a word of complaint. The figure of this great poet sets a noble example to all artists.

I quoted just now a simile George Moore found for Yeats. Here is one that Yeats heard for George Moore:

'I dined with Lady Gregory last night. Moore was there, looking, as some friend of Miss Farr's said, like a boiled ghost.'

The other night James Bone said to me that George Moore looked like a poached egg. They are both perfect similes.

There is an enchanting letter to Lady Gregory in 1912 about a committee meeting of the newly formed British Academy:

'I never look at old Prothero[5] for five minutes without a desire to cut his throat; he frequently takes the chair and is a very bad chairman. We are getting up a Browning celebration, he will probably deliver the oration. In the middle of his last Maurice Hewlett[6] said to Henry James: "This is dull," to which Henry James sternly replied, "Hewlett, we are not here to enjoy ourselves."'

Does the British Academy still exist?

I was hoping to find some letters about the Tailteann Games in Dublin in August, 1924, when with G. K. Chesterton, Edwin Lutyens, Augustus John and others I was a guest of the nation, but there is only one. No doubt Yeats was too busy in his position as a Senator to write letters. He was an impressive figure dressed in formal black clothes and playing the part of a Senator to perfection. I recall meeting him in the lobby of the Theatre Royal as we emerged together from a concert of John McCormack's before it was over, to go on to some function.

'A wonderful concert and a wonderful house,' I observed.

'Wonderful, wonderful,' Yeats replied in the voice of one who has just been initiated at Eleusis. 'But oh, the clarity of the words,' he almost moaned. 'The damnable clarity of the words!'

My last memory of him is of his picking up from a table in the Savile morning room a copy of Professor Hogben's *Mathematics for the Million*.

'Ah,' he murmured, with a kind of Druidical disapproval, 'more religion for the suburbs.'

NOTES

Sir Compton Mackenzie (1883–1972) was an English novelist who also wrote *Poems* (1907) and plays including *The Gentleman in Grey* (1906), *Columbine* (1920) and *The Lost Cause* (1931). Among his novels are *The Passionate Elopement* (1911), *Carnival* (1912), *Sylvia Scarlet* (1918), *The Parson's Progress* (1923), *Vestal Fire* (1927), *Gallipoli Memories* (1929), *The Four Winds of Love* (1937–46), *A Musical Chair* (1939) and *The Monarch of the Glen* (1941). He also wrote books of reminiscences.

1. Sir Edmund Gosse (1849–1928), poet and man of letters. Among his several works are *Collected Poems* (1911), *Father and Son* (autobiography; 1907) and many volumes of literary criticism, surveys and biographies.

2. Gosse was Librarian to the House of Lords from 1904 to 1914.

3. Sir Edwin Ray Lankester (1847–1929), English scientist who attained distinction as a morphologist.

4. *The Letters of W. B. Yeats*, ed. Allan Wade (London: Rupert Hart-Davis, 1954).

5. George Walter Prothero (1848–1922), English historian and editor.

6. Maurice Henry Hewlett (1861–1923), English essayist, novelist and poet.

Reminiscences of W. B. Yeats*

L. A. G. STRONG

I first met W. B. Yeats in the autumn of 1919. He had come to live in Oxford, and, as secretary of a college literary society, I besought him to address us. The reply was an invitation to come and see him one night after dinner in a tall house in Broad Street,[1] opposite Balliol. The room into which I was ushered was dimly lit, and there, in a loose-fitting suit of a faintly pinkish tint and a blue soft shirt, was the tall legendary figure. He greeted me in a low tone, introduced me to Mrs. Yeats, put into my hand a strange-shaped glass—I was too much overcome to notice what was in it—and then, in a surprisingly brisk and business-like fashion, asked me what sort was our society and what we would like him to talk about.

After that I saw him a few times only until the appearance of my first book of verse nearly two years later. He sent for me one Monday evening after dinner, and told me he was now obliged to look at me in a different way: 'I have had to readjust my mind. I had thought of you as Strong the schoolmaster. Now I must think of you as Strong the poet'.

At the end of the evening, Yeats told me that I was to come every Monday night as long as he was in Oxford. It can be imagined what this meant to a young man in poor health, unsure of himself and of his future. During these years in Oxford he was sought out by all manner of young people, and gave most generously of his consideration and his time.

* Extracted from *Listener* (London) LI, 22 Apr 1954, 689–90. Broadcast on the BBC Third Programme.

Theological students came to the pagan poet and were confirmed in their belief. We asked him one day how he had dealt with a very solemn young man who had Doubts. 'The Doubts are allayed', he replied. 'I read with him through all the Forty-nine Articles'.

To another he said, 'I would have you take Holy Orders that you may make your thought historical'. And to a third, 'In religion, never leave your father's house till you are kicked down the steps'. This was the Yeats who said, surprisingly to those who did not know him, 'Every human soul is unique, for none other can satisfy the same need in God'.

The conversations on these Monday evenings stretched over a wide range of subjects. About the magical side of Yeats' beliefs I must say something, even though critics have tended to by-pass this side of his work. These beliefs were at the centre of all his work and all his philosophy. They were never what Mr. Edmund Wilson has called 'the detritus of genius'. A price that had to be paid for what the world valued so clearly. There has been much talk, too, of Yeats' credulity. I had the opportunity to see as much of this side of his mind as anyone of my generation, and I know that he was anything but credulous in his approach to so-called psychic and occult phenomena. He had reconciled his findings with a formidable intelligence, and—once more to quote Edmund Wilson—with a sense of reality inferior to none in Europe. He *had* his credulous phase, but that was long before this Oxford sojourn. It belonged to the days when, under the guidance of A.E., he invited visions, and accepted them at their face value. 'This went on for some time, until one day I saw in a vision the lower half of John Bull. And as I could not conceive of John Bull as an inhabitant of eternity, I decided from that moment to scrutinise and interpret all that I saw'.

From this experience came the axiom on which he insisted to me more than once: 'The thing seen is never the vision, the thing heard is never the message'. Both were images, like the images of persons seen in dreams, which according to Yeats were always the results of a substitution. This theory, as you will see, was important, because it meant that Yeats aligned the images seen in dreams with poetic imagery, fitting both into his theory of symbolism, and claiming that both needed to be interpreted.

The view of reality which enabled Yeats to make a harmony of his various experiences was fundamentally simple.It was not an abritrary theory, adopted in arrogance or despair. Like all intelligent men, Yeats was concerned to make sense of the things that happened to him. 'The stronger your philosophic belief, the more rigorously should you investigate scientifically the apparent evidence for it; for one is a truth of the will, the other is concerned with intellectual truth'. He had to find a hypothesis which would include his experiences on all levels.

By this time, between 1920 and 1923, advances in scientific thought seemed to give additional support to the kind of view which Yeats' experience was pressing upon him. He saw that the universe extended far beyond the range of direct human perception, and that the finality of matter, as the Victorian scientist saw it, was challenged. What we perceived by means of our senses was roughly determined by our biological needs, and there was therefore a measure of agreement as to what might be called 'material' and what might not. Yeats' experience, and that of many people whose word he trusted—including A.E.'s—showed that human perceptions might be extended, spontaneously or experimentally, beyond the agreed average range, so as to apprehend in material form things to which the label was not applied. As I heard him put it, 'Nowadays the subjective can walk about the room'. He met this problem by believing that all material forms were interpretations put by our senses upon eternal reality. True to his nature, he called them dramatisations; images.

> Hardly is that thought out
> When a great image out *of spiritus mundi*
> Troubles my sight . . . [2]

*   *   *

Magic by Candlelight

These years at Oxford were a period of intense creative work for Yeats, both in prose and verse. He was writing his autobiographies, and read to us on many occasions from the unfinished drafts. Yeats' method of reading verse is well known, but the recordings which exist do not give any idea of the quality of voice which he had at this time. There was a vibrant singing note, a virility in the diction which, by the time the records were taken, had become unsteady, and the tone itself had worn thin. He did not only read his own poems but those of various friends, or anything else he happened to admire or like; and I was often disappointed afterwards to see the poems in print, and realise that magic had been vouchsafed to them by candlelight, an immense personality, and a chanting voice. Best of all I remember the reading of one poem, which did very well bear inspection afterwards, Frank Pearce Sturm's 'Eternal Helen', with its opening lines which Yeats repeated over and over again:

> Dread are the death-pale kings
> Who bend to the oar,
> Dread is the voice that sings
> On the starless shore
> Lamentations and woes:
> Cold on the wave
> Beautiful still heart goes
> To the rock-hewn grave.

Yeats' view of the act of writing a poem came up very clearly in his comment on an argument I had with A.E. A.E., reviewing my second book, complained that intellect was bullying imagination, and that I did not surrender to my vision. Yeats said that poetry was written by all the faculties fused in one by the white heat of inspiration. Intellect had an essential place in it. Challenged to define intellect, he turned in a flash and replied: 'Intellect—the man that judges' and amplified this by saying that he meant the entire personality expressed in an act of choice. The poet, writing in this incandescence which fused his powers into one, must then put the poem away, and return to it later as cold as ice, an enemy, implacable. The cold intellect must dispassionately scrutinise what had been written in the blazing conjunction of intellect and imagination. And there were so many occasions when inspiration did not come. 'That is why I write regular hours like a man in an office. Inspiration will be more apt to visit a man who keeps his house ready to receive her'. Four lines of a lyric was a good morning's work, or ten lines of blank verse.

Then came another favourite axiom: 'No work is ever wasted. Often, when in the morning my work has been in vain, and I have been baffled by a problem, I sit down at five o'clock to some quite different task, and solve its problems without difficulty, because of the struggle in the morning'. With hands on knees he looked round at each of us in turn. 'No work is ever wasted'.

This insistence on the function of intellect in the writing of poetry is of particular interest to us today, when poetry has tended to divide itself into two camps, with purely cerebral work at one extreme and dithyrambic excitement at the other. Yeats would never allow this division. I remember telling him one evening about a phase in the work of that fine lyric poet, Wilfred Rowland Childe, who died less than two years ago. Childe was devoutly religious, and a medievalist. He had been favoured with a number of visionary poems during a period of strong inspiration, in which he seemed to have little to do but record what presented itself so splendidly before him. The period passed and, hoping to regain it, Childe formed the habit of inducing in himself a kind of trance, a suspension of the faculties almost like that of a medium.

Wrestling with the Angel of Inspiration

Yeats strongly condemned this passive approach to the problem of poetic composition. 'The only legitimate passivity is that which follows exhaustion of the intellect. Then guidance comes'. He saw the whole thing as a struggle in which all the poet's faculties were united in order to grasp, receive, and wrestle with the visiting angel of inspiration. Intellect could never be left out, at any stage of the process, and it always had the final task of editing and polishing the poem so that it could stand the world's inspection. One had to remember the world and do all that integrity allowed and courtesy enjoined in order to meet it. The thought of the poem might be difficult, but the syntax should be clear. The poet was bound to give what help he could, but it must stop far short of compromising the vision.

One evening must be recorded after Yeats had left Oxford and returned to Dublin. I went across in the summer of 1924, my first visit for ten years, and was bidden to Yeats' house.[3] Seldom can a young writer have been more favoured by the fates. For the first part of the evening, the only other person present was A.E., and we were joined later by James Stephens. It was the year when, in order to celebrate the founding of the Free State, Eire renewed the legendary Taileann Games, and invited distinguished people from all over the world to be her guests. Yeats plunged into all this festivity, wearing a morning coat, and having his hair cut so that it would fit inside a top hat. A.E. rallied him on this, saying that he seemed to enjoy attending social functions, whereas he himself would go miles to avoid them. Yeats looked up at once:

'In my youth I read, in that book which I still think the wisest of all books, *Wilhelm Meister* by Goethe, these words: "The poor are, The rich are, but are also permitted to seem". I at once set myself to acquire this necessary technique of seeming. I was a shy young man tongue-tied and awkward, but I forced myself to go to soirées and salons and tea-parties and gatherings of every sort, until I, too, acquired this necessary technique of seeming'.

This experience, combining with Oscar Wilde's theory of the mask helped to shape Yeats' thought and governed his social practice. I gave the poet a share in shaping the image that should dramatise his reality to the world.

NOTES

Leonard Alfred George Strong (1896–1958), poet, novelist and journalist, the child of Irish parents, was born in England. His volumes of verse include *Dublin Days* (1921), *The Lowery Road* (1924), *At Glenan Cross* (1928), *Northern Light* (1930) and *Call to the Swans* (1936). Among his novels are *Dewer Rides* (1929), *The Jealous Ghost* (1930), *The Garden* (1931), *Sea Wall* (1933), *Corporal Tune* (1934) and *The Bay* (1941). He also wrote studies of Tom Moore (1937), J. M. Synge (1941) and James Joyce (1949).

1. The Yeatses held Monday 'at homes' at 4 Broad Street to which undergraduates were invited.

2. W. B. Yeats, 'The Second Coming', *Michael Robartes and the Dancer* (1921).

3. After leaving Oxford, the Yeatses purchased a Georgian house at 82 Merrion Square, Dublin.

Yeats at his Ease*

L. A. G. STRONG

W. B. Yeats came to live at Oxford in 1919. The years he spent there were productive and happy. He wrote a number of poems, including *All Souls' Night*[1] and *A Prayer for my Daughter*,[2] and a great part of *The Trembling of the Veil*,[3] which he read aloud on many occasions, often having difficulty with his own handwriting. Above all, he was at his ease; removed from the insistent acerbities of Irish politics, but able to reassure Englishmen in authority, as he was later loyally to do when De Valera came into power and politicians in London feared some kind of dramatic show-down. He could live the unharassed life of a man of letters in an ancient university, enjoying the company of scholars and, especially, of undergraduates; among whom he had a legendary status.

He invited undergraduates to his rooms, and accepted their invitations. I remember, as secretary to a college literary society, calling with two other officials at his house in Broad Street to collect our guest. Short though the distance was, we had a taxi. Yeats had changed into a kind of informal dinner jacket and a soft white shirt. He glanced sharply at us, noting that we had not changed, and for the moment we were afraid that he would feel we were not treating him with proper respect; but he made no comment, ate his dinner with us on a bench in Hall, and delighted everyone within range by his vigorous, quick-darting talk and his stories. The official part of the evening was just as successful, and he disconcerted a don by dating within thirty years a piece of very early Greek sculpture.

All the time he was in Oxford Yeats showed an extraordinary readiness to interest himself in the doings of the young.

One instance of his kindness suggests the reputation he held in the university. A girl undergraduate had committed the sin of taking a book away from the Bodleian. Overcome with horror, she rushed to the fountain-head of wisdom, and presented herself sobbing to the astonished poet. He gave her his complete attention, and, satisfied on the facts, sent for Mrs Yeats, who comforted the girl with tea and aspirin. Yeats then took the book back to the Bodleian and handed it to a stupefied official with a long and flamboyant explanation which, if it conveyed anything to him at all, suggested that the book had arrived at the Broad Street house in the form of a spiritualistic apport. Yeats then departed, well satisfied, leaving the

* *London Magazine*, II, no. 3 (Mar 1955) 56–65.

official to eye the book and restore it, rather gingerly, to its place on the shelves.

Yeats's relationship to the University as such was rather equivocal. Certain of the dons looked on him with suspicion as a rebel. He himself attributed their hesitation to other causes.

'No sooner does a period in which I have been seen to be harmless encourage them, and they decide that though I am an Irishman I have no plan to overthrow the British Empire, and their wives plan to ask my wife to tea, than the red heels of Lady Ottoline Morrell[4] are seen gleaming upon my doorstep, and all shudder and retreat once more.'

The liveliest were not deterred, however, and if the staider sort kept away, I think the poet's criticisms of university education perhaps had as much to do with it as the bizarre elegance of Lady Ottoline. Yeats in my hearing remarked to two English dons, 'I can't see what you think you are achieving. You seem to be busy with the propagation of second and third and fourth hand opinions upon literature. Culture does not consist in acquiring opinions, but in getting rid of them.'

But there was no doubt of his success with undergraduates. He was invited to speak at the Union, and brought that most formidable of audiences cheering to its feet with a torrent of oratory on the wrongs of Ireland. And on Monday evenings he kept open house—but only for the invited. I saw a gate-crasher turned out with glacial finality.

The themes that recurred most frequently on these Monday evenings were, naturally enough, magic and the occult: writing in general and stories about particular poets. Of Yeats's interest in magic I have written elsewhere,[5] and mention it here only because it leads to one of his stories. One afternoon William Sharp came into the house where Yeats was staying, and pounced on the cabalistic symbol of death, which Yeats had purposely left lying on a table. A week afterwards Sharp complained of terrible experiences and visions to do with death. This I am afraid is discounted as evidence of the symbol's evocative power by the fact that Yeats would often amuse himself, when out walking with Sharp, by transferring thoughts to the older poet's mind.

'I would be out upon a walk with him, and would decide to myself "Now from the third bush along the path a red devil will rush out and attack Sharp": and sure enough, when the third bush was reached, Sharp would clutch me in terrible panic, seeing a red devil making upon him from the bush.'

Yeats talked a great deal of Sharp, whose dual personality strongly interested him. He believed that the Fiona McLeod imposture arose in the first place from an encounter with a living actual person, who captured Sharp's imagination and was translated into this legend. Sharp was a man who lived in a land of dream. Yeats used to send him folk tales from Ireland, and in course of time would hear from him that Miss McLeod had found the same story in the Highlands, and a much elaborated version would duly appear in her next work.

'Once he went so far as to introduce a beautiful girl to George Meredith as Fiona. Meredith was furious when he discovered the deception. Sharp's sister used to write the Fiona letters for him. The whole thing flattered his vanity: this beautiful and gifted person who adored him was a conquest which did him credit. So far was Fiona a secondary personality that his wife would ask him each morning "Are you William or Fiona today?"'

'He used to say that Fiona was interiorly a man and he a woman: and told a story, that in Italy once he dreamt that she visited him as a man and had connection with him as a woman, with the result that for several days after he woke his breasts were swollen almost to the size of a woman's.'

Sharp was a tall, very handsome man. Later in life he used to speculate as to the identity of Fiona, suggesting that she might be this or that great lady: still suggesting always a conquest creditable to himself.

He told a tale once of how, when a boy of eighteen, he had loved madly and had been madly loved by a beautiful girl. They decided to die together.

'We got in a boat and I rowed out for miles and miles into the Atlantic. Then we embraced one another, and I put my foot through the bottom of the boat, and the girl was drowned.'

'Yes, but what about you, Sharp?' demanded Yeats.

'It was terribly sad: the water came rushing in through the hole and she was drowned.'

'Yes, yes, Sharp, but what about you?'

'Well, you know, when a man goes through an experience like that, it makes a great difference to him: it—'

'Yes, but, Sharp, what happened to YOU?'

'. . . SWUM ASHORE!'

He had started his story and entirely forgotten how to end it.

As I said, Yeats was busy during these years on his Autobiographies, and puzzled often over the doom that seemed to have encompassed the Rhymers' Club. For reasons of my own, I had been reading the poems of Ernest Radford.

'Did you find anything?'

'Not much.'

'I thought not': and he went on to list the other members and their fate.

'They all followed Rossetti in his absolute withdrawal into the world of art. Radford, a talker and a man of the world, went mad. Hilliard, whose published verses were dull, burnt all his manuscripts, which were said to contain good things, and went mad for no apparent reason. Arthur Symons went out of his mind for two years, but recovered, to live on with impaired faculties. Dowson reached such a state of lassitude through drink that he starved to death. Lionel Johnson fell down in the street when he was drunk, cut his head open, and died.' He looked from one to another of us. 'Each one calamity may easily be accounted for, but how explain so many in a club of twelve?'

Rossetti came often into Yeats's talk, nowhere more memorably than in his account of an incident told him by his father, the painter John Butler Yeats. The painter was a close friend of Rossetti. One day, when they were walking together, a chaffinch by the roadside showed signs of agitation, and fluttered along beside them from bush to bush as they walked. Rossetti stopped, and nodded towards it. 'That is my wife's soul,' he said sadly—and immediately the chaffinch came and perched on his shoulder.

Yeats stated many times, in talk and in print, that if he could have chosen a life to live, it would have been the life of William Morris. One night, an undergraduate was present who professed a very fastidious taste in literature, and looked pained when he was advised to read a certain popular author. Yeats was always extremely tolerant of young men's opinions, unless they affected superiority. Then he could flatten them as well as anyone.

He turned on the young man, telling him that if a thing was good the setting did not matter.

'William Morris used to say, to the people who claimed that they could only read Shakespeare. "Rubbish. Flame is flame wherever you find it".'

He spoke with affection of W. E. Henley,[6] and was sad that he could not praise Henley's poems.

'When I was a young man, for all my admiration of him, I could not greatly admire his poems. The other day I read them again, and I do not think them very good.' He was silent for a moment, peering into the dimness of the room through his thick lenses. 'We all loved Henley, because he was plainly not on the side of our parents.'

Another figure from these early days whose name often arose was Aubrey Beardsley.

'Some time before his death Beardsley became converted. The first symptom or intimation we had of it was the submission of drawings of an astonishing blasphemy. It began gently, with a Madonna and Child—the Child in a long nightdress covered with fripperies.'

Here is Yeats's own version of the famous story about his first encounter with James Joyce. This story has been denied by one of Joyce's biographers, but I do not think Yeats invented it. The stories which he did invent, or embellish beyond recognition, had always a wealth of circumstantial detail, and the figures in them spoke a little too appropriately, with a quickness of wit which too much resembled Yeats's own, or an obtuseness which no one else could have devised for them.

The first time I heard this story was during a discussion of *Ulysses*. On its first appearance, Yeats had dismissed it as mad. Now, less than a year later, he was recanting, and acknowledging a grave mistake. His first judgement may well have been coloured by memories of the author.

'James Joyce was one of the maddest young men that ever came out of Dublin. After calling on A.E. from 12.30 to 4 a.m., and opening the conversation by telling him that he disliked his poetry intensely, he called upon me, to read me some of his poems.

'"I must tell you, to begin with, that I consider your opinion of no value."

'"All right," I said. "Go on."

'He read, and certainly many of his poems are beautiful. At the end he said, "How old are you?"

'I told him, deducting a year or two, to be on the right side.

'"I thought so," he said. "I have met you too late."'

Yeats had a tenderness for the foible of concealing one's age.

'A certain French artist was very tolerant of his wife's amours. Of one he said "I always told my wife that Persian would turn out badly": and after her death he caused her age to be understated upon her tombstone.'

Of American writers I do not remember him to have spoken often although for two at least he had a deep respect. Whitman and Emerson were dismissed on grounds which may surprise their admirers. 'Their work ultimately loses interest for us through their failure to imagine evil.'

Yeats's debt to Ezra Pound was freely acknowledged, but there was at least one retort to him. 'What you are trying to make speech is punctuation marks without words between them. That,' he added to us, raising his head abruptly, 'is my conception of a mathematical world.'

If he disliked the notion of a mathematical world, he showed no dislike of mathematical symbols: and it was possibly the fourth American writer who reconciled him to their use. This was the philosopher Henry Adams, who caught Yeats's attention with a view of human development embodied in the image of the cones. Adams saw our progress in alternate cones or spirals, narrowing towards subjectivity, or widening towards objectivity and the totality of nature. 'The cones may be one inside the other, but one is the complement of the other. We are at present at the extreme objective width of the base of the cone. We have spiralled outwards a civilization of apparatus, and are due now to turn inwards again towards the subjective, self, the spirit.'

Yeats was fascinated too by the fanciful parallel which Adams drew between man's progress towards the totality of nature and a stone falling towards the earth, alleging that the rate of acceleration was measurable and exactly similar. His explanation of the ice age was a deduction from the second law of thermo-dynamics. It is probable therefore that such tolerance as Yeats extended towards mathematical imagery he owed to Henry Adams.

There was less talk of the theatre during these Oxford years than I heard from Yeats afterwards, perhaps because, removed from the Abbey and its problems, he had turned his mind in other directions. Talking one night of tragedy, he quoted with glowing approval Lady Gregory's dictum 'Every true tragedy must be a joy to the man who dies.' His voice quickened with passion as he elaborated. ' "Absent thee from felicity awhile"—it is a cry of joy, a triumph.' Then he added, 'I resent a painful tale if the painfulness is an arbitrary invention. *Othello* is the only tragedy in Shakespeare I resent, because, though he is glad to die, it is only at the end that he is glad to die.'

We went on from that to definitions of tragedy, which Yeats defined as the struggle of the soul with an obstacle which can be escaped only in death.

'In farce, the soul is struggling against a ridiculous object: in comedy, with a removable object: in tragedy, with an irremovable object.'

Passing to lighter matters, he began to talk of the Abbey.

'Peace in the Abbey company varied with the size of Sara Allgood's waist. When she did herself well, this increased, and it was no longer necessary to cast her for all the young heroine parts: instead she would readily play the old peasant women for whom she had especial genius. But whenever she was ill, and returned· with a waist reduced, immediately there was turmoil and confusion.'

For music he had no aptitude, and he said so. One day some Indians called, asking that he should come with them to hear an Indian musician. Yeats promised that his wife should go. He himself could not tell one note from another, and had very little opinion of musicians. They could not talk.

'I was once with Arthur Symons in Paris, and he excused himself to go and talk for a minute to a man sitting on the far side of the café. When he came back I said, "Who is that musician?"

'Symons was surprised. "How did you know he was a musician?"

' "You know none but artists—no artist but a musician could have such a foolish face." '

Yeats was very critical of settings of his own words, with the criterion that one note should represent one syllable. For this reason he liked particularly Thomas Dunhill's[7] setting of *The Cloths of Heaven*.[8] Shaking with laughter, he complained of hearing a lullaby sung by three men with stentorian voices, and of a composer who said to him 'I wish you could have heard my setting of your *Innisfree*,[9] sung in the open by two thousand boy scouts.'

He laughed again, and quoted, 'And I shall have some peace there.'

Because of the seriousness of so much of his thought, and the dignity of the practice, the way in which Yeats wore his poetic mantle, there is a danger of supposing him to have been solemn. Far from it. In many moods he loved ribaldry. No man took more pains to perfect a good story. A great deal of ingenuity was devoted to paying back old scores against George Moore, and the final selection of stories arrayed against him was exquisitely calculated to make him appear limp and ridiculous.

'George Moore came to me one day and said, "O Yeats, I wish you would advise me on a matter that has been troubling me for years. How do you keep up your little pants that are inside your trousers" And I said to him, "Moore, if you look at the tops of your little pants that are inside your trousers, you will see that they have small tapes fastened to them. And if you put the ends of your braces through the small tapes before you fasten them to your trouser buttons, your little pants will stay up inside your trousers." Moore thanked me and went away, and the next time I saw him he came up to me and said, "O Yeats—God bless ye".'

Once in America Moore was found in a state of deep depression. It transpired that he had set his affections on a lady—that they had got along splendidly, and that at last he had made an offer and been turned down.

'But you must have said something wrong to her.'

'I didn't say anything wrong.'

'What did you say?'

At last Moore growled, 'I told her I was clean and healthy, and that she couldn't do better.'

The statement was logically unimpeachable. Logic was Moore's dominating quality.

At the end of a long discussion of his character, Yeats said, 'I have dropped Moore because he is so dangerous. He will take to you most violently, and exalt you to an embarrassing degree. This is the naïf simple primitive benevolent side of him. But his life is made up of this benevolence, and reactions from it to a calculated malice. So, after about five years, you will become the victim of some such piece of malice.

'The trilogy (*Ave, Salve, Vale*) was written when Moore's admiration of A.E. was at its height: but it is not his fault that the third book does not contain a blow at his hero. One day Moore exclaimed, "Yeats, there must be a flaw somewhere in that perfect soul." So he went down one Sunday night, when A.E. sits surrounded by his friends, to discover the flaw.

'He was back full of dark whisperings. "Yeats, I have discovered the flaw—suppressed wife"; and set off to write a chapter for his book to the effect that A.E. neglected his wife for Miss Mitchell, who happened to work in the same office with him.

'Quite apart from the fact that the suggestion was absurd only a person of Moore's naïveté would have supposed that such a publication would be allowed. A.E. at once took proceedings and stopped the chapter. "You know, Yeats," said Moore, "he's such an egotist!"'

Another story involved Dr Gogarty.

'One day George Moore woke up with an indigestion spot on his face. He went to Oliver Gogarty, who said, "Memories of your dead past, Moore!" Moore then became voluminously autobiographic, whereupon Gogarty said, "I can't treat you for it, you know, because I'm an aurist and Dublin doctors are so jealous: but I'll send you to a man." He thereupon sent Moore to the stupidest doctor in Dublin.

'Moore arrived, coruscating with autobiography, and was treated on the strength of his memoirs. Gogarty then procured invitations for him to houses which had hitherto refused to receive him. Finally, when the joke had gone far enough, the eruption luckily spread to his ear, and Gogarty, saying "I can treat you for it now," gave him a harmless blood mixture which speedily cured him.'

I have a whole hat-full of stories against George Moore, most of which I am afraid I do not believe, and a great many others which illustrate Yeats's delight in mischief; a sheer high-spirited humorous delight, which sometimes went to absurd lengths. There is no room to tell them here, and readers may feel that such things are trivial compared to his importance as a poet. I mention them only because the interest in his work, and the books that are being written about him, may throw on the mind's screen a monumental figure, out of touch with common humanity. This is distressing to those who knew him, like the persistent legend of his aloofness, and it may hinder a just appraisal of his work.

One story which shows the lighter side of his mind may be welcome. Yeats reported amusingly on one of the official functions which he attended at the celebration of the Tailteann Games in the summer of 1924. The presence of so many distinguished foreign guests demanded a banquet; but when all preparations had been made, the new and wholly inexperienced government held no one who knew the order of precedence in which the guests should be seated. While they were discussing the problem, there came forward a certain noble lord, a member of the old guard, who offered to arrange the matter in accordance with protocol.

The offer was accepted; but when the list was taken for approval to the Governor General, he discovered that he would have to sit next to a distinguished Frenchman.

'I will not sit next to um. Sure I wouldn't know what to say to um.'

Deadlock. To the rescue came Dr Oliver Gogarty, and offered to make a list based upon human interest, seating those people together who could be expected to enjoy each other's society. Dr Gogarty's list was approved, and everyone was happy.

An hour before the banquet, the noble lord looked in, saw what had happened, and in high rage went around the tables restoring his own list. Ten minutes before the official hour, Dr Gogarty looked in and had just time to rearrange the seating in *his* way before the guests came in, the customary half hour late.

Under this new, liberal arrangement, Yeats found himself next to a Persian poet. The Persian spoke no English, but an interpreter stood behind his chair. The rest I can tell as Yeats told it to me.

'As soon as the preliminaries were over, I turned to the interpreter and asked the Persian about his work. The Persian replied by means of the interpreter: "In my youth I was court poet to my Royal Master the Shah, and it was my duty to praise in my verses the charms of whatever lady my

Royal Master the Shah might admire. But as I was in no way permitted to show any personal interest in those charms, or to suggest that I myself might be moved by them as a man, my poems remained models of propriety, and are used as text books in all the girls' schools in Persia." Then I said to the interpreter, "Ask him what he is writing now?" And the Persian replied by means of the interpreter, "Now I only write useful things." And I said to the interpreter, "Ask him what on earth he means by that." And the Persian replied, "Being bidden by my Royal Master to attend the meetings of the League of Nations, I submit my reports in rhyme." '

Those who knew the mischievous side of Yeats had no lack of reverence for his work. They did not honour him less because they hurried to him with the latest Rabelaisian story. He was shy, but there was a clear way through his shyness; and, though he said little on directly personal things, he could make a word or two mean a lot. I shall never forget going over to Dublin for a dinner given him to celebrate his seventieth birthday. There were many people there, some of whom had known him all his life. A crowd stood round him at the reception before the dinner, and it was some time before I could get near to greet him. Presently he turned and saw me. He put a hand on my shoulder: 'Ah, Strong. You came.'

No man deficient in human kindness, on a night of triumph and acclaim, could thus have greeted one with so small a title to his regard.

NOTES

1. In *The Tower* (London: Macmillan, 1928).
2. In *Michael Robartes and the Dancer* (Churchtown, Dublin: Cuala Press, 1920).
3. *The Trembling of the Veil* (London: T. Werner Laurie, 1922).
4. Yeats used to go to Garsington, the beautiful manor house of Lady Ottoline and Philip Morrell, where undergraduates mixed with distinguished folk on Sunday afternoons. The first section of his poem 'Meditations in Time of Civil War', written in 1921, was in part inspired by Lady Morrell's house and gardens. See Robert Gathorne-Hardy, ed; *Ottoline at Garsington; Memoirs of Lady Ottoline Morrell* (London: Faber and Faber, 1974).
5. 'Reminiscences of W. B. Yeats', *Listener* (London) LI, 22 Apr 1954, 689–90.
6. William Ernest Henley (1894–1903), English poet and critic. His best-known poems are 'Invictus' and 'England, my England'. The young Yeats received encouragement from Henley, who sometimes revised the young poet's work. 'I . . . began under him my education.' The editor of the *Scots Observer*, afterwards the *National Observer*, lived not far from Bedford Park; Yeats, after a few calls on Sunday evenings, began to contribute to the *Scots Observer*, where appeared what he afterwards called 'my first good lyrics'.
7. Thomas Frederick Dunhill (1877–1946), English composer.
8. 'He Wishes for the Cloths of Heaven', *The Wind among the Reeds* (London: Elkin Mathews, 1899).
9. 'The Lake Isle of Innisfree', *Poems* (London: Fisher Unwin, 1895).

A Day with Yeats*

R. F. RATTRAY

There is in Leicester one of the leading Literary and Philosophical Societies. While I was Principal of the University College in that city in the 1920's, a lecturer due to the Society was ill and notified the secretary that he could not come. The latter resorted to a lecture agency, which replied, 'Would Mr W. B. Yeats do?' Would W. B. Yeats do, indeed? My wife and I were asked to put him up.

I of course went to meet him at the station. Crowds came off the train but I could not see anyone answering to the man I wanted. I had noticed a tall gentleman, but he was superintending a large stock of luggage, so it could not be he. When, however, there was no one else to answer, I looked again at the tall gentleman. He was wearing a 'wideawake' hat, eyeglasses on a ribbon, and a large bow tie of soft material. He had white hair and an aquiline nose. I asked and it was. I thought to myself, 'He is on the way to Ireland and will leave his luggage at the station, taking only a suitcase.' But no, the whole stack was piled on the car.

When he had changed, I noticed that he had donned white socks. When you really saw Yeats, he was an impressive figure. He gave me the impression of being very tall: he was erect and straight as a lath. He had a somewhat imperious mien and a step like a king. He wore a large enamelled ring, made for him (so he told us) by Edmond Dulac. When he spoke, it was as one having authority, and not as the scribes, but nevertheless he talked humbly and with humour.

I heard afterwards that Yeats was capable of forty minutes' silences, but throughout his visit he was entirely gracious and spoke easily and naturally and fully. It happened that we had staying with us Mr and Mrs Vacher Burch. (The former was later to become Dr Burch, lecturer at Liverpool Cathedral, and published learned books.) Mr Burch, with his wellstored mind and charming address, was a great help in drawing Yeats out. What Yeats said was always worth while. He spoke with a deep, booming Irish voice and accent.

Between dinner and lecture my wife seized an opportunity to take me to see Yeats's room, to which a maid had invited inspection. It was like a battlefield. The stack of luggage was now explained. He had three

* *Poets in the Flesh* (Cambridge: The Golden Head Press, 1961) pp. 5–8.

dressing-gowns. Clothes were strewn all over the room; there was a row of medicine bottles on the mantelshelf. Yeats had laughingly drawn attention to the fact that his wife had insisted on his carrying a kitbag of the kind formerly carried by the forces in which to stuff articles which he could not get into his suitcases.

The lecture was his standing single lecture and was a great success. He held the large audience easily, and what he said was a delightful mixture of poetry, autobiography and humour. He told us that when he was a little boy, he spent holidays on the lake isle of Innisfree, an earthly paradise. Later, when he lived in London (he lived in an attic and rare spirits climbed the stair to hold converse with him), he was one day walking along a street when suddenly he heard the sound of water falling. As a matter of fact, it came from a fishmonger's window from a jet on which was poised a celluloid ball. The sound of the splash of water, however, probed Yeats's heart and took him back to the lake isle of Innisfree. He at once wrote the poem. 'Now,' said Yeats, 'I am going to say to you the only poem of mine you know.' He recited it with great sincerity and feeling, ending with great emphasis as he said:

'I hear it in the deep heart's core.'[1]

Yeats, of course, uttered poetry in a kind of chant. He told that after a lecture in America, a lady said, 'Will Mr Yeats kindly infarm us why he utters his poetry in that fashion?' Yeats replied, 'Every poet, from Homer down to today, has uttered his poetry in that fashion.' The lady then asked, 'Will Mr Yeats kindly infarm us how he knows that Homer uttered his poetry in that fashion?' Yeats's reply was, 'The answer to that question is the one given by the Scotsman on being asked whether Shakespeare was Scotch—"The ability would warrant the supposition".'

When we got home and sat round the fire there began one of the most remarkable conversations in which I have ever participated. Yeats told us that as a young man he studied magic under a sister of Bergson. He found that, by placing certain symbols on his pillow before he went to sleep, he got visions during sleep. I asked, what sort of vision? Yeats became dramatic and said most impressively, 'I saw between sleeping and waking a galloping centaur and a moment later a naked woman of incredible beauty standing on a pedestal and shooting an arrow at a star.' Mr Burch said, 'O but you know what that is. These symbols occur in ancient Greek mythology.' 'You don't mean it,' said Yeats in astonishment. I recalled that Freud, analysing the mind of a patient, dug out symbols which to him were meaningless and that later, in casual conversation with an anthropologist he mentioned the symbols and was amazed to find that they belonged to antiquity. Yeats was deeply interested and continued to tell his visions. When he had recounted another, Mr Burch said, 'O but you know that occurs in the folklore of Cornwall.' (It has been made out that the Yeatses came from Cornwall.) Yeats was thrilled and it was a wonderful experience to hear him recount in his most dramatic and expressive way his experiences.

I remember that Yeats was grimly amused by Joyce's *Ulysses*, which had recently appeared in the original Paris edition. I remember too that he told us that in his home in Dublin, for his little girl they had a Catholic nurse. Ireland was still suffering active unrest and bombs were being thrown. One evening the little girl, in bed, was startled by an explosion, sat up and cried out, 'Sacred Heart! What on earth was that?'

The next day Yeats was due to go to Birmingham and asked if he might stay over lunch. He confided that he was due to stay with one of the Cadburys but did not remember which. So in the morning I took him to the public library. On the way, Yeats, absorbed in conversation, would stop in the middle of the street and, with hands behind his back, hold forth. At the library I got out the Birmingham directory and ran over the Cadburys to see if he could identify the one. Rather doubtfully he did think that he recognized one, and I wrote down the address. On the way to the station after lunch I found that Yeats had lost the address, but fortunately I had kept a copy and put it into his hand. When I got home I found that he had left behind him his shaving brush and a book.

NOTE

1. W. B. Yeats, 'The Lake Isle of Innisfree', *The Rose* (1893).

Four O'clock Tea with W. B. Yeats*

NANCY PYPER

Dublin, Oct. 20, 1924.—For a long time when I have thought of Dublin I have thought of W. B. Yeats, poet and playwright, the creator of beauty in verse and prose, the Irishman who has made the English language music, co-founder of the famous Abbey Theatre, one of the leading spirits in the Irish Renaissance, and now a member of the Senate of Ireland. I had longed to meet the man himself, and when I arrived here I determined to have a shot at interviewing him.

At first the chances seemed poor—everywhere I spoke of him I heard of his inaccessibility—'he's a very hard man to get hold of,' I was told. I learned that he was in town, however, as the Senate was sitting, and with

* *Musical Life and Arts* (Winnipeg, Manitoba), 1 Dec 1924, pp. 161–5.

no little trepidation presented myself at his home, 82 Merrion Square.

The maid who answered the door was very dubious when I asked if I might see Mr. Yeats—'he doesn't see anyone in the mornings.'

'May I see Mrs. Yeats?'

She took my card and went off, leaving me in a very large hall, the olive-tinted walls of which were hung with clever rough color sketches in narrow gilt frames. As I was admiring these, the deep orange curtains at the foot of the stairs parted, and the maid returned to take me up to the dressing room. I have rarely seen a more distinctive room than the Yeats drawing room. Tall pale green bookcases filled with inviting looking books caught my eye first, and then a series of beautiful portraits in oils which hung on the walls. A log fire crackled in the large open fireplace. Deep easy chairs were everywhere—one beside the fireplace had a tiny stool before it on which stood a small portable typewriter with paper in it—one leaf had fluttered to the floor. A large carved table laden with books, flowers in a stand in the middle of the floor, tall candles everywhere!

Suddenly Mrs. Yeats came in, a very good-looking and charming woman, tall and well built, with delightfully fresh coloring and red brown bobbed (not shingled) hair. She made me feel at ease at once, and we talked for some minutes. She told me they had had to make it a rule not to let anyone see her husband in the mornings—he simply had to rest then—but—'was I staying in Dublin long?'

'Only a day or two,' I replied, and then, bless her, she said, 'will you come to tea tomorrow afternoon at four?'

I could only say 'thank you' and shake the hand she held out to me. She waved the maid away—'I think I'll see you downstairs myself,' she said, and we went down the broad stairs together to the door where we shook hands again and I went away happy, my mind filled with the friendliness and graciousness and 'hominess' that made the atmosphere of the 'inaccessible' home of the poet.

On the following afternoon I was ushered straight in and up the stairs where people were passing and repassing. The study door was thrown open, and as I stepped across the threshold a tall man rose from an easy chair before a redly glowing electric fire, and with outstretched hand greeted me. And then Mrs. Yeats came forward with a smile and said, 'This is Lady Gregory,' and I was bowing to another very famous Irish playwright—an elderly lady in black, who rose to greet me with a very delightful smile. 'What piercing eyes she had,' I thought; they flashed into you almost.

We chatted for a few moments, and then Lady Gregory said, 'I had better go and get off my things, I am very travel-stained and wet, I have just come in from the country.' She and Mrs. Yeats went, and I was left alone with W.B. himself.

I looked at him as he came back from the door, and thought how much younger he appeared than his photographs, not a bit like his 59 years.

He is very tall, and his shoulders are broad, hair wavy-brown, slightly streaked with gray, deep brown eyes, well shaped nose, and an oddly small mouth. His voice is delightful, half Irish and half English, his speech a sort of 'silver' somehow. And his hands are beautiful. He has a great dignity, his bow is so curtly, and the little gracious bend of the head comes so naturally to him.

He sat down, pushed back his wavy hair and as I looked at him I thought 'I hope you like me as much as I like you.'

'You'd like a cigarette,' he said, and I took one from a silver casket which he took from his desk.

'Now a match—there were boxes here, but there have been some men before us—you know I don't suppose a man ever sees a box of matches without putting it in his pocket,' and away he went with a jolly smile to get another.

'Now,' he said, as we sat facing each other again, 'I suppose you want to ask me questions.'

'I had much rather listen to you talk,' I replied, and he laughed—a low, most infectious little laugh.

He talked of poems, of the work of the American poet Davies, 'delightful, just delightful,' and the man himself a very charming personality, 'being Canadian you'd enjoy meeting him.'

As he spoke he pushed his hand through his hair, a little gesture that is habitual with him. His soft brown eyes have a far-away look; he plays with his pince-nez constantly, suddenly puts them on, leans slightly forward and looks at you for a few moments as he talks, then relaxes and takes them off again.

He mentioned Lascelles Abercrombie's 'Mary and the Bramble'[1] as being a favorite of his. 'A delightful man to meet, Abercrombie,' he said.

He talked of his own poems, the reviving of the old ballads and legends he loves most—his beautiful play, 'The Countess Cathleen' came to him in a dream, he told me.

He talked of the Abbey Theatre, the subject of which I most wanted to hear him speak. I had been to 'The Abbey' the previous evening, and had seen two comedies: 'Apartments,'[2] by Fand O'Grady, in which Sara Allgood and Michael Dolan took the chief parts, and 'Insurance Money,'[3] by George Shiels.

'Yes, we have Miss Allgood back with us again for some of our recent plays; there have not been many suitable parts for her lately, she suits the "folk" parts best, you know—of course, you will be seeing her in "The White-headed Boy"[4] to-night.'

I spoke of our Little Theatre in Winnipeg, and he was immediately interested.

'What Irish plays have you done?' he asked.

I told him that we had done the 'Shadow of The Glen,' 'Hyacinth Halvey,' and Eugene O'Neill's 'Beyond the Horizon.' I mentioned 'The

Pine Tree,' which seemed to interest him, for he went to his bookcase and, with fingers that seemed to love them, turned over some volumes of Japanese plays, translated by a friend of his. 'The Pine Tree' was not among them, and he made a note of it.

'There are some delightful little Spanish plays you should look over,' he said, 'especially those of Bonaventure, so simple and yet so telling.'

'Have you any more Irish plays in mind,' he asked.

I said I had been reading 'The Building Fund.'

'Oh, yes, Boyle has a strong stage sense—dramatic sense—but he is uneducated in other ways.'

I said I should like to try my hand at producing his own 'Countess Cathleen,' and he gave me some very helpful suggestions.

Of it he says: 'When I wrote it I thought of course chiefly of the actual picture that was forming before me, but there was a secondary meaning that came into my mind continuously, I thought. It is the soul of one who loves Ireland, plunging into unrest, seeming to lose itself, to bargain itself away to the very wickedness of the world and to surrender what is eternal for what is temporary.'

He was glad to feel that his meaning seemed natural to many, although the play was greatly criticised—'even the very girls in the shops' complained that 'to describe an Irishwoman as selling herself to the devil was to slander the country.'

A knock at the door and the maid brought in the tea tray. Mr. Yeats made room for it on a little table beside me, and poured out two cups of fragrant China tea. We sat silent for awhile, and for myself I don't think I have ever enjoyed afternoon tea as much as I did in this delightful room. He lighted another cigarette for me—he doesn't smoke himself—and I let my eyes wander round his working room. A beautiful shade of blue was the predominant note, with splashes of orange here and there—I remember he had said 'a certain shade of blue always affects me'—the armchairs on which we sat were of a willow pattern blue, the hangings of the same beautiful color and on a little table near him was an orange vase filled with beautiful blue spikes of larkspur. In front of the long windows was a very wide bird cage, in which lived some five or six lovely little yellow birds, which sang and twittered softly all the time. On the wall near my chair hung the original of Sargent's charcoal drawing of the poet, and I thought how like it was, though it was done in 1908.

I laid my cup down—such beautifully vivid Sevres china—and, leaning back in my chair, wished with all my heart I could put all I longed to know and ask into words.

Suddenly a book I had recently read—'Set Down in Malice'—came into my head.

'Do you remember speaking to Gerald Cumberland', I asked.

He laughed. 'Yes, I remember saying "good afternoon" to him. A dreadful man, published a lot of interviews which never took place. You ought to go and see a friend of mine whom he called on. My friend had not time to see him, and the only words he said were: "Good morning, I haven't time to talk just now." Cumberland made a wonderful interview out of that, you know.'

Then: 'You know we're very easy people here—or, perhaps, I ought to say, were—and one doesn't expect a man to prowl around trying to make up interviews out of a chance remark which he overhears. Cumberland didn't mention to any of us that we were being interviewed, and one feels his methods were hardly—well, cricket.'

Our own talk was, to me, so terrifyingly unlike an interview that I felt suddenly panicky and afraid I should have nothing whatever to record. Then two questions suggested to me by the master of one of the large public schools in Dublin came into my head in all their precise and correct form—'Will Irish ever become the everyday language of Ireland?' I heard myself say.

'I don't know, one can't tell that, it's for the people themselves to decide, isn't it?'

'Then if not,' I persisted, 'what is to be its part in the development of an Irish national culture'

'Well, the movement is trying to restore what is called a more picturesque way of life—that is to say a way of life in which the common man shall have some share in imaginative art and culture. That, I feel sure, is the decisive element in the attempt to preserve the Irish language. If Ireland had not lost the Gaelic she would never have had this sensitiveness as of a parvenu presented at court for the first time. When she had the consciousness of her own antiquity her writers praised and blamed according to their fancy—she kept her own identity.'

'Do you think the Free State government should endow a national theatre?' I asked.

'Oh, yes, that will come in time. We work slowly here, you know—and there isn't much money—but we hope greatly.

He asked me how it was with our Little Theatre, had we a standing cast of principal players, and were the principals paid? I hadn't known till he told me that the Abbey players were paid.

We discussed the problem of how to do good plays with very little money. Mr. Yeats was insistent that every increase in expenditure lowered the quality of dramatic art itself by robbing the dramatist of freedom in experiment and by withdrawing attention from his words and from the work of the players.

'Absolute simplicity of the form and coloring of scenery and costumes are necessary. As a general rule the background should be but a single color, so that the persons in the play, wherever they stand, may harmonise with it and preoccupy the attention.'

I had felt this very strongly at The Abbey on the previous evening when

I saw the effect of the admirable simplicity in the costumes and setting of 'Insurance Money.'

'We have, at least,' said Mr. Yeats, 'got away from bad painting, with innumerable garish colors.'

I mentioned that the incidental music at The Abbey didn't seem to me to be very well suited to the plays, and asked him did he not think that well-chosen music had a great effect in producing the needed 'atmosphere' both before and during the performance.

'Oh, yes,' he said, 'undoubtedly it has, but, unfortunately, I don't know much about music, and I have to trust a good deal to my friends.'

If songs were to be brought into plays, he said, it mattered little to what school the singer belonged, so long as every word, every cadence, was as audible and expressive as though it were spoken.

It was getting late, and I felt that I had been taking up a great deal of his time. I had brought with me my old copy of 'Plays and Controversies,' and as I rose to go asked him if he would autograph it for me.

'Certainly,' he said, 'I shall like to.'

He took the book, turned to the page opposite his picture, struck out the printed 'By W. B. Yeats,' and wrote his name in with the date, October 20, 1924.

'This,' said he, with the whimsical smile which fairly lights up his face; 'is, I assure you, the correct way to autograph one's own book. You see your name is unchallenged on the first page—isn't it so?'

Then as I tried to thank him he said, 'It's been most pleasant, you have told me a great many interesting things. Now we are friends and have talked together about the things we both care for.'

He told me to be always sure of his sincere interest in the Little Theatre in Canada, and especially from now on in the one in Winnipeg.

Then Mrs. Yeats came in smoking a Russian cigarette, tall and gay, with blue sparkling eyes and firm, quick step.

As I was saying good-bye Mr. Yeats said, 'perhaps you would like to have Charles Ricketts' water colors explained—you may have noticed them in the hall.'

We went down together and he pointed out the special beauty and purpose of each one. One very beautiful picture of a tall, graceful woman in the legendary, Irish clothes of long long ago was designed for 'The Countess Cathleen.'

'You like it,' he said. 'Yes, Ricketts is wonderful. He has designed all the scenery for Shaw's St. Joan.'

He showed me out himself, and, as we shook hands at the door, I felt that I had spent one of the most enjoyable afternoons of my life. My only regret is that you have not someone clever enough to tell you all about it.

NOTES

1. Lascelles Abercrombie (1881–1938), English poet and scholar. His first volume of verse *Interludes and Poems* (1908) was followed by *Mary and the Bramble* (1910).

2. *Apartments* was first produced at the Abbey Theatre on 3 September 1923.

3. *Insurance Money* opened at the Abbey Theatre on 13 December 1921.

4. *The Whiteheaded Boy*, a comedy by Lennox Robinson, had its first production at the Abbey Theatre on 13 December 1916.

The Plough and the Stars;
Mr Sean O'Casey's New Play*

'The Plough and the Stars,'[1] a new play by Mr. Sean O'Casey has been put into rehearsal at the Abbey Theatre, where it will be produced for the first time in about a month.

The play, which is in four Acts, deals with tenement life in Dublin in the period of the 1916 rebellion. The lengthy cast includes all the Abbey company, with the exception of Miss Sara Allgood, who is playing in London in Mr. O'Casey's 'Juno and the Paycock,' which promises to hold the stage of the Royalty Theatre for many weeks to come.

*   *   *

Mr. W. B. Yeats, speaking of 'The Plough and the Stars' to an *Irish Times* representative, said that it is a much finer play than 'Juno and the Paycock'; more profound and more original, as much an advance on Juno as 'Juno'[2] is on the 'Gunman.'[3] 'In this play we have O'Casey more entirely himself. He is no longer hampered by traditional plot elements. The writing is as original and as profound as a novel by Dostoievsky.'

* Extracted from *Irish Times* (Dublin), 12 Jan 1926, p. 9.

NOTES

Sean O'Casey (1880–1964) was a leading Irish dramatist, whose earlier work, remarkable for its realistic observation of people and circumstances, its rich dialogue, and its blend of humour and the tragic sense of life, includes *The Shadow of a Gunman* (1923), *Juno and the Paycock* (1924) and *The Plough and the Stars* (1926). In his later work, O'Casey wrote in a more expressionistic vein. This period includes *The Silver Tassie* (1928), *Within the Gates* (1933), *The Star Turns Red* (1940), *Purple Dust* (1940), *Red Roses for Me* (1942), *Oak Leaves and Lavender* (1946) and *Cock-a-Doodle Dandy* (1949). He also wrote six autobiographical books, reprinted as *Autobiographies*. Although Yeats admired O'Casey's early work, his refusal, with the concurrence of Lady Gregory and Lennox Robinson, of *The Silver Tassie*, which was a new departure, created a sensation.

1. When *The Plough and the Stars* was first performed at the Abbey Theatre on 8 February 1926 it created the most celebrated riot since Dublin playgoers erupted over Synge's *The Playboy of the Western World*. Its obvious censure of methods of revolution angered the diehard Republicans; a small number of men attempted to rush the stage, and police protection had to be sought for the players. Yeats thought the row 'horrible' yet showed his old determination to see things through. Joseph Holloway's *Impressions of a Dublin Playgoer* records: 'A great protest was made tonight, and ended in almost the second act being played in dumb show . . . to-night's protest has made a second *Playboy* of *The Plough*, and Yeats was in his element. . . . Some of the players behaved with uncommon roughness to some ladies who got on the stage, and threw two of them into the stalls. . . . The chairs of the orchestra were thrown on the stage, and the music on the piano fluttered, and some four or five tried to pull down half of the drop curtain, and another caught hold of one side of the railing in the scene in Act 3.' (Thursday, 11 Feb 1926) The *Irish Times* for 12 February 1926 reported that when the play was at a standstill Yeats shouted at the rioters from the footlights rebuking them: 'Is this', he asked, 'going to be a recurring celebration of Irish genius? Synge first, then O' Casey . . . Dublin has once more rocked the cradle of genius.'

2. *Juno and the Paycock* was first produced at the Abbey Theatre on 3 March 1924.

3. *The Shadow of a Gunman* opened at the Abbey Theatre on 12 April 1923.

With the Poet in Merrion Square*

SEAN O'CASEY

Coming close to the first night,[1] Sean's eyes filled with inflammation, and in-growing eyelashes made the inflammation worse. Dr. J. D. Cummins, now an intimate friend, did all he could to lessen the searching pain; but on the night of the first performance, Sean found it hard and painful to keep his eyes fixed on the bright zone of the stage. The theatre was packed to the doors; the curtain went up; the play began. Though some of the actors didn't seem to strive very earnestly to swing themselves into the drama, most things went well, and the audience sat still, intensely interested in what they saw before them—the mimic, but by no means unimportant, portrayal of a part of Dublin's life and feeling. When the end came, the audience clapped tumultuously, and shouted applause. They shouted for the author, and Sean went on to the stage, quietly glad that the play had succeeded. He took the appreciation of those there nicely, though the flame of pain in his eyes pricked like red-hot needles. But all was pleasant, and the loud applause flowed from the serenity of agreement with, and appreciation of, the play. Tightening the belt of his rubber trench-coat tight around him, he went home settled in mind, happy in heart: the worst was over. He was very much the innocent gaum.

* Extracted from *Inishfallen Fare Thee Well* (London and New York: Macmillan, 1949).

The next night he sauntered into a storm. Holy Murther had come again on a visit to the Abbey Theatre. When he entered the foyer, he was hurried up to the Secretary's Office, where W. B. Yeats was waiting for him. Listen to my tale of woe. There he was told that the theatre was in an uproar, and that the play could not go on, if something definite wasn't done; that missiles were being flung at the actors, and that it looked as if the stage would be stormed.

—We think it necessary that the police should be sent for immediately, so that the mob may be kept from preventing us carrying on the work we have set our hands to do, said Yeats. We want your consent, O'Casey, to send for the police, as you happen to be the author of the play.

The police! Sean to agree to send for the police—never! His Irish soul revolted from the idea; though Yeats and others reminded him that the police were no longer in a foreign service, but were now in Ireland's own. That the tricolour waved over their barracks, and that it even graced the big drum of their band. Even so, Sean couldn't see his way to ask them to come. No, no; never! But a wild roar heard in the theatre, seeming to shake the room where they all stood, told him to make up his mind quick; and swearing he could ne'er consent, consented.

The police were summoned, and the play began again—two plays, in fact: one on the stage, the other in the auditorium. Yeats tore down the stairs and rushed on to the stage to hold the fort till the constables came. The whole place became a mass of moving, roaring people, and Yeats roared louder than any of them. Rowdy, clenching, but well-groomed hands reached up to drag down the fading black-and-gold front curtain; others, snarling curiously, tried to tug up the very chairs from their roots in the auditorium; while some, in frenzy, pushed at the stout walls to force them down. Steamy fumes ascended here and there in the theatre, and a sickly stench crept all over the place, turning healthy-looking faces pale. The high, hysterical, distorted voices of women kept squealing that Irish girls were noted over the whole world for their modesty, and that Ireland's name was holy; that the Republican flag had never seen the inside of a public-house; that this slander of the Irish race would mean the end of the Abbey Theatre; and that Ireland was Ireland through joy and through tears. Up in the balcony, a section was busily bawling out *The Soldier's Song*, while a tall fellow frantically beat time on the balcony rail with a walking-stick. Barry Fitzgerald became a genuine Fluther Good, and fought as Fluther himself would fight, sending an enemy, who had climbed on to the stage, flying into the stalls with a flutherian punch on the jaw. And in the midst of the fume, the fighting, the stench, the shouting, Yeats, as mad as the maddest there, pranced on the stage, shouting out his scorn, his contempt; his anger making him like unto an aged Cuchullain in his hero-rage; his long hair waving, he stormed in utter disregard of all around him, confronting all those who cursed and cried out shame and vengeance on the theatre, as he conjured up a vision for them of O'Casey on a cloud, with

Fluther on his right hand and Rosie Redmond on his left, rising upwards to Olympus to get from the waiting gods and goddesses a triumphant apotheosis for a work well done in the name of Ireland and of art.

Then the constables flooded into the theatre, just in time. Rough and ready, lusty guardians of the peace. They filed into the theatre as Irish constables for the first time in their life; mystified, maybe, at anyone kicking up a row over a mere play. They pulled the disturbers out, they pushed them out, and, in one or two instances, carried them out, shedding them like peas from the pod of the theatre, leaving them in the cold street outside to tell their troubles to their neighbours or to the stars. Then the play went on, halting often, and agitated to its end. For the first time in his life, Sean felt a surge of hatred for Cathleen ni Houlihan sweeping over him. He saw now that the one who had the walk of a queen could be a bitch at times. She galled the hearts of her children who dared to be above the ordinary, and she often slew her best ones. She had hounded Parnell to death; she had yelled and torn at Yeats, at Synge, and now she was doing the same to him. What an old snarly gob she could be at times; an ignorant one too.

He left the auditorium where the people were watching the play, subdued and nervous, hedged in by the silver-plated helmets of the police, and strayed out into the foyer, right into the midst of a group of women squealers, members of Cumann na mBan—the Society of Women. They shot remarks at him from where they stood or lounged. They said he was a renegade, a friend to England, and that he would soon have a government pension. They said he had held up Ireland's sacred name to ridicule for the sake of the money he'd get for doing it; that it was he who, sooner or later, would feel the shame, and not Ireland. They said he was one now with those who had always hated Ireland, and that the Union Jack was his flag now, and not the Irish tricolour that he had defamed.

—Yes, said one, leaning against the wall, an' I'd like you to know that there isn't a prostitute in Ireland from one end of it to th' other.

Cathleen ni Houlihan was talking. Drawing her patched and fading skirt close around her, she was talking big. Through these women, she was talking. There wasn't a comely damsel among them. Sean noticed this with some surprise. They were all plain, provoking no desire in him to parley words with them, as a pretty face would have done, had one been among them. So after listening for awhile, and saying a few words, he left them to go up to the office to see how things were going. Yeats was shaking hands with an Inspector of Police who was introducing Sergeant Bantry Bay to the poet. The sergeant had developed into a mood of hilarious nervousness. He bowed to the poet, took off his hat, offered his hand, and when Yeats offered his, shook it vehemently, bending Yeats forward with the power of his hand's pull, blurting out a greeting that he must have been practising all the way to the theatre: *It is to be greatly regretted, sir, that I have had the honour and pleasure of meeting you for the first time undher such disthressing circumstances!*

The Inspector looked silly to hear this greeting, and its unexpected eloquence stunned Yeats out of his senses for a few moments, so that he stared at the sergeant till he summoned enough thought to mutter confusedly, Yes, yes; quite. It is, it is.

*   *   *

But Ireland was full of folly, seeking, probing even, for a good opinion. He remembered once when he was in Coole, sitting by the huge fire in the library, the great logs throwing up lusty golden and scarlet flames, doing a fine dance on the coloured bindings of the books marshalled around the walls, with Lady Gregory sitting opposite chatting away; while she, at times, prodded the logs with a brass poker into greater energy and glow. In her smiling chat she had told him how shocked she had been to discover that Yeats had read nothing written by Dostoievsky; how she had cried shame on him for his neglect of so great a man; and how she had given him *The Idiot* and *The Brothers Karamazov* only a week ago to take away with him so that he might read them, and be delighted with the images of a great and spiritual mind. Then she told Sean how Yeats had written to say he had read one, and how great the work was, and how he enjoyed it . Just then, Sean had had his third play taken by the Abbey, and it was to go into rehearsal in a week or two. When he got back to Dublin, he was told that Mr. Yeats wanted to see him to talk about the play.

The next day he set out for the poet's home in Merrion Square. This will be the second time, he thought, I have set a foot within a house in this place which still treasures the secluded brocade and perfume of the past. An awesome place, for the top achievement for many years in Dublin had been a residence in Merrion Square. The glory of living here was next to the glory of living in one of the Big Houses of the country: a glory reached only by the lonely few. As he came closer to it, the streets became more refined, as if aware of their greater neighbour; and those that were closest to this elegant dot of life began to assume an air of importance, and bravely tried to look imposing.

He entered the Square, and halted to stand and stare at the gracious houses. The Square looked as if it had been knighted by king exclusion and queen quietness, separating it from the lumbering, trade-tired streets of Dublin. He entered it with a bow and a murmur of Yer servant, Sir Merrion; for it was a holy place, to poverty unknown; unknown, save by name, to the distant proletariat of the tenements. If a proletarian ventured to pass through it, he would go quiet and quick, without lounging, or sending a disparaging spit into its kennels. He would lift his passing feet carefully, and set them down intelligently, so as to provoke no noise from the footway. He would pass through with the circumspection he'd show while passing by a rich bed in which a noble or a bishop lay sleeping; pass by slyly and rapidly, without commotion, eager to get to a place where he could walk with ease, hands in pocket, and spit in comfort, the poorer world before him, ready to fulfil his hardier will and lustier pleasure.

How stately the houses looked with their gleaming windows, the brightness of them muffled in the brief modesty of costly curtains, concealing secrets of private life from the eyes and ears of the street outside; their cleverly-painted, highly-polished front doors, each side pillared stiffly, as if petrified footmen stood guard there to see that no dirty hand was stretched out to soil a dazzling knocker, or imprint a slum-speck on the bell-push, that shone like a brassy jewel on a cheek of the opulent doorway.

—Here, the houses would quiver in pain, thought Sean, if a hawker went by chanting, Strawberries, penny a leaf, penny a leaf, the ripe strawberries! And the houses would swoon in shame if the cry changed to, Fresh Dublin Bay herrin's, thruppence a dozen; thruppence the dozen, the Dublin Bay herrin's fresh from the say!

Sean mounted the wide steps to the door which was Yeats's dwelling-place. Two Free State C.I.D. men stood in the shadow of the pillared doorway, planted there to prevent the assassination of the senator-poet by some too-ready Republican hand. Guns guarding the poet, thought Sean, though he knew that the Republicans had as much idea of shooting Yeats as they had of shooting Lady Gregory or the Catholic Archbishop of Dublin.

—Are yeh goin' in to see himself? asked one of them who knew Sean well; but as what he asked was half a statement, he went on. I don't envy yeh, Sean, for I wouldn't like to be alone with him long. His oul' mind's full of th' notion of oul' kings and queens the half of us never heard of; an' when he's talking', a fella has to look wise, pretendin' he's well acquainted with them dead an' gone ghosts. It's a terrible sthrain on a body whenever he stops to talk. Wait till yeh hear, though, and his hand put down Sean's as it stretched out towards the bell-push. Yeh know Jim Errishcool, don't yeh? Yes, well, of course. Well, what d'ye think th'bugger's done, an' him on guard over Senator Fedamore's residence, some doors down? What d'ye think he done, disgracin' th' whole of us? Th' second time he's done it, too! Guess what th' boyo done?

—Fired at a shadow he thought a Republican?

—Aw, no, not that. What d'ye think th' goboy done but got acquainted with th' upper housemaid, an' when th' genthry were away, got into th' house quiet, an' lo and behold yeh, he gets th' girl in th' family way as cool as bedamned through th' medium of th' best bed in th' best bedroom. Now, what d'ye think o'that! A cool customer, wha'? Th' best bed, no less, for a fella only just up from th' bog, in Fedamore's own house, mind yeh, an' th' upper housemaid, too. They found th' bed all knocked about an' th' girl on it in a half-dead daze, cryin', an' murmurin', He's after nearly killin' me! An' th' boyo come on duty th' same night to take over guard, cool as you like. Now you'll be talkin'!

—Oh, well, he could do worse, said Sean.

—Sure I know he could, said the guard impatiently; but what about us? Everyone of us is misthrusted now. Th' way they look at us when they're passin' as if we all had th' same failin'.

—And I'm afraid we have, said Sean.

—We know all about that! snappily said the guard; I know we all have th' failin', but we all haven't got it in th' direct fashion of a fallin' thunderbolt overthrowin' an innocent girl!

When Sean stepped by the neatly-dressed maid, who held the door open for him, and entered the study, he was met by a blast of heat that nearly drowned him. He had entered a den of heat. Never before had he experienced such an onslaught of venomous warmth. The hot air enveloped him, made him sink into a chair, to silently gulp for breath; and it was soon forcing him into an unpleasant sense of sickness. On the chair, he wrenched his will towards feeling calm, towards trying to breathe easy. There it was, at the end of the room, the devil of heat, a huge, squat, black anthracite stove, belching out its invisible venom quietly, threatening Sean with an embarrassing display of faintness. Overcrowded or overheated rooms tended to make Sean's brain buzz, and his stomach feel queer, and already he could feel everything in his belly trying to turn over; the power of his will alone preventing it from happening.

And what was that sound of piercing shrillness, like the ear-splitting scream of a hundred fifes playing in a room at the same time, in dire disharmony together? Birds! A golden-barred cage, half filling a big window, swung there, swung and fluttered there with the shrill tuning of half a hundred canaries. Rich yellow ones, some of them streaked with creamier lines, some with dark satiny patches on them; active, alert, darting from side to side of the cage, from top to bottom, and back again, over and over again, never stopping, singing without cessation, singing, singing all the time, splitting the thick and heated air of the room with a mad, piercing melody of noise! These were the canaries that Lady Gregory had called Dose derrible birds! And through the heated air, and through the savage whistling, the noble voice of Yeats boomed out a blessing on the new play.

What was he saying, what was the man saying? Could Sean fashion the words from the booming, disentangle them from the violent chittering, mould them from the heavy air, and fold them into making sense within his own mind? No. Surely Yeats wasn't saying what he was saying! But Sean's will caught the words, and made sense of them, out of the heat, and through the mad fifing of the canaries; and he listened with an exquisite desire to laugh out loud, as he listened to the voice, the deep, fine voice booming out through the sweating air and the jeering whistle of the uncalmable birds; the majestic voice of Yeats, as he paced up and down the room through the moist haze, came booming to the din-dulled ears of Sean: O'Casey, you have written a great play; this play is the finest thing you have done. In an Irish way, you have depicted the brutality, the tenderness, the kindling humanity of the Russian writer, Dostoievsky; O'Casey, you are the Irish Dostoievsky!

Moving homewards, gasping into him the cool air of the street, faint still from what he had suffered in the red, ruthless heat from the anthracite stove, his shirt sticking to back and breast, Sean felt ashamed of Yeats and ashamed of himself. Wait, now, till he grew a little cooler. Sean had worked within the airless chamber of a boiler, helping to fix a furnace, but it never gave him the languishing feeling of sickness he had suffered in that room. Why was Yeats afraid of a cooler air? He had, Sean knew, a tendency to chest or lung complaints. But the heat in that room would be bad for one even in the throes of bronchitis. It will do the man harm. Now why hadn't he had the courage to tell Yeats that? Sean, when his second play was in rehearsal, had walked, with a temperature from bronchitis, and a sense of suffocation, from North Circular Road to Nelson's Pillar, in falling snow; had there taken a tram to St. Vincent's Hospital, and had never felt the worse for it. It wasn't a sensible thing to do, of course; but less dangerous than to live and sleep in such a torrid heat endured by the poet Yeats. It will do the man harm. And the piercing chatter of those yello-clad birds—how can Yeats, the delicate-minded poet, stand that chirruping turmoil? He had no ear; he was tone-deaf—that was the reason. Now Sean realised that there were different kinds of bliss: what was heaven to one man might be hell to another.

Another Dostoievsky! An Irish one, this time! And Yeats only after reading the man's book for the first time the night before. If it hadn't been for his battle with the blast and the birds, Sean would have had a battle with laughter. Yeats was trying to impress Sean with his knowledge of Dostoievsky. That was a weakness in the poet. But why hadn't Sean the courage to tell Yeats that he knew damn all about the Russian writer? That was a weakness in Sean. It was a cowardly omission. He should have told Yeats he knew Lady Gregory had given him two of Dostoievsky's books only a night or so ago. And, instead, he had put a smile of appreciation on his heat-strained face when Yeats had said it. Christ Almighty, what a world of deceits! Sean's father would have said how he felt and what he thought without a hesitation. He had let his father's memory down. He'd try to be braver the next time. Some had said he was another Chekhov, others, a Dickens, and another Ben Jonson. He knew himself that he was like Sean O'Casey, and he was determined to be like no-one else; for better or worse, for richer or poorer, so help him God!

*   *   *

It was time for Sean to go. He had had enough of it. He would be no more of an exile in another land than he was in his own. He was a voluntary and settled exile from every creed, from every party, and from every literary clique, fanning themselves into silence with unmitigated praise of each other in the most select corners of the city's highways and byebye-ways.

* * *

One thing that was good—he would never be in contact with any controversial literary Dublin clique. One of these cliques, not long ago, had tried to entangle him into an effort to undermine the literary influence and authority of Yeats; and he had been shocked to watch this mean and reprehensible envy of the poet's literary standing bubbling up in the minds of educated and cultured, but lesser men, who had been so safely and so comfortably nurtured in cradle and in school.

Yeats didn't praise them enough; he saw through them, but said nothing. Some of them were the fame-fleas that A.E. wanted Yeats to recognise with a little, or, maybe, substantial praise; pointing out that the poet had praised what others had sung or said, forcing from the lordly Yeats the little verse,

> You say, as I have often given tongue
> In praise of what another said or sung,
> 'Twere politic to do the like by these;
> But was there ever dog who praised his fleas?

Masked pompously he was, in style and manner, but under all was the poet immortal who will be remembered forever. Friendship with Yeats was something Sean couldn't reach yet, for the poet was almost always hidden from view by this group of Gaeligorian guards who, now and again, wrote an article for *The Irish Statesman*, or sent an occasional poem to the Journal to fill a vacant corner. Wherever the poet stood, there they stood too, and followed meekly where he led, though secretly hating the man's true greatness. All that one could see from the fringe of this guard was the noble head of the poet, wearing now the mask of Sophocles, then the pompous one of Plato; again, the mask of contemplative Robartes, and, anon, the wild, warlike one of Red O'Hanrahan; and, to Sean, the deep, medieval voice, seeking impressiveness, however it might sound in laughter, or whatever it might say, always seemed to be murmuring, *Regina, Regina, Pigmeorum, Veni*. Though Gaumalfry followed him everywhere, Sean felt sure that Yeats, without his guards, could be simple and childlike, ready to gambol seriously, and would be inclined to gossip about, and laugh at, the follies and fripperies of men. So Sean kept away from the poet and his guards, for he was captivated by his own work, had been made a prisoner by himself, and his captivity had set him free.

Sean always felt a rude desire to laugh whenever he found himself among this group of guards; he felt that most of them realised this; sensed a sound of silent laughter somewhere. He remembered once when he went to the house of Yeats, in Merrion Square, to see *The Hawk's Well* played in the drawing-room. The room was full of them, dressed in their evening best, the men immaculate in shiny sober black, the women gay and glittering in silk sonorous, and brilliant brocade, all talking animatedly and affectionately together, like teachers and children waiting for trams to come to bring them away on a Sunday-school excursion. Sean tried to attach himself to the conversation by listening, but there was nothing to hear. No-one spoke to him, and, right or wrong, he felt that they were uncomfortable with a tenement-dweller in their midst. Yeats suddenly caught sight of him, came quick to him, and guided Sean to the front, where he wheeled over a deep and downy armchair as a seat for Sean.

—You'll be able to see well here, he said.

NOTE

1. *The Plough and the Stars* opened at the Abbey Theatre on 8 February 1926.

Profiles of a Poet*

GABRIEL FALLON

The year nineteen hundred and twenty-one was not the best of times for the Abbey Theatre. Its finances were at their lowest ebb. Ireland's war of independence was rising to a peak-point; the notorious Black-and-Tans[1] were loose upon the land; the streets of Joyce's Dublin were pocked with daily and nightly ambushes; a British curfew declared that citizens must be within their dwellings by 8:00 p.m. When a 9:00 p.m. curfew closed all the other theatres, the Abbey had remained defiantly open, but the additional hour was just one hour too much. Shaw, Yeats, and Lady Gregory, taking advantage of this temporary closure, gave lectures in London to help to keep the Abbey's doors open and to pay off its debt to the bank. Most of the Theatre's leading players had gone off to the U.S. on a tour of Lennox Robinson's *The Whiteheaded Boy* leaving behind a handful of part-time players—of whom I was a junior member—a promising School of Acting and a seasoned actor from the main company who remained behind to direct the School. A gift of £500 from Lady Ardilaun, added to the takings from the London lectures, gave the Theatre a new lease of life and, as soon as the British lifted their curfew to a more reasonable hour from the Theatre's point of view, Lady Gregory left the Black-and-Tan terror of Coole Park, Galway, for the Black-and-Tan terror of Abbey Street, Dublin, and ordered rehearsals to commence.

These she attended in person, primly sitting—a better looking version of Queen Victoria—in the middle seat of the front row of the stalls. The

* *Modern Drama* (Lawrence, Kansas) VII, no. 3 (Dec 1964) 329–44.

rehearsal over she would gather us around her in the Green Room and distribute her praise and blame. She wanted a little more of this or a little less of that; as for the other thing, it ought not to be even mentioned amongst us if we wished to retain our places in the Abbey Theatre Company. One afternoon she told us that she was bringing Mr. Yeats to the following afternoon's rehearsal. William Butler Yeats, she informed us, was a very great poet; and to make clear this fact she drew our attention to the framed Cuala Press copies of his poems that adorned the Green Room's walls. There, for instance, was 'The Pity of Love,'[2] there 'The Lover tells of the Rose in his Heart,'[3] and there 'The Lake Isle of Innisfree.'[4]

She read them for us in her ageing quavering voice with its intriguing habit of transforming 'th's to 'deh's. We duly looked impressed, and with some of us our looks did reflect our inner feelings. I couldn't help wondering how the author of these poems would react to *The Lord Mayor*,[5] the semi-political farce by Edward McNulty (a bank manager relative by marriage of George Bernard Shaw) which we were then rehearsing.

The next afternoon we assembled for rehearsal at the usual time and as we stood in the wings were told that Lady Gregory and the poet were out front. The rehearsal went through with a little more vigour than usual, the effect of an upsurge of nerves, undoubtedly due to the fact that we were acting in the presence of two-thirds of the Abbey Theatre's Directorate (Lennox Robinson, the remaining third, with whom we always felt much more at home, being on holidays in Paris). Our acting ability wasn't helped by the report of a small-part player (who had surveyed the auditorium through a hole in one of the flats) that the poet had spent most of the time with his head bent over the pages of some literary journal. The rehearsal over we trooped up the stairs to the Green Room and tried to compose ourselves while we awaited the arrival of that Director whom most of us knew only by sight. Soon we heard a familiar voice saying, 'Now, Willie, I want you to meet the players.' (Good Heavens, she was calling the man 'Willie'; she was one of the few—if indeed there were any others—who had the right to do so.) Our first impression of Lady Gregory's 'Willie' could be summed up in two words 'dignity' and 'distance.' He had a way of looking at you as if he did not see you. His glance seemed to penetrate and go beyond you as if he were intently examining your aura which had somehow slipped round to the back of your neck. He heard our names as Lady Gregory introduced each one of us as if he were standing on the outer edge of the world we inhabited. She did all the talking; he occasionally inclined his head in acquiescence. He took a step forward and boringly examined the Cuala Press copies of his poems. He looked towards the sloping ceiling of the Green Room as if examining it for the first time. He then looked at Lady Gregory, as if to say, 'I take it this interview is at an end.' With a final word of commendation to the respectfully silent group of players Lady Gregory touched the poet's elbow and they left the Green Room together. When the sound of their footsteps died away on the concrete floor that led through the scene-dock to the stage there was an immediate buzz of conversation in the Green Room. Out of it came, with an unmistakable Dublin accent the voice of a small-part player, a not-so-promising member of the School of Acting: 'So that's the man who talks to fairies. Be God, he looks it!'

Later I was to see much more of William Butler Yeats and to learn that the impression given by him of looking through and beyond a person was due to a defect of vision. This, with the up-tilted head, the mane of silvered hair, the pince-nez with its flowing black ribbon, the now habitual hieratic gestures of arm and hand, tended to make him a man apart; alone, aloof, and palely wandering. Yet the man behind the mask, though shrewd and subtle, was one with a sly sense of humour, one whose humanity peeped out at odd and unexpected moments. He was a member of a select dining club which once a month brought to its honourable table some artist who had gained recent distinction, a painter it might be who had been hung on the line in the Royal Hibernian Academy, or a writer whose play had been presented—at the Abbey Theatre, of course. Only once in its history had the club honoured the acting profession, and I, on the strength of my performance as Old Hummel in Strindberg's *The Spook Sonata* happened to be the actor concerned. The club dined in a small but select Dublin hotel. Sean O'Casey in one[6] of his autobiographical volumes (of which, a Dublin wit has said 'ninety-five per cent is delightfully pure O'Casey; the rest, unfortunately, is the truth') condemns the cooking as not being up to his mother's standard. I did not find it so dreadful and neither did the half-a-dozen members whose culinary taste was, I would have said, rather superior to Sean's.

The evening I was there Yeats apologetically arrived late. Distantly asking how far we had progressed with the meal, he sat down on hearing Lennox Robinson's monosyllabic: 'Fish-ish!' Finding himself opposite me, he addressed me as if I was Harry Clarke, our distinguished stained-glass artist, to whom I bore a certain likeness. As it happened Clarke was sitting two places away from Yeats on Yeats's side of the table. Clarke signalled to me to accept the challenge and for the best part of two minutes I answered Yeats's questions on the stained-glass business briefed by signals flashed to me by Clarke. Realising that the tables were being turned against him, Yeats brought his little joke to an end by identifying me as Fallon, adding: 'You do rather resemble Clarke; except, of course, that *you are ever so much better-looking.*' Whereupon Clarke signalled: '*Touché!*'

At that time I knew little about the history of the Abbey Theatre and less about Yeats's stature as a poet. The art of acting and that of the playwright in relation to it held all my interest. I had acted in a number of the poet's plays—*The Shadowy Waters,*[7] *The Countess Cathleen,*[8] *The Hour Glass,*[9] *The King's Threshold*[10]—and I had been a pupil (one of the last) of Frank Fay, to whose 'beautiful speaking' the poet had dedicated *The King's Threshold.*

Through Fay I glimpsed something of the poet's intentions in founding the Abbey Theatre. So far as I could see the time was out of joint; there was a wind blowing across the sea from Norway and the 'joyless and pallid words' (Synge's phrase)[11] of the sociological half of Ibsen was having its effect on Anglo-Irish letters. The scripts that in the name of the 'deeper thoughts and emotions of Ireland' were submitted to the Abbey Theatre were far removed from those dreamt of by Yeats. It is true, as Eric Bentley points out, that 'the Abbey Theatre provided the soil for *some* kinds of drama but not for Yeats's kind.[12] A great poet but a dramatist *manque*.[13] 'My blunder has been' he wrote, 'that I did not discover in my youth that my theatre must be the ancient theatre that can be made by unrolling a carpet or marking out a place with a stick, or setting a screen against the wall.' It was an experience to play in those early plays, all myth and mist, but it was a poetic experience rather than a dramatic one.

I have always believed that it needed the dynamic personality of Mrs. Pat Campbell to make Yeats's *Deirdre*[14]—beautiful to read—come to even half-life in the theatre. I encouraged him on one occasion to speak about her. He described her as having 'an ego like a raging tooth' and of her habit of 'throwing tantrums' at rehearsals. At one rehearsal after a particularly wild 'tantrum' she walked to the footlights and peered out at Yeats who was pacing up and down the stalls of the Theatre. 'I'd give anything to know what you're thinking,' shouted Mrs. Pat. 'I'm thinking,' replied Yeats, 'of that master of a wayside Indian railwaystation who sent a message to his Company's headquarters saying: "Tigress on the line; wire instructions"!' By the time I joined the Abbey Theatre Yeats had long given up the practice of conducting rehearsals. I remember Arthur Sinclair,[15] that great instinctive player, who, like all his tribe, could perfectly act a part without understanding it, telling me that on one occasion Yeats shouted from the stalls: 'That's it, Sinclair . . . magnificent! You've got it!' Sinclair retired to the Green Room and spoke to his colleagues: 'Well, Mr. Yeats says I've got it. What it is I've got, I couldn't for the life of me tell you: but I hope to God I don't lose it!' 'Dossie' (Udolphus) Wright,[16] who was a member of the company both in Sinclair's time and my own, told me of an experience he had with Yeats during a lighting rehearsal. 'Dossie,' who for a time had been a rival of Synge for the affections of Maire O'Neill, was both actor and stage electrician. Abbey Theatre lighting in those days was of the most primitive kind. While Yeats paced the stalls, 'Dossie' was engaged in putting one coloured gelatine slide after another into a kind of biscuit-tin 'flood' off stage. Nothing seemed to satisfy the poet. A thoroughly fed-up 'Dossie' decided it was time for a smoke. Having lighted his cigarette he accidentally flicked his still-lighted match into the box of gelatine slides. The whole thing flared up into a five-foot blaze. As 'Dossie' rushed for the nearest fire-extinguisher he heard Yeats shout from the stalls: 'That's it, Dossie; that's the colour I want!'

By the middle twenties it was increasingly clear to me that whatever the Abbey Theatre had become it was very far from being what Yeats had professedly wanted it to be. Yet I felt that if Yeats had had his way there would be no Abbey Theatre. It would have faded away in the mists of a Celtic Twilight. Some think that that might have been a good thing; some think otherwise. At all events, Yeats himself had written: 'The mere growth of the audience will make all useless, for the Irish town mind will by many channels, public and private, press its vulgarity upon us. If we should feel that happening, if the Theatre is not to continue as we have shaped it, it must, for the sake of our future influence, for the sake of our example, be allowed to pass out of our hands, or cease. We must not be responsible for a compromise.'[17] And again: 'We were to find ourselves in a quarrel with public opinion that compelled us against our will and the will of our players to become always more realistic substituting dialect for verse, common speech for dialect.'[18] It occurred to me at the time I read them that these statements called for an explanation. It looked as if on Lady Gregory's side at all events that the compromise had been made; for the Theatre had not escaped vulgarity; yet Yeats still remained on its Directorate. And now with the coming of Sean 'Casey the audience was growing as never before in the history of the Abbey Theatre. It is true that in 1919 in an open letter[19] to Lady Gregory Yeats had protested against the Abbey's commonplace realism, saying: 'We did not set out to create this sort of theatre, and its success has been to me a discouragement and a defeat.' He wanted, he said, to create for himself 'an unpopular theatre and an audience like a secret society where admission is by favour and never too many.'

I wasn't the only one who was puzzled by this attitude of Yeats. A young Irish poet, Valentin Iremonger,[20] writing some years afterwards in a special number[21] of *Irish Writing* wanted to know if Yeats was 'ever interested in the theatre as we understand it to-day in its development over the last four hundred years?' 'The theatre, as we know it,' he wrote, 'is a place of public entertainment which creative writers use to express their reflections and interpretations of the behaviour of people under the stress of idea or emotion. By its nature, it vulgarises: However pure or finely imagined an idea or emotion in the mind of an author, he cannot allow that idea or emotion full play or give it all his attention since he is and must be conscious that he himself cannot transmit the idea or emotion unalloyed to each member of the audience.' Acknowledging that within the limited terms of reference which Yeats set himself in the theatre his success as a dramatist was considerable, Mr. Iremonger concludes that he had no interest whatsoever in the theatre as we know it.

As for Yeats's attitude in linking up the will of the players with the will of the Directors in the lamented transition from poetry to dialect and from dialect to common speech I'm afraid it fails to stand up to examination. It is true, of course, that the early players under the invaluable tuition of

Frank Fay could and did speak poetry and dialect with ease and beauty, nevertheless their basic training as actors was in the naturalistic tradition. This naturalism can be traced to the revolution in acting carried out by André Antoine[22] in his Théâtre Libre in Paris with whose work the brothers, Frank and Willie Fay, as well as Yeats, were familiar. Michel Saint-Denis in his work *The Re-discovery of Style* has pointed out that Antoine, almost eleven years before Stanislavsky,[23] had already achieved what the Russian set out to achieve in his so-much-misunderstood 'Method.' It is this 'Method' derived from Antoine and re-modelled to fit the Irish temperament by Frank and Willie Fay which has come to be known as the Abbey Theatre acting tradition. It has been formally taught in the Schools of Acting which the Abbey has set up from time to time and it has been traditionally handed down from company to company, until to-day one can trace it back to the Fays. And just as Aristotle derived the theories outlined in his *Poetics* from the practice of contemporary Greek dramatists so Yeats derived most of his theories of acting from the work of Frank and Willie Fay. Yeats wanted actors who would help to restore words to their sovereignty, make speech even more important than gesture, and delight the ear with a continually varied music. 'Greek acting,' he wrote, 'was great because it did everything with the voice, and modern acting may be great when it does everything with voice and movement. But an art which smothers these things with bad painting with innumerable garish colours, with continual restless mimicries of the surface of life is an art of fading humanity, a decaying art.'[24] Yeats remained faithful to his text, and so a quarter of a century later in his poem 'The Old Stone Cross'[25] we find the man in the golden breastplate in angry mood

> But actors lacking music
> Do most excite my spleen
> They say it is more human
> To shuffle, grunt and groan,
> Not knowing what unearthly stuff
> Rounds a mighty scene.

All very well but the truth was that the Abbey Theatre lacked the authors capable of supplying the music as well as audiences willing to listen to it. Indeed, his own plays excepted, Abbey Theatre dramaturgy from the days of the foundation had all the marks of Zola and the naturalists upon it. Yeats had failed only where he could not have succeeded. In an early poem entitled 'At the Abbey Theatre'[26] he had been compelled to write:

> When we are high and airy hundreds say
> That if we hold that flight they'll leave the place,
> While those same hundreds mock another day
> Because we have made an art of common things,

So bitterly, you'd dream they longed to look
All their lives through into some drift of wings.

The art of common things had to have its way; the flight could not be held. Those 'same hundreds,' in reality a pretentious minority, pay lip-service to poetry, were outnumbered by audiences—never at any time large enough to keep the Abbey from teetering upon the edge of bankruptcy—content to accept what the rising forces of naturalism had to offer. It was this audience which increased a hundredfold with the coming of O'Casey. This increase which delighted Lady Gregory had a depressing effect on Yeats. It was this increase which urged some of Yeats's literary imitators and camp-followers to declare that with the coming of O'Casey the Abbey Theatre had been 'given over to the mob.'

While Lady Gregory rejoiced in the Abbey's new 'house-full' audiences, Yeats busied himself with his 'Plays for Dancers.' As far back as 1915 Yeats had joined with Ezra Pound, Arthur Waley, and Edmund Dulac in their enthusiasm for the Japanese Noh play which none of them, incidentally, had ever seen. As in the days of the foundation of the Abbey Theatre when the poet George Russell had induced him to look in on the Fays and their group of amateurs, Yeats now found in Ito[27] just what he was looking for. He immediately began to develop a new form of drama with music and dancing, European in form, but influenced by the Japanese Noh. 'I have invented a form of drama,' he said,[28] 'distinguished, indirect, and symbolic, and having no need of mob or press to pay its way—an aristocratic form.' It was natural, he said, that he should go to Asia for a stage convention 'for more formal faces, for a chorus that has no part in the action and perhaps for those movements of the bodies copied from the marionette shows of the 14th century.' 'I seek, not a theatre,' he said in a later essay,[29] 'but the theatre's anti-self, an art that can appease all within us that becomes uneasy as the curtain falls and the house breaks into applause.'

Lady Gregory, wise woman that she was, held her peace. O'Casey was bringing the crowds into what she always referred to as her 'liddle dea-other' and she was satisfied. On the Friday of a week in which we were playing *Juno and the Paycock*[30] to crowded houses a notice appeared on the Call Board to the effect that Miss Ninette de Valois,[31] would, between the matinee and the evening performances of the following day, Saturday, give a lecture in the Peacock Theatre on the fundamentals of ballet. To this lecture the players were cordially invited. 'The Peacock' was the one-hundred-and-one-seater experimental theatre constructed as an adjunct to the Abbey on Abbey premises with money provided by the first Government grant to the Theatre. It had been christened by Yeats. It was not easy to persuade the players to attend Miss de Valois's lecture, but I was determined not to miss it and I managed to lure my dressing-room companion, Barry Fitzgerald, to come along with me. We had had a substantial lunch before the matinee, and I pointed out that we would just have time to get a snack of something before the evening performance.

When we got to the Peacock we found Lady Gregory there before us. As soon as she saw us, she indicated the vacant seats to the right and left of her own. Whatever we thought about the situation this was a royal command which we daren't turn aside. As soon as we were comfortably seated, she told us that this lecture idea was merely one of Mr. Yeats's 'foolish notions' but that it provided a grand opportunity for the players to rest themselves between the two Saturday performances! I found the de Valois lecture both fascinating and useful, particularly that section of it in which the lecturer carefully worked out for us the positions of importance on the stage. Since I was at the time directing plays for the Dublin Drama League (founded by Yeats, James Stephens, and Lennox Robinson for the purpose of staging Continental and American masterpieces on Sunday and Monday evenings at the Abbey—and thoroughly hated by Lady Gregory) I found that this lecture helped me considerably in the business of determining position and movement in staging a play. Barry Fitzgerald was bored and since Lady Gregory insisted on being facetious whenever the occasion presented itself, he made no attempt to conceal his boredom. When the lecture was over, we invited Lady Gregory to tea, half hoping she wouldn't accept, but she told us she would only be too delighted. Tea over, we walked back slowly with her to the Theatre. By this time the queues for the evening performance of *Juno* were stretching out in length from the Theatre's entrances. She made us stop at the corner of Abbey and Marlboro Streets to admire the increasing rush of patrons. 'There are times,' she said, 'when I find I can love my fellow-man with much more ardour than usual; and this'—she pointed to the queues—'is one of them.'

She then told us of those far-off days in the Theatre's history when in a desperate attempt to attract people to the Abbey she used to pretend she was a patron by putting on a hat and marching from the Stalls entrance to the Pit entrance through which she popped after pausing, as if to pay, at the Box Office. She would then wait inside for a few seconds and repeat the procedure this time moving from the Pit to the Stalls entrance. Looking at us both with tears in her eyes, she managed to squeeze up a smile as she said: 'What a joy to think that those bad days will never come again.' There had been no references whatsoever to the de Valois lecture. I began to see for the first time how much Lady Gregory and William Butler Yeats differed on this all-important subject of audiences. Lady Gregory clearly wanted them in the mass; Yeats yearned for the select few. I began to wonder how it was with them both in the days of the foundation of the Abbey Theatre. Yeats had begun by talking of a return 'To the people—as in Russia!' What had happened to disillusion him? Was it the attitude of the public to his own poetic plays, or was it the rioters at Synge's *The Playboy of the Western World?* Whatever the reason it was clear that by the middle' twenties, if not long before, he had fallen out of love with audiences. I wondered if this had been a cause of contention between Lady Gregory and himself during the early days. Long after I left the Abbey Theatre I felt I had found an answer when on looking into Maurice Browne's[32] *Too Late to Lament* I read of the foundation of the Chicago Little Theatre and Browne's first meeting with Lady Gregory.

In 1911 the Abbey Theatre Company on its first U.S. tour visited Chicago. At that time Maurice Browne and his friend Nellie Van Volkenberg were striving hard to found a little theatre in that city in which one Al Capone (with whom Browne discussed the view at sunset from the Greek theatre of Taormina) was referred to as 'a coming man.' Browne and his friend went to see the Abbey Theatre Company and were enthralled with what they saw. They met Lady Gregory and told her of their hopes and plans. 'By all means start your own theatre but make it in your own image.' They pointed out that they had no experience, no money, no players, no place to play. 'We had none of these things either,' Lady Gregory replied. 'It is true that we were not so poor as you; but you have one asset which we lacked: youth. And we had one liability which you will not incur: we confused theatric with literary values.' 'One of you'—she glanced at Nellie Van Volkenberg—'already sees that these values are different; the other—she glanced at Maurice Browne—will learn it, slowly and painfully. He will learn that poetry must serve the theatre before it can again rule there.' Then she left them to it with the remark: 'Strike out, my children. And God bless you.' They struck out and the Chicago Little Theatre—the father of all the little theatres in the U.S.—was the result. It is not unreasonable, I think, to claim that Lady Gregory was the god-mother of the little theatre movement in America. But the confusion of 'theatric with literary values'—the lesson that 'poetry must serve the theatre before it can again rule there!' Were these things born out of her early experience with William Butler Yeats and the Abbey Theatre? I believe they were.

I have often wondered to what extent William Butler Yeats acted upon the advice given him by his father, that artist and philosopher who early in life made the discovery that the vocation of law 'isn't for a man of genius.' 'The best thing in life,' he told his son, 'is the game of life, and some day a poet will find this out. I hope you will be that poet.' On the establishment of the Irish Free State the poet was made a Senator. This distinction was followed by the award of the Nobel Prize. At the awarding ceremony at Stockholm he impressed the members of the Swedish Royal Family by having the manners of a courtier, which was not surprising to those who knew him. He joined the Kildare Street Club, at one time the stronghold of British conservatism, a symbol of all that Ireland hated. He took his Senatorship duties seriously. He had now settled down in Dublin and was to be seen more frequently at the Abbey Theatre. Needless to remark his Senatorship and his Club did nothing to endear him to Republicans in a country still bleeding from the wounds of Civil War. But he was deeply involved in the game of life and thoroughly enjoying it.

In mid-January 1926 the Abbey Theatre Company was invited by Senator and Mrs. Parkinson to their house and training-stables on the wind-swept Curragh of Kildare. The purpose of the invitation was the presentation of Sean O'Casey's two-act play *The Shadow of a Gunman* in the gymnasium of the Curragh Military Camp in aid of an educationally charitable body of which Senator Parkinson's wife was a member. Senator William Butler Yeats accompanied us on this visit. After the performance the players who had been entertained royally throughout the day assembled in the Parkinson drawing-room. Much of the conversation concerned horses, jockeys, races, and trainers, prompted by an extensive visit to the Parkinson stables which had taken place between lunch and the performance at the gymnasium. Yeats, whose knowledge of horses and racing was as negligible as mine, sat in a high-backed chair beside the fireplace. It so happened that I sat directly opposite to him chatting with the youngest daughter of the Parkinson household who hoped that the poet might be persuaded to write some verse in her autograph book. I knew by the gleam in the poet's eye that he was in good talking form and would need little encouragement to make himself heard above the din of pedigrees, weights, and distances that crowded in upon us from every side. Seeing that Miss Parkinson and I were whispering together (about the poet as it happened), he elected to scent an amorous intrigue and leaned forward in our direction with a knowing smile. 'Fallon' he said, 'an old farmer in the West of Ireland once said to me: "There were eighteen of them and I loved any one of them better than the woman I married."'

This set him off. Miss Parkinson was delighted. I got him to talk about the Rhymer's Club, about Ernest Dowson, Lionel Johnson, and Oscar Wilde. His stories about Wilde were fittingly tempered to Miss Parkinson's hearing. I lured him on to Synge and *The Playboy of the Western World* and the rioting at its first production. Here he was in his element as he re-lived his fight before a growing audience, for some of the players had dropped their racing talk and had brought their chairs nearer to Yeats and the fireplace. His eyes shone as he concluded his story of the fight with the remark: 'I fought them, Fallon; my father did a finer thing—he forgot them!' At this point Barry Fitzgerald's brother, Arthur Shields, suddenly asked what I thought was a rather pointless question. 'I wonder, Mr. Yeats' he said in that soft persuasive, slightly unctuous, voice of his, 'I wonder if we will ever see scenes like that in the theatre again?' The question seemed to prick Yeats into increased vitality as a rider's spurs prick a lagging horse. He rose in his seat and raising his right hand in its familiar pontifical gesture he smiled broadly as he said: 'Shields, I shall tell you that in a fortnight's time!'

'In a fortnight's time?' Good Lord! In a fortnight's time—on February 8th.—we were due to present for the first time Sean O'Casey's *The Plough and the Stars.*[33] And here was Yeats actually looking forward to trouble. My mind raced back to Sean O'Casey's qualms about the second act and the speech outside the window, which was based on a speech made by Padraic Pearse the leader of the 1916 Rebellion. It was O'Casey's opinion, expressed when he read the scene to me in his tenement room at 422 North Circular Road, that ultra-nationalists might find some cause for offence here. I had dismissed these qualms of his as being unimportant, assuring him that the entire scene was a magnificent piece of theatre and that it would be ruinous to interfere with it. Yet here was Yeats actually looking forward to another theatre riot. Could it be, I wondered, that Yeats in his role of Free State Senator was hoping to use O'Casey's play to score over Republican enemies? It certainly looked as if something like that was afoot.

Rehearsals of *The Plough and the Stars* were far from being happy. A conspiracy against the author—triggered off by his outspoken criticism of a presentation of Shaw's *Man and Superman*—had divided the players into a small pro-O'Casey party (of which I was a member) and a large anti-O'Casey one. There were some 'scenes' at rehearsals and one or two refusals to speak certain lines on 'moral' grounds.[34] The subsequent publication of Lennox Robinson's selected passages of Lady Gregory's *Journals* reveal much of the atmosphere of unco-operativeness in which rehearsals were held. Yeats in a letter to Lady Gregory referred to the situation as 'an aggravating comedy'[35] and left it at that.

On Monday, February 8th., 1926, *The Plough and the Stars* opened at the Abbey Theatre to a 'booked out' house. That evening Senator Yeats had invited certain members of the Executive Council of the Irish Free State, including its Vice-President, its Finance Minister, and its Lord Chief Justice, to dinner. They accompanied him to the theatre and occupied seats in the stalls. The play seemed to go reasonably well though a number of us thought we detected a certain air of over-tenseness in the auditorium. At the second interval Yeats led his party of Ministers to the Green Room to meet the players. As they mounted the stairway on the lefthand side of the stalls leading to the pass-door, Joseph Holloway, that inveterate theatregoer whose voluminous diaries now repose in our National Library, was heard to voice his Republican sympathies in the clearly audible remark: 'There they go, the bloody murderers!' Otherwise things went as they usually do on a first night. There was generous applause at the end. The author was called for and appeared.

On the Tuesday night there was a certain amount of indiscriminate hissing, the purpose of which we couldn't accurately estimate. On the Wednesday night the hissing was louder in violence and seemed to be directed against the young prostitute, Rosie Redmond. On Thursday night, February 11th., the storm broke in earnest. Only one reasonably accurate version of the main events of that night reached the public eye. In the London *Observer* of Sunday, February 14th., 1926, Stephen Gwynn[36] published an eye-witness' account sent to him by a friend who was present. This opens as follows: 'Back from a very rowdy evening, having heard with difficulty two acts (first and last of the four that there are) and much of a Republican demonstration, curiously illogical, headed by Mrs. Sheehy-Skeffington,[37] and also a threat that the Abbey might be blown up, as a cinema was, on the charge of Free State propaganda.'

Various accounts have been written about what took place that evening. Some of these have been magnified beyond recognition. Reading them I have been reminded of the Duke of Wellington's reaction to another's description of Waterloo: 'My God, was I there at all?' I have had to listen to exciting recitals of the affair by people who were not even within the vicinity of the Abbey Theatre on the evening in question. Realising that I was, so to speak, in the midst of history in the making I decided to note down the important things and to ignore the rest. What was supremely important was the attitude of Yeats to the whole affair. Lady Gregory was at her home in Coole, Co. Galway. Lennox Robinson, the Abbey Director who had directed the play could not be located anywhere. Yeats, I was told, was already on his way to the Theatre. This would be exciting. I thereupon made up my mind to note everything he said and did.

One would have imagined that the senior Director of a theatre at which rioting was taking place would have looked somewhat perturbed on arriving there in the middle of the riot. Not so Yeats. He was smiling broadly as he came through the stage-door and down the seven wooden steps leading to the stage itself. I happened to be standing at the centre of the stage-curtain which had been lowered on the Manager's instruction. Yeats began to pace up and down the stage his eyes gleaming behind their glasses. He seemed to be thoroughly enjoying himself. From the auditorium came a confused medly of sounds in which it was possible to distinguish such words as 'shame,' 'scandal,' and 'insult.' Early on in the rioting it was obvious that the rioters were divided on the issue at stake. The politicals, led by Mrs. Sheehy-Skeffington were objecting to the play on patriotic grounds—contending that the whole thing was a studied insult to the heroes of Easter 1916. Their sticking-post was that point in the play towards the end of the second act where Clitheroe, Lieutenant Langan, and Captain Brennan excitedly enter the public-house carrying the banner of The Plough and the Stars and a green, white, and orange Tricolour. This was considered to be an outrage perpetrated on the national flag. Another party inflamed by the reflection that this was a public row in which anyone could join decided to make a protest on 'moral' grounds. Poor Rosie Redmond became the target of this particular group. I can still hear the Joxer-Daly-like accents of that fruity Dublin voice demanding that 'that wumman be taken offa th' stay-age.'

When Yeats stopped his pacing, I said to him: 'This looks like a rather serious state of affairs, Mr. Yeats; what do you propose should be done about it?' He threw back his head, ran his hands through his flowing white hair, looked at me with the light of battle in his eyes, smiled and said: 'Fallon, I am sending for the police; and *this time* it will be *their own* police!' The significance of this emphasis was not lost on me. The old war-horse was hearing once again trumpets sounding the vindication of Synge. This time, too, he was going to fight the rioters however much his father's memory might have counselled him to forget them. By now the author of *The Plough* was in the vestibule of the theatre surrounded by a crowd of patriotic women to whom he was appealing for 'one at a time, please; one at a time!' The upshot of this clamour was that they were begging him to write plays that would honour Ireland's heroes not defame them. Knowing that he would be violently opposed to the idea of sending for the police, I managed to get word to him that Yeats had already taken that step. Leaving the women in the midst of their clamour he made his way back-stage and told Yeats that he did not want police-protection for his play. Yeats pointed out that such protection was needed for the Theatre. In any case the protest came too late. The police were already on their way.

As coolly as if he were pacing his eighteenth century drawing-room in Merrion Square, Yeats walked up and down the stage still smiling to himself apparently oblivious to the pandemonium that raged beyond the curtain. Suddenly he approached me and said: 'Tell O'Malley [the stage electrician] to raise the curtain the very moment I give the signal.' I told O'Malley. Yeats then placed himself close to the curtain and after a moment's pause gave the signal. Now actors are trained by instinct and experience in such matters as gesture, tempo, and the effective rise and fall of intonations. Armed with this technique they meet dramatic situations on the stage and transmute them for an audience into unforgettable shining moments. That night at the Abbey Theatre even the finest of actors would have stood transfixed in admiration of Yeats's performance. Every gesture, every pause, every inflection, was geared to a tolerance calculated to meet an angry mob. From his well-considered opening, with flashing eyes and upraised arm 'You have disgraced yourselves again!' to the final hammer-blow: 'This is his [O'Casey's] apotheosis!' it was a performance of genius; regally contemptuous, an emperor rebuking slaves.

There are those who hold that Yeats was not interested in defending O'Casey, that he was merely using this occasion to attack his political enemies and incidentally to defend the liberty of the theatre. This may well be so. In a few years time he was to reject contemptuously (and some think foolishly) *The Silver Tassie* written by the man whose apotheosis he was now proclaiming. The fact that he anticipated trouble, as indicated by his remark in Senator Parkinson's drawing-room, and his flamboyant associ-ation with members of the Free State Government on the opening night of the play, in an atmosphere still charged with the anger of civil war, lead me to believe that he used both the play and the occasion for the purpose of whipping his political enemies. Since I left the Abbey Theatre not very long after that occasion (which had its outcome in Sean O'Casey's departure for London) I had no opportunity for any further conversation with the poet. In fact with the exception of one or two fleeting glimpses I never saw him again.

Such were the major profiles of the man as they presented themselves to me during my membership of the Abbey Theatre company. There were minor outlines too—his reciting his own poetry in the Green Room before the assembled company and a group of visiting American journalists. An unforgettable experience with Lady Gregory telling him to 'Stand up, now, Willie, and do it properly.' Or the dignity of his speech at the supper given to him by the players on the occasion of his return from Sweden after receiving the Nobel Prize. It had been a rather Bohemian affair and someone (I have never found out who dared) had affixed a coloured balloon to the lapel of the poet's dove grey jacket. Everyone wondered what he would do when he rose to speak. 'Before I begin' he said, 'perhaps you will kindly allow me to *remove*'—he detached the baloon—'this—symbol of frivolity.' Then there was the end of that festive occasion with the guests arranging to depart when I saw for the first time the mask slip revealing the man beneath. I had come to tell him that the car in which we were to return to Dublin was now ready. With a conspiratorial grin he whispered: 'Fallon, I hear some talk of whiskey and sandwiches. I propose we wait.' And so we waited and we got our whiskey and sandwiches. Many years afterwards when staying in Gort, Co. Galway, and using it as headquarters for explorations of Lady Gregory's Coole Park and Yeats's Tower of Ballylee, I had the good fortune to meet the last of Lady Gregory's coachmen who had some wonderful stories of the poet walking through the Seven Woods or down by the Lake beating out the rhythms of a poem—'lettin' powerful moans and groans out of him' was how the old man put it. Somehow I felt it would be useless to explain how these same 'moans and groans' so nurtured by Lady Gregory had made William Butler Yeats the greatest poet of our time.

NOTES

Gabriel Fallon (1898–   ) joined the Irish Civil Service and worked in London as a young man. In 1920 he returned to Dublin, where he joined the Abbey Theatre Company as a spare-time actor (the general practice then) and acted in the first productions of Sean O'Casey's plays. He left the company in 1928, but remained interested in the theatre as a critic and since 1959 as a director of the Abbey Theatre. His writings include *Sean O'Casey: The Man I Knew* (1965), *The Abbey and the Actor* (1969) and several articles on the theatre in various periodicals.

   1. Auxiliaries, British forces sent to Ireland in 1920.
   2. 'The Pity of Love', *The Rose* (1893).
   3. 'The Lover Tells of the Rose in His heart', *The Wind among the Reeds* (1899).
   4. 'The Lake Isle of Innisfree', *The Rose* (1893).
   5. *The Lord Mayor* opened at the Abbey Theatre on 13 March 1914.
   6. *Inishfallen Fare Thee Well* (London and New York: Macmillan, 1949).

7. *The Shadowy Waters*, the least successful of Yeats's verse plays, had its première at the Molesworth Hall, Dublin, on 14 January 1904.

8. *The Countess Cathleen*, a miracle play in four acts, was first performed by the Irish Literary Theatre at the Antient Concert Rooms, Dublin on 8 May 1899.

9. The Irish National Theatre Society opened at the Molesworth Hall, Dublin, on 14 March 1903 with the first production of Yeats's morality play *The Hour Glass*.

10. *The King's Threshold* was first produced by the Irish National Theatre Society at the Molesworth Hall, Dublin, on 8 October 1903.

11. J. M. Synge, 'Preface', *The Playboy of the Western World* (1907).

12. Eric Bentley, *The Modern Theatre; A Study of Dramatists and the Drama* (London: Robert Hale, 1948) p. 160.

13. Eric Bentley calls Yeats 'another dramatist *manqué*', ibid., p. 159.

14. The first performance of *Deirdre*, a play in verse, was at the Abbey Theatre on 24 November 1906.

15. Arthur Sinclair (1883–1951), husband of Maire O'Neill, made his first appearance on the stage in Yeats's *On Baile's Strand* (1904) with the Irish National Theatre Society, and was with the Abbey Theatre until 1916, playing in all the notable productions of that time. Then he formed his own company and toured Ireland and England, subsequently appearing in variety theatres in Irish sketches. He built up a great reputation as an Irish comedian.

16. 'Adolphus Wright has been with the Theatre for . . . many years . . . He acted very often in the earliest productions, he knows our Theatre through and through, since he first appeared as a mere helper in Camden Street, then he followed the little Company to Molesworth Hall, then to the Abbey Theatre, and today, February 1950, I have seen . . . Dossie Wright directing how our new piano should be placed.'—Lennox Robinson, *Ireland's Abbey Theatre* (London: Sidgwick and Jackson, 1951) p. 66.

17. 'Estrangement: Extracts from a Diary Kept in 1909.' Reprinted in *Autobiographies* (London: Macmillan, 1955) p. 484.

18. 'The Irish Dramatic Movement; A Lecture Delivered to the Royal Academy of Sweden.' Reprinted in *Autobiographies* (London: Macmillan, 1955) p. 562.

19. W. B. Yeats, 'A People's Theatre; A Letter to Lady Gregory', *Irish Statesman* (Dublin) 6 Dec 1919, pp. 572–3. Reprinted in *Dial* (Chicago) (Apr 1920) pp. 458–68.

20. Valentin Iremonger (1918–   ) was trained in the Abbey Theatre School of Acting and joined the Abbey Theatre Company (1939–40) and the Dublin Gate Theatre (1942–4). He entered the foreign service in 1946, and in 1964 was accredited Ambassador to Sweden, Norway and Finland. In 1945 he won the AE Memorial Award. His volumes of poetry include *On the Barricades* (1944) and *Reservations* (1951).

21. *W. B. Yeats. A Special Number of Irish Writing*, ed. S. J. White, no. 31 (Summer 1955).

22. André Antoine (1858–1943), French actor, producer and theatrical manager. He founded the Théâtre Libre in Paris in 1887, which began as an amateur company for the presentation of new plays of the realistic school. Inspired by the example of the Meiningen Company, Antoine worked for an integration of the various production elements and revolutionised French theatrical style by the introduction of naturalism in acting and scene design.

23. Constantin Stanislavsky (1863–1938), Russian actor and one of the greatest directors and teachers of the modern theatre. His attempt to codify the art of acting through a lifetime of observation and study of the methods of great actors of the past, resulted in the famous 'Stanislavsky method', the system by which he trained his students. By the last decade of the nineteenth century, he became convinced that the general run of contemporary acting did not represent life, but merely a set of cut-and-dried makeshifts. Accordingly, in partnership with Nemirovich-Danchenko, he formed the Moscow Art Theatre in 1898. Begun as an experiment and a protest, its influence spread far beyond Russia.

24. 'The Reform of the Theatre', *Samhain*, (Sep 1903) p. 10. Reprinted in *Collected Works*, vol. IV (Stratford-on-Avon: Shakespeare Head Press, 1908) p. 116.

25. In *Last Poems and Plays* (London: Macmillan, 1940).

26. In *The Green Helmet and Other Poems* (Churchtown, Dublin: Cuala Press, 1910).

27. Mr Ito was a Japanese traditional dancer who helped Yeats to evolve the stylised movements for *At the Hawk's Well*, the first of his *Plays for Dancers*. He had attracted considerable notice at the London Zoo by prancing about outside the cages of the birds of prey, and Yeats was often seen beside him, all attention. See W. B. Yeats, *Essays, 1931–1936* (Dublin: Cuala Press, 1937) p. 277.

28. 'Certain Noble Plays of Japan', in 'The Cutting of an Agate', *Essays and Introductions* (London: Macmillan, 1961) p. 221.

29. 'A People's Theatre', op. cit., p. 573.

30. Sean O'Casey's *Juno and the Paycock* was first performed at the Abbey Theatre on 3 March 1924. Gabriel Fallon played the part of Charlie Bentham, a school teacher.

31. Dame Ninette de Valois, an Irish dancer and original member of Diaghilev's famous Russian ballet. She came to Dublin to found a school of dancing at the Abbey Theatre. Yeats valued her art highly. In a letter (7 August 1934) to Olivia Shakespear on the production of his *The King of the Great Clock Tower*, in which Ninette de Valois played the role of the Queen, he said that it was 'magnificently acted and danced' (*Letters*, p. 826). See interview with Ninette de Valois, who talks about the Abbey Theatre and Yeats, *Trinity News*, 13 Feb 1964, p. 5.

32. Maurice Browne (1881–1955), English producer, actor and dramatist. He went to America and was Director of the Little Theatre, Chicago, from 1912 to 1918.

33. *The Plough and the Stars* opened at the Abbey Theatre on 8 February 1926. Gabriel Fallon played the part of Captain Brennan, of the I.C.A. (Irish Citizen Army). See O'Casey's account of the riots the play caused in his *Autobiographies*, vol. II (London: Macmillan, 1963), pp. 147–51. See also *Lady Gregory's Journals 1916–1930*, ed. Lennox Robinson (London: Putnam, 1946) pp. 94–101. In a letter to Ethel Mannin Yeats described *The Plough and the Stars* as 'almost our best play' (*Letters*, p. 914).

34. 'Then a whisper in Sean's ear told him that Miss Crowe had decided not to play the part of Mrs. Gogan. . . . Miss Ria Mooney, chosen for the part of the prostitute, was bombarded with barbed beseeching to rise out of the part. . . . F. J. McCormick was hesitant, and seemed to be responding reluctantly to his part. Then, in the midst of the anxiety, Gabriel Fallon, whom Sean had selected to play the part of Peter Flynn, came stealing up to beg this part be taken from him, and the part of Captain Brennan given in its stead.'—Sean O'Casey, *Autobiographies*, vol. II (London: Macmillan, 1963) p. 147.

35. *Lady Gregory's Journals 1916–1930*, ed. Lennox Robinson (London: Putnam, 1946) p. 95.

36. Stephen Gwynn, 'The Dublin Play Riots: Accounts by Eye-Witnesses', *Observer* (London) 14 Feb 1926, p. 16.

37. See Mrs H[annah] Sheehy-Skeffington, 'Letter to the Editor', *Irish Independent* (Dublin) 15 Feb 1926, p. 8; O'Casey's reply, 20 Feb 1926, p. 8; Mrs Sheehy-Skeffington's counter-reply, 23 Feb 1926, p. 9; and O'Casey's rejoinder, 26 Feb 1926, p.8.

A Contact with Yeats[*]

ARTHUR POWER

It was in the Arts Club which was then housed at 44 St. Stephen's Green that I first came in contact with Yeats when during dinner time he used to appear in the long, dark, white-pillared dining-room and as the evening progressed would wander from table to table to talk with his friends: Maire O'Neil, Cruise O'Brien[1] and others.

At that time he was at the height of his powers; was a particularly fine looking man, tall and distinguished with hieratic features, with those famous hawks' feathers running through his hair while his pale complexion made a dramatic contrast to the solid and black intensity of his eyes. Detached and critical he could be very haughty at times. However, when talking with his old friends he used to relax, as far as he was able to that is, for his haughty manner was not so much assumed as it was natural to him, for in 'On the Boiler,'[2] a collection of poems and essays written late in life, he says: 'I was born arrogant, and had learnt an artist's arrogance.' 'Not what you want but what we want.'

But to get some idea of the hostile and confused atmosphere which surrounded him at that time one must remember that the English were still in control here and that the upper social crust was strongly pro-British and regarded anything Irish with disfavour, and contempt even, for it threatened their imagined political and social superiority. This opinion was universal among them and anyone who differed was immediately ostracized in a Dublin which was still steeped in a delayed Victorianism, and dominated by the Castle Government and the British Army, and, in which Irish Nationalists with a few exceptions only existed among the lower middle classes and the peasants, while the upper classes gyrated around the Lord Lieutenant and the Castle entertainments; or in their own circle in Fitzwilliam and Merrion Square.

In the schools only English history was taught; the glory of the Battle of Agincourt; and the glory of Elizabeth's reign tempered with a few bits of kindly folklore; King Alfred burning the cakes; Bruce and the Spider; and the Pretender hiding in the Oak tree. While for poetry one was given Wordsworth's 'We are Seven' or his 'Ode to Immortality'; Macaulay's 'Days of Ancient Rome,' and Tennyson's 'Idylls of the King.'

* *Irish Tatler and Sketch* (Dublin) (Dec 1964) pp. 34, 61. Condensed as 'My Visit to W. B. Yeats', *Irish Digest* (Dublin) LXXXII (Feb 1965) 54–6.

>   In came Sir Ray, the seneschal, and cried,
>   'Aboon, Sir King! ev'n that thou grant her none,
>   This railer, that hath mock'd thee in full hall.
>   No: or the wholesome boon of gyve and gag.'

—All of which might have meant something to an Englishman but which meant little to us.

But when one read:

>   And from the woods rushed out a band
>   Of men and ladies, hand in hand,
>   And crying, singing all together,
>   Their brows were white as fragrant milk,
>   Their cloaks made out of yellow silk.[3]

one's mind rose into a timeless world, not of the aristocracy of turret or tourney-field; of position or achievement; but into one of emotion and freedom: of the lake, wood, and seashore. For as one reads Yeats' 'The Wanderings of Usheen,' the lost Celtic world gradually rose to the surface:

>   O Patric! for a hundred years
>   We went a-fishing in long boats
>   With bending sterns and bending bows,
>   And carven figures on their prows
>   Of bitterns and fish-eating stoats.

images which recalled the remnants of our Gaelic life; the currachs coming in across the reeded lakes, the stark and massive castles their broken towers standing up against the sky: the slim, delicate and bare-footed girls who gazed at one passing as though you were a foreigner, and the wild-looking young man in home-spun boneen and pampooties who stood around with their cattle in the market square on a fair-day in Galway—a civilization which has been lost under the layers of English conquest.

Published in 1899, this poem was all the more remarkable; for out of curiosity I once checked the chief events which were recorded in that year. In Ireland the main interest then was in the new and much debated Social Government Act, a tentative step towards self-government introduced by Lord Salisbury. In the West there was another failure in the potato crop which incidentally may have given Yeats his idea for his play 'The Countess Cathleen.' While abroad, Spain was at war with the United States: and France was in the toils of the Dreyfus affair.

Also in that year Meredith had published a new book of poems which made considerable impression, and Henley and Newbolt had brought out new volumes: while William Watson had published his collected poems which were sold out.

But Yeats was determined to form his own style when he put aside the political aspirations of Swinburne, and the psychological searchings of a Browning, and the cardboard world of Tennyson's 'Idylls of the King,' for he has written somewhere: 'You cannot give a body to something that moves beyond your senses unless your words are subtle and complex, as full of mysterious life as the body of a flower, or a woman.'

One day in Paris I got Arland Ussher's[4] translation of 'The Midnight Court': and in the preface which Yeats wrote for it, to my surprise he mentioned a play of mine,[5] though in fact the Abbey had rejected it some time previously. I was advised to get it re-typed and send it to him again—which I did, when he wrote back to say that he would produce it.

I crossed over to Dublin to see it, and after the performance Lennox Robinson took me to visit Yeats in his house in Merrion Square, of which he had his own latch-key to let himself in. The house was in total darkness when, as we ascended the stairway, a white Borzoi came down to meet us.

In a back room on the first landing we found Yeats and Lady Gregory, Lady Gregory sitting apart in an upright wooden chair reminding me of a smaller version of Queen Victoria. It was with difficulty she rose out of the chair to shake hands with me when Yeats led me beside the fireplace. While down the centre of the room my eye wandered to a very long table on which books and manuscripts were placed at intervals.

After a while Lennox left, and then Lady Gregory went to bed, when a discussion rose between us on Swift. In the argumentative mood of youth I maintained that Irish wit was playful and fantastical but Swift's was typically English—a hammer blow to kill. But Yeats maintained that Swift was Irish by residence and environment and sympathy.

'His mother came from Leicestershire and his father from Yorkshire, and even if you accept that Sir William Temple was his father he was still English,' I replied, for one was nothing if one was not obstinate.

In the end, however, Yeats smiled and said with a sigh: 'Anyway we try and claim him for our own.' Then as midnight approached he rose and said that he had some work to do, and very graciously led me down the stairs followed by the white Borzoi into the hall. But I remembered how as I had sat talking he had constantly reminded me of Sean O'Sullivan's portrait as he leant forward on one side in his chair with one arm projected downward and his head slightly forward when he gave the impression that his poetic demon never let him rest, for even when one saw him walking around Dublin in the afternoons, a tall and distinguished figure in his grey tweed coat and black hat with hands behind his back, his fingers continually twisting and re-twisting as he unravelled the intricacies of some new poem—this constant and exhausting effort of literary creation which Dante Algieri complained in his 'Vita Nuova'—had reduced him to a shadow.

It was some years later when travelling through Sligo that I stopped at the cemetery at Drumcliffe, a place which must always have been a sacred spot, with its ruined Round Tower, the black phallic stone, and that beautiful ancient Irish Cross carved with biblical stories of Adam and Eve, and of Cain Killing Abel, and the Lion of St. Mark carved out on one of its arms, while to the left of the gaunt Protestant Church, where an ancestor had been rector, the countryside stretched away to the distant Ben Bulben which owing to its peculiar rock formation gives one the impression that a line of hieratic gods have been carved across its summit.

As the old gate-keeper led me through the iron gate he told me that some people came over from London lately clad in white robes and held a ritual chanting around the grave one night—a grave so severe and formal that even though he had so instructed it to be, nevertheless one wished it had been something more magnificent for even some of the tombs around, of the local gentry, were more imposing.

As I left the cemetery I remember the old gate-keeper stopped me and said about those famous lines:

> Cast a cold eye
> On life, on death,
> Horseman, pass by!

'There is one who can put a meaning on them.'

NOTES

Born in Waterford, Ireland and early educated in Hampstead, London, Arthur Power was fourteen years of age when his family moved to France. He fought in World War I, and on his release from the army at the end of the war he went, via Florence, Rome and Pisa, to Paris where he first met James Joyce and his family in the early twenties. It seems that Joyce offered oblique thanks for Power's friendly conversation by allowing him to double, in *Finnegans Wake*, with Frank le Poer ('Ghazi') Power, under the pseudonym 'gas-power'. In Paris, Power worked for some time as art critic for the *New York Herald*. He returned finally to Ireland in the thirties, and looked after the family estate in County Waterford for a few years. A well-known artist, he now lives and works in Dublin. See his *Conversations with James Joyce* (London: Millington, 1974).

1. For a note on Conor Cruise O'Brien see p. 53.
2. *On the Boiler* (Dublin: Cuala Press, 1939).
3. *The Wanderings of Oisin and Other Poems* (London: Kegan Paul, Trench, 1889).
4. Arland Ussher (1897–   ), author of *The Face and Mind of Ireland* (1949), *Journey Through Dread* (1955), *The Thoughts of Mr. Wong* (1956), *The XXII Keys of the Tarot* (1957), *Spanish Mercy* (1959) and *Sages and Schoolmen* (1967).
5. *The Drapier Letters*, which had its première at the Abbey Theatre on 22 August 1927.

Memory of Meeting Yeats*

RICHARD EBERHART

After my first year at Cambridge I made a trip to Ireland. I went to Limerick to see if I could locate any Ghormleys. I had been given this middle name for my maternal grandmother, who had thirteen children in America. I found no Ghormleys. I walked and bicycled on the west coast. Returning to Dublin I met James Stephens and Miss MacNie, AE, Miss Sarah Purser,[1] Gogarty, and Yeats. After a lapse of twenty-eight years I discovered a letter written upon returning from Ireland to Cambridge (October 13, 1928), apparently never sent and probably written as a diary to preserve these early literary memories. The letter follows:

'My bag was still lost, and I was staying at 84 Lower Baggot Street, wherein I was flea bitten beyond the point of tolerance, until I had a hide in motley, and it was while the flea was omnipotent that I suffered martyrdom but recreated my Valencia island afternoon and wrote a poem by candlelight to forget the jumping army.

'At Ely Place I called on Oliver St. John Gogarty. He showed me his first editions, pointed out of the window to the garden in which George Moore used to write, showed me a personal picture (and a sword) just received from the Kaiser, and when I saw a shelf of Nietzsche I rejoiced, for we had considerable in common. Gogarty asked me if I would like to meet his friend Lord Dunsany, and said he would send me to him at once, but asked if I knew his works, and when I said no, he made a jest and said it would be impossible, for odd Dunsany talks only of himself. I liked Gogarty's frankness and his wit: he said all Yeats needed was a mistress, that Yeats was a cult like Rossetti and (more important, I add) that Ireland's literary renaissance would die out surely, and that proud as they were, Ireland was but a part of Great Britain. Gogarty was reading Pindar. He talked intelligently about Greece and Rome. Would you like to meet Yeats? He's leaving for Rapallo[2] soon,as he is supposed to be an invalid. Come to my house at nine o'clock Thursday, Yeats and AE will be there . . .

'At nine in the evening, Thursday, I knocked several times. The maid let me into the drawing room upstairs. A fat man was sitting in a chair, and a man with his back to me was sitting on a divan before the fire. Gogarty

* Extracted from 'Memory of Meeting Yeats, AE, Gogarty, James Stephens', *Literary Review* (Rutherford, New Jersey) 1 (Autumn 1957) 51–6.

arose, greeted me, the gray-headed man turned, and I was introduced to Yeats. I noticed the shortness of his fingers and the soft texture of his hand when he made the polite gesture, and was struck by the height and physique of Yeats. He wore glasses, a soft blue shirt with a bow tie, his coat was open and one button of his waistcoat was unbuttoned. A magnificent head! His voice had a querulous quality in it. Sometimes he ran his hand through his long iron-gray hair, which lay back from his temples in gentle strands. Coffee was brought, and I was sitting beside Yeats on the divan. The conversation, after Yeats had asked me two civil questions about America and Cambridge, became at once animated concerning the Censorship Bill to be brought up in the Dail Eireann.[3] The Catholics want to censor everything from birth control to 'immoral' literature, and even propose, like ostriches with their heads in the sand, to allow no printed mention to be made anywhere of venereal disease, thinking, in a most peculiarly Irish illogic, that they can do away with an evil by refusing to see any mention made of it. Senator Yeats made a jest about contraception. The party was indeed animated with serious discussion of all points of the bill. The intelligentsia of Ireland is limited to a few. These members of the Senate were the center of that group which upholds tolerance and a desire for widespread education. Yeats said that nothing about the body was evil, he pleaded for the Doric[4] discipline, and wanted practical education. The fat man, some editor, left, and Gogarty brought a bottle of claret. There was a knock below, and Gogarty went to welcome AE.

'Yeats had been anxious for AE to come, as he wanted to get him to write some editorial apropos of the Censorship Bill in his *Irish Statesman*. It was about 9:45 and while I was alone with him he said it would do no good. Impassioned he arose and made an impetuous gesture with his arms, yet there was ennui in it, saying he was to give his last speech in the Senate on October 10, but that it would do no good, that 'he would only make another of his impassioned speeches' and the unenlightened would rule. It was touching to realize the meaning of this. Yeats had given years to the service of his State; it was futile; he must retire to Italy and have no longer an active part either in the Government[5] or in the Abbey Theater.[6]

'AE came in, I retired from the divan to a proper chair farther off, Gogarty gave AE a cigar and the talk became so fervent that the tea was forgotten when it was brought. AE sat in a chair near the fireplace. I could see his right profile, and noted the fine texture of his skin, and the little depression the frame of his glasses made from ear to eye socket.

*   *   *

'When the war was over, quelled by excellent tea, the conversation turned to scholarship, poetry, and the humanities. I only remember Yeats' views on two persons. Speaking of Baldwin[7] he said he was much more intelligent than he had expected him to be; and after sincerely lauding

Baldwin, he turned to Gogarty and said, "Gogarty, he has studied politics as you and I have never studied poetry." And about T. E. Lawrence,[8] after lauding his self-effacement after heroism, he said, "That act should be a great thing in history." But these sentences appear a little absurd out of full context.

"We looked at our watches, it was near midnight, AE had gone a while before, so Gogarty helped us on with our coats, and I felt as little as possible as if I were with the poet Yeats. We walked into the night, and went the same way for a few blocks together, and there was nothing to say. Yeats was to make his last speech in the Senate, he was going from his island to Italy, and if I had thought of it, when I turned and walked into the night, I would have said, "Sweet joy befall thee".'

It is circumstantial to be old enough to try to psychoanalyze one's former self. I give the letter as it was written, with minor changes. Yet I know that I was afraid to express fully my feelings at the end of the Yeats episode. I remember these feelings very clearly. At that time I had not yet published a book. I had boundless belief in poetry and wanted more than anything to be a poet. I had already begun, but knew that Yeats could not know of my early, just sprung work. I idolized Yeats, and AE and James Stephens, all the literary men who were kind to me and were interested in me in Dublin, beyond the telling. I worshipped them. So that while I was walking a few blocks from Gogarty's house with Yeats in the dark night, I had an intense perception of his greatness and immortality. I had whirling words to say, to tell him how much I enjoyed his poetry, but this frenzy was quieted by common sense. I hated to take each step for I knew that up the street soon he would go one way, I another. I would turn off and go alone in the dark to my own place and dispensation. He would go straight on and I knew I would never see him again, as indeed turned out to be the case. I was having high drama walking along. Yeats seemed in deep thought, heavily meditating, looking straight ahead and saying nothing. We spoke no word. How thrilling it was! I was speaking millions of words to him. I was so sensitive I wondered nervously about the common civilities. Should I say goodnight? Should I mutter some polite phrase? Actually, the most eloquent thing happened, an eloquence of silence. When we came, walking together in the Irish night of literary time, to the predestined corner, he did not look at me and I did not look at him. I turned off right-face on my street and we parted forever without a word.

NOTES

Richard Eberhart (1904–) is an American poet. He was professor and poet-in-residence at Princeton University and Dartmouth College and served as the first President of the Poets' Theatre in Cambridge, Massachussets, in 1950–1. From 1959 to 1961 he was poetry consultant to the Library of Congress. Collections of Eberhart's poems include *A Bravery of*

Earth (1930), *Burr Oaks* (1947), *Undercliff: Poems 1946–1953* (1953) and *Collected Poems, 1930–1960* (1960).

    1. Sarah Purser (1848–1943), Irish artist who founded a co-operative society of artists known as An Tur Gloine [The Tower of Glass] in 1902. She was a friend of the Yeats family. See Elizabeth Coxhead, 'Sarah Purser and the Tower of Glass', *Daughters of Erin* (London: Secker and Warburg, 1965) pp. 125–66.

    2. In 1928 Yeats was advised to spend his winters out of Dublin and to avoid public life.

    3. [Assembly of Ireland] Irish Parliament.

    4. Pertaining to Doris, an ancient region in central Greece.

    5. The fact that Yeats's term of office as a Senator would end in 1928 made it seem easier for him to withdraw from public life.

    6. Yeats, though, wrote to Olivia Shakespear on 28 February 1928: 'Once out of the Senate—my time is up in September—and, in obedience to the doctors, out of all public work, there is no reason for more than 3 months of Dublin—where the Abbey is the one work I cannot wholly abandon.'

    7. Abraham Baldwin (1754–1807), American political leader.

    8. Lawrence of Arabia [T. E. Shaw] (1888–1935).

Did You Know Yeats?*

DENIS JOHNSTON

When I returned from London around 1927 I was called to the Irish Bar. I continued to direct plays for the Drama League. I directed Barry Fitzgerald and F J McCormick and actors of that sort and was subsequently to direct them in *King Lear*[1] at the Abbey Theatre. That was the Abbey's first effort at Shakespeare. Some people said that Yeats invited me to direct *Lear* because he had refused to present *The Old Lady Says No!* But it wasn't for that reason at all. It was because the Abbey had never played Shakespeare and wanted a director who could approach the play from a new angle; at least that is what Yeats told me. I used to sit near him in the Abbey Theatre. To me he was a major poet with a floppy tie. It never occurred to me at the time how remarkable it was to be sitting beside him. George Russell was just a nice old man with a beard: the 'hairy fairy' as he was called. I don't drop names as a rule, but in America, where I have been teaching for a good many years, I find myself being regarded with awe by people who ask: 'Did you actually know Yeats? Did you really have lunch with Shaw? What was Lady Gregory like? What was George Russell like?' It must have been an unusually interesting time, but to me all these people were merely citizens of Dublin like myself.

    When I wrote *The Old Lady Says No!* in 1926 nobody would stage it. Eventually it was Shelagh Richards[2] who persuaded Hilton Edwards and Micheál Mac Liammóir to produce it. They had to be persuaded, because

* *A Paler Shade of Green*, ed. Des Hickey and Gus Smith (London: Leslie Frewin, 1972) pp. 63–4.

the play was hard to follow on the page. It wasn't written with any idea other than that a director would want to see what would happen if he attempted certain techniques on the stage. The play was written without any didactic motive; the last thing that emerged from the writing of *The Old Lady* was the point of the play. I had already written a couple of one-act plays as an experiment but *The Old Lady* was the first play I sent to anybody with the idea of having it produced. I had originally submitted it to the Abbey and they received it in a very friendly fashion. Yeats did a lot of work on the script. One of my precious possessions is the first draft of *The Old Lady* with Yeats's marginal notes all the way through and lines crossed out and other lines substituted. He told me that audiences would not accept more than an hour and a quarter of the play, so I got it down to an hour and a quarter. Eventually Yeats said to me, 'The play has too many scenes.' Then he thought for a long while, and added, 'And the scenes are too long.'

Yeats did his best for *The Old Lady*, but I have never resented the fact that the Abbey turned the play down. I don't think it was their kind of play; it was definitely a Gate play. I had a deep respect for Yeats for his canons of good taste. When one is young one tends to overwrite. In the first draft of *The Old Lady Says No!* there is the line, 'I have written my name in letters of fire across the page of history.' Yeats crossed this out and substituted, 'I shall be remembered.' I didn't use his corrections, but I recognised the fact that I was over-writing. Despite my respect for Yeats's good taste, I had no particular respect for him as a constructive dramatist. I was aware that he had attempted techniques on the stage which could not be done. Lady Gregory was a much better dramatist, but I didn't much like her personally.

NOTES

In 1918, Yeats, Lennox Robinson and others, feeling a certain parochialism in the almost solely Irish repertoire of the Abbey Theatre, formed the Dublin Drama League. It used the Abbey stage and many of the Abbey players to present a wide variety of works from the world theatre. The League ceased to exist in 1928, when Hilton Edwards and Micheál MacLiammóir arrived with their plays and their ideas. However, it had prepared a path for them, had perhaps inspired a dramatist or two, notably Denis Johnston, and, not being a money-making concern, gladly stepped aside to make room for the Edwards–MacLiammóir Dublin Gate Theatre. Johnston, who was not totally involved with the Abbey Theatre, became a director of the Gate Theatre in 1931.

1. *King Lear* was produced by Denis Johnston at the Abbey Theatre on 26 November 1928. The text of the interview given by Denis Johnston suggests that both Barry Fitzgerald and F. J. McCormick took part in the play, whereas actually only McCormick played the role of the King. See Lennox Robinson, *Ireland's Abbey Theatre* (London: Sidgwick and Jackson, 1951) p. 143.

2. Shelah Richards was Denis Johnston's first wife. She played the part of Cordelia in his production of *King Lear*.